Born in Chatham in Kent, **Henry Stedman** didn't learn to walk till the age of two but enjoyed the experience so much that he's been on his feet ever since. Over the past ten years Henry's legs have taken him up and down the Himalaya in Nepal, the Yellow Peak Range in China, the Karakoram in Pakistan, the Chouf in Lebanon, the Cordilleras in the Philippines, Gunung Leuser in Sumatra and round the Ramonafana National Park in Madagascar.

He is the author of Trailblazer's *Istanbul to Cairo Overland*, the *Bradt Guide to Palestine*, and he is the co-author of the *Rough Guide to Indonesia* and the *Rough Guide to Southeast Asia*.

Trekking in the Dolomites
First edition 2001

Publisher
Trailblazer Publications
The Old Manse, Tower Rd, Hindhead, Surrey, GU26 6SU, UK
Fax (+44) 01428-607571
info@trailblazer-guides.com
www.trailblazer-guides.com

British Library Cataloguing in Publication Data
A catalogue record for this book is available from the British Library

ISBN 1-873756-34-8

Editor: Patricia Major
Typesetting: Anna Jacomb-Hood
Layout: Bryn Thomas and Henry Stedman
Cartography: Nick Hill and Jane Thomas
Illustrations: Nick Hill
Index: Jane Thomas

Warning: mountain walking can be dangerous.
Please read the notes on mountain safety on p31-3 and information on
vie ferrate on p24-5. Every effort has been made by the author and publisher
to ensure that the information contained herein is as accurate and up to date
as possible. However, they are unable to accept responsibility for any
inconvenience, loss or injury sustained by anyone as a result of the
advice and information given in this guide.

Printed on chlorine-free paper from farmed forests by
Technographic Design & Print (☎ 01206-303323) Colchester, Essex, UK

TREKKING
IN THE
DOLOMITES

HENRY STEDMAN

TRAILBLAZER PUBLICATIONS

This book is dedicated to my mum,
because she puts up with a lot.

Acknowledgements

In Italy, thanks must go to Sisto Menardi at the tourist office in Cortina; Nadia at the tourist office in Santa Stefano; Frank and Claude Ernzer (Lux); Hunter Lenihan, Fiorenza Micheli and Christiana Ghiandelli for helping me to complete the via ferrata at the Croda Rossa; the staff at the Fondo Valle for looking after my stuff; Stefan Reiche (Leipzig) for the company through the Vette Feltrine, and for the string to hold my boots together; Gianni Pertusio (Torino) for his knowledge and enthusiasm for all things Dolomitic; Alex Timillero of the Rifugio Treviso; Brian and Linda Waldie (Lanarkshire) for their advice and company in the Passo di Valles; and Renata Osterwalder for translating the German menu; and last but most definitely not least, Barbara Ganzarolli (Italy) for translating the signs.

At Trailblazer, thanks to Patricia Major for editing the text, Jane Thomas for drawing the trail maps and indexing the book (twice – sorry!), Nick Hill for the town plans and illustrations and Anna Jacomb-Hood for typesetting.

A request

The author and publisher have tried to ensure that this guide is as accurate and up to date as possible. If you notice any changes or omissions please contact Henry Stedman at Trailblazer (henry@trailblazer-guides.com or to postal address on p2). A free copy of the next edition will be sent to persons making a significant contribution.

Cover photograph: Civetta: Torre di Valgrande and NW face from Col Negro di Coldai © John Cleare (Mountain Camera) 2001.

CONTENTS

INTRODUCTION

'I crossed many passes, I found many unknown sites of great beauty, I discovered many of those wild peaks. They attracted me with their apparent inaccessibility, and appeared even more desireable (sic)'.
  Paul Grohmann, conqueror of the Dolomites' highest peak, the Marmolada.

In 1789, the celebrated mineralogist Deodonne Sylvian Guy Tancrède de Gratet de Dolomieu (or Deodat to his friends) embarked on a journey to Rome from his native France. By all accounts, the trip wasn't particularly eventful, certainly by the standards of the eighteenth century. Nevertheless, it was this journey that led Dolomieu to discover the mineral that today bears his name; a discovery that not only brought him both fame and fortune during his lifetime but which would also, long after his death, result in an entire mountain range being named after him. For while passing through a valley in what was then part of the Austro-Hungarian Empire, Dolomieu's attention was caught by some unusually vivid rocks and stones that lay in abundance on the ground by the side of the road. Unable to identify the rocks, Dolomieu paused to collect some samples, and on his return to France ran a series of tests that proved that these rocks were composed of calcium magnesium carbonate, a previously unidentified mineral.

In honour of Dolomieu's discovery, a few years later both the mineral and the rock were named after him. Then in 1864, a full 95 years after his journey, two itinerant English geologists, J. Gilbert and G.C. Churchill, published *The Dolomite Mountains*, an account of their explorations in a mountainous region that had previously been known by a whole series of names, including the Venetian Alps and, more poetically (if a little less accurately) the *Monte Pallidi*, ('Pale Mountains'). The book's title caught on, and ever since this small yet sublimely beautiful range has been known as the Dolomite Mountains, or simply, the Dolomites. There's a certain irony in the fact that though the mineral that he identified exists in abundance in these mountains, and though the entire range is named after him, Dolomieu himself never actually visited the Dolomites, his rock samples having been taken from the Valle Isarco, to the north-west of the range.

Gilbert and Churchill's explorations, along with those of other British pioneers such as John Ball and Amelia Edwards and the Austrian climber Paul Grohmann, paved the way for the tourist industry of the late 1800s. Before the century was over, mountaineers, skiers, trekkers and thrill-seekers from all corners of Europe were flocking to this small, mountainous part of the Austro-Hungarian Empire. Few would have been disappointed by what they found. The Dolomites may not be the largest range in Europe, nor are its mountains particularly massive when compared to the giants of neighbouring Austria and Switzerland. But what these mountains lack in scale, they more than make up for in both beauty and diversity. It is in the Dolomites that you find some of nature's boldest designs: sheer pinnacles of pink and grey soaring above grumbling glaciers and windswept, karstic plateaux. Here, too, you can witness the natural phenomenon of Alpenglow – or *enrosadira* as it's known in the local Ladin language – where the mountains seem to glow a vivid pink and orange in the late afternoon sun. While down in the valleys that separate these massifs, you'll come across any number of enchanting little villages, each huddled around over-sized mediaeval churches.

The Dolomites is also the region where the neatly-manicured gardens and lovingly-tended window boxes of the Southern Tyrol meet the renaissance-inspired glories of Italian architecture; sandwiched between these two cultures we find the Ladin people, one of the smallest ethnic minorities in Europe who, despite a history in which they have been the subjects of one vainglorious empire after another, have managed to retain their own language and identity. Their folktales, too, have received widespread recognition, which in turn have helped to perpetuate the notion that the Dolomites is the haunt of a whole host of sage old wizards, greedy goblins, despotic mountain kings and innumerable lovelorn princesses. It is a notion that the mountains' wild and primordial landscape, its lonely peaks and deep, dark forests, does little to dispel.

Thankfully, the mountains' charms are not just for the adventurous and intrepid. As well as an extensive network of well-maintained footpaths, the Dolomites are also renowned for their **vie ferrate**, steep and/or exposed trails where assistance – in the form of iron cables, metal rungs and ladders – has been provided along parts of the trail. This allows those with little or no climbing skills a chance to see the kind of awesome panoramas that were once the sole preserve of accomplished climbers.

I give the last word of this introduction, as I gave the first, to the 19th-century Austrian climber Paul Grohmann and hope that when you, too, feast your eyes upon these extraordinary mountains, you'll experience the same sense of awe and wonder as he did over a century ago:

'When from the peaks and heights of the Tauri Range, which I had explored up to that moment, I cast my gaze southwards, I saw a brand new world of beautifully-shaped mountains which even the best book could not describe in detail. It was an alpine world still covered in mystery. I decided to go to the Dolomites and work there.'

ABOUT THIS GUIDE

This book makes no claims to being a complete rundown of all the walking trails in the Dolomites. Such a project would run to many volumes and you probably wouldn't be able to fit them in your rucksack, let alone lug them up and down the mountains described. Instead, what we have done is take two major trails running right the way through the range – one from west to east and one north to south – and described each in detail. We have also pointed out and described a number of shorter walks, varying in length between one and five days, thus allowing you to choose the length and area of your trek.

All of the routes in this book have been chosen because a) they offer the best variety of terrains and scenery, and b) because they can be completed by anybody of average fitness with very little technical climbing skills required. In the three places in this book where the vie ferrate are of a slightly more advanced level, alternative trails have been suggested.

In other words, if you don't want to do anything technically challenging, you don't have to. And you don't have to be an expert mountaineer to go trekking in the Dolomites.

This point is worth emphasizing. Though I've done a fair bit of mountain trekking, including in Nepal which, I have to say, is a bit of a cinch compared to some of the trails in the Dolomites, I had never used a rope or karabiner before I came to Italy; in fact, if the truth be told, I had to look up the exact definition of 'karabiner' before I first set out to research this guide. I don't walk particularly fast, indeed I was overtaken en route by most people, some elderly and others quite young. Compared to the locals, most of whom have the sure-footedness of mountain goats, I'm hardly nimble either; nor am I entirely comfortable with heights.

If I can do these walks I'm sure most people can. Don't be put off by the Dolomites' reputation as a Mecca for the macho. Some of the walking is strenuous because the paths tend to climb and fall with great regularity and often very sharply; but if you're reasonably fit and don't suffer from chronic vertigo, I dare say you'll be completing the trails a good deal more quickly than I did.

About the maps in this guide

All the trekking maps in this guide are drawn to the same scale, 20mm to 1km. Only the town plans are drawn to larger scales, and some of these plans are simply rough sketches.

Though we have tried to make the trail maps in this book as useful and accurate as possible, they are designed as an accompaniment to the locally produced trekking maps, rather than as a substitute. These maps can give you better information on adjoining trails (useful if you have to

❏ Place names

In the Dolomites most places, particularly in the autonomous Südtirol province, have at least two names, one in Italian and one in German. Sometimes you'll also find a third, Ladin version of the name too. In this book, the Italian name is the one we use in the text, though when a place in the German-speaking part of the country is mentioned for the first time, the German name is also given (separated from the Italian name by '/').

make an emergency descent from the trail) and they can also help you identify the various mountains and other geographical features you'll pass en route.

The times that I have indicated on the maps should be used as an approximate guide only. They refer to **walking times only**, and do not include any time for breaks and food; don't forget to add on a few minutes when estimating the total time for a particular stage.

Lastly, if you're planning to do any of the walks in the opposite direction to that given in the book, remember that you'll be walking uphill where I was walking downhill, and vice versa, so that these estimated times need to be adjusted.

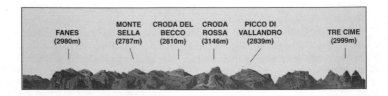

FANES (2980m) MONTE SELLA (2787m) CRODA DEL BECCO (2810m) CRODA ROSSA (3146m) PICCO DI VALLANDRO (2839m) TRE CIME (2999m)

PART 1: PLANNING YOUR TRIP

With a group or on your own?

INDEPENDENT TREKKING

Camping . . . ?

Few people bother to camp in the Dolomites and there are good reasons for this. Camping can be a very lonely experience, especially outside the high season, and it is illegal in Italy's national parks, which together cover a wide area in the Dolomites. Furthermore, as accommodation in the region's numerous *rifugi* (mountain huts, see below) is so cheap, many trekkers consider a tent or bivouac an unnecessary burden to lug up and down mountains. Instead, most trekkers prefer to plan their itinerary to begin and end at rifugi, foregoing the need to stay overnight in towns.

That said, there are those who love the freedom of carrying their own shelter around with them. There are also those who swear by camping gear for safety reasons and they have a point: should you find yourself stuck on a mountainside overnight, you'll consider the effort expended in carrying your camping equipment with you all the time to be a small price to pay. Furthermore, in some towns such as Cortina and Bolzano, camping is the only cheap accommodation option – and the campsites in these towns are often superb, with excellent facilities and good restaurants to boot!

. . . or rifugi?

All the main trails in the Dolomites are well served by rifugi. These are mountain huts offering both food and accommodation at very reasonable prices. The advantages are obvious: cheap, warm, sociable, and with all the latest information about the neighbouring trails, rifugi also allow trekkers to cut down on the amount of gear they need to carry with them. Of course there are disadvantages too – the loss of freedom engendered by the necessity to reach a rifugio or town before nightfall, the lack of privacy, the high probability that for at least one night you'll have to share a dormitory with a heavy snorer and so on.

Nevertheless, most trekkers feel these are outweighed by the advantages listed above. As a result, this book caters more for those who don't have any camping gear by starting and finishing each stage at a rifugio or a town.

GROUP/GUIDED WALKS

The **Scuola di Alpinismo**, which has offices in Cortina and most other large towns, organizes a variety of short guided treks in the mountains. Unsurprisingly, with their excellent safety record and unparalleled experience in the Dolomites, they are the best people to sign up with should you decide not to do your trek independently.

Programmes include *vie ferrate* courses (currently starting at around L85,000 per day), a rock-climbing school (a basic three-day course will set you back around L350,000), and a number of starter lessons for children. Unfortunately, in the high season, particularly in August, they are often booked out months in advance, so do plan and book well ahead. Details of their latest programme can be found at ▱ www.mnet-climb.com/guidecortina. The address of the Cortina branch is: Guide Alpine Scuola D'Alpinismo (☎ and ▤ 0436-868505; ▱ guidecortina@mnet-climb.com), Corso Italia 69a, 32043.

TREKKING AGENCIES IN THE UK

● **Exodus Walking Holidays** (☎ 020-8673 0859, ▱ sales@exodustravels.co.uk, www.exodustravels.co.uk), 9 Weir Rd, London SW12 0LT. Huge London-based outfit currently offering a 13-day holiday, including trekking in the Fanes group and a brief via ferrata taster around the Cinque Torri.

● **Marmot Trails** (☎ 020-8469 0127, ▱ marmot.trails@cwcom.net, www.marmotdolomite.mcmail.com), 12 Hazeldon Rd, London SE4 2DD. Organizes small group walking holidays, including a Discover Dolomites tour which takes in a couple of easy ambles around the Val Pusteria, including a taste of via ferrata, and a more challenging via ferrata tour. The price includes all necessary via ferrata equipment and guides.

● **Naturetrek** (☎ 01962-733051), Chautara, Bighton, Nr Alresford, Hampshire SO24 9RB. Naturetrek organizes guided birding and botany holidays to destinations worldwide, including an eight-day botanical holiday around the Fassa Valley.

● **Sherpa Expeditions** (☎ 020-8577 2717, ▤ 020-8572 9788, ▱ sherpa.sales@dial.pipex.com), 131a Heston Rd, Hounslow, Middlesex TW5 0RD, offers a 14-day trek around the Dolomites.

● **Ramblers Holidays** (☎ 01707-331133, ▤ 01707-333276, ▱ ramhols@dial.pipex.com), Box 43, Welwyn Garden City, Herts AL8 6PQ, offer Dolomites walking holidays.

● **Cox & Kings** (☎ 020-7873 5000, ▤ 020-7630 6038, ▱ www.coxandkings.co.uk), Gordon House, 10 Greencoat Place, London SW1P 1PH. A nine-day guided Dolomites botanical and wildlife walking holiday costs £855 including full board and flights (ex-London).

TREKKING AGENCIES IN CONTINENTAL EUROPE

Germany
● **Baumeler Travel** (☎ 0761-380 570, 🖹 0761-380 5730, 💻 www.baum eler.de), J Baumeler Wanderreisen GmbH, Engelbergerstr 21, 79106 Freiburg, offers one-week tours with accommodation in three-star hotels.
● **Wikinger Reisen GmbH** (☎ 02331-9046, 🖹 02331-904875, 💻 mail @www.wikinger.de, www.wikinger.de), Kölner Str. 20, D-58135 Hagen. Wikinger offers eight-day walking tours in the Dolomites.

Italy
● **Guide Alpine Scuola D'Alpinismo** (☎/🖹 0436-868505, 💻 www.mnet -climb.com/guidecortina), Corso Italia 69a, Cortina 32043. See Group/ Guided Walks opposite for more information.

Netherlands
● **SNP Travel** (☎ 024-327 7000, 024-327 7099, 💻 www.snp.nl), PO Box 1270, 6501 BG Nijmegen. SNP Travel have two eight-day treks in the Dolomites and also offer individual walking and cycling tours in several other parts of Italy.

TREKKING AGENCIES IN NORTH AMERICA

USA
● **Ferrate Tours** (☎ 570-675-7835, 💻 jresio@ptdprolog.net, www.fer-ratetours.com), 19 Old Grandview Avenue, Dallas, PA 18612. Offers a challenging two-week holiday, including over a week of via ferrata around Cortina, Lagazuoi and the Lago di Braies, as well as some side-trips to Venice and Austria.
● **Going Places** (☎ 216-566-0600, 💻 www.goingplacestravel.com), 120 Huron Rd, Cleveland, Ohio 44115. Offers a one-month walking tour that takes in the Cinque Terre region, some easy trekking around the castles of the Val Gardena.
● **Trips n' Trails** (☎ 530-994-3575, 💻 trails@psin.com, www.ps ln.com/trails), PO Box 210, Calpine, California 96124. Small US-based outfit offering a two-week jaunt between Lake Garda and the Dolomites, where you'll visit the WWI battlefields around Sesto.
● **Cox & Kings Travel** (☎ 800-999-1758, 🖹 813-258-3852, 💻 www.cox andkings.com), 25 Davis Blvd, Tampa, Florida 33606. Cox & Kings offer a nine-day guided Dolomites botanical and wildlife walking holiday.

Canada
● Butterfield & Robinson (☎ 416-864-1354, 🖹 416-864-0541, 💻 www.butterfield.com), 70 Bond St, Suite 300, Toronto, Ontario M5B 1X3. Butterfield organize a walking tour in the Dolomites ('Italian Alps' on their website).

Getting to the Dolomites

BY AIR

There are three major international **airports** serving the Dolomites: **Venice** and **Milan** in Italy, and **Innsbruck** in Austria, as well as the smaller Trento, Verona and Bolzano (in Italy) airstrips which almost exclusively serve domestic traffic. Of the international airports, Innsbruck is convenient for both Bolzano and Bressanone, the starting points of both our main trails, as is Milan, while Venice is the closest airport to Cortina and the eastern Dolomites.

Scheduled airlines, including British Airways and Alitalia, offer open-jaw tickets, where you can fly in to one airport and leave from another, though often they insist that the two airports are in the same country.

From UK

Milan and Venice are your best bets for cheap flights. Fares to Venice in particular, served as it is by a number of charter companies, can often be extremely low off-peak. Check with Ryanair too; in 2000 they were selling tickets to a number of Italian destinations for as little as £5 from London! If they can't help, and it's a cheap flight that you're after, have a quick scan through the flight-only adverts on Teletext and you should be able to pick up a return to Venice or Milan for less than £100.

Recommended agencies to try in the UK include: **STA Travel** (London ☎ 020-7937 9962, Bristol ☎ 0117-929 4399, Manchester ☎ 0161-834 0668, Cambridge ☎ 01223-366966, Oxford ☎ 01865-792800); **Trailfinders** (London ☎ 020-7938 3366, Manchester ☎ 0161-839 6969, Glasgow ☎ 0141-353 2224, Bristol ☎ 0117-929 9000, Dublin ☎ 01-677 7888), and **Campus** (London ☎ 020-7730 3402, Manchester ☎ 0161-273 1721, Edinburgh ☎ 0131-668 3303).

From USA

In the US, check out **Air Brokers International** of San Francisco (☎ 1-800-883 3273), **Sky Link** of New York (☎ 212-599 0430) and **STA Travel** (New York ☎ 1-800-777 0112).

From Australia

In Australia try **Flight Centre** (Melbourne ☎ 03-9650 2899), **Thomas Cook** (Sydney ☎ 02-9248 6100) and **Trailfinders** (Sydney ☎ 02-9247 7666, Brisbane ☎ 07-3229 0887).

❏ TO THE DOLOMITES FROM VENICE, INNSBRUCK AND MILAN

From Venice to Cortina

There is one bus daily (at 5.30pm) in the high season from the airport direct to Cortina. Failing this, the easiest and cheapest way to reach Cortina is to go by a combination of bus and train. Begin by catching an Atvo bus from the airport to Mestre train station. Tickets (L4000) can be brought from the kiosk next to the exchange counter, which must then be validated in the machine by the driver's seat. Buses run every 30 minutes from 7.21am to 00.20am. The journey time is approximately 20 minutes.

From Mestre there are very occasional buses to two Dolomite towns, though these operate in high season only and are quite expensive; you're better off taking one of the reasonably frequent trains (L11,500). These run to Ponte Nelle Alpi-Polpet (93 mins), from where you change for Calalzo – Pieve di Cadore (43 mins). Once again, tickets must be validated, this time in the machines on the platform before you board. From Pieve Di Cadore, it's another L5200 (with baggage) to travel the 33km by bus to Cortina. The total journey time from Mestre to Cortina is about three hours.

From Innsbruck to Bressanone/Bolzano

Arriving at Innsbruck airport, the easiest and quickest way to reach the Dolomites is to take one of the shuttle buses straight from the airport to Bolzano railway station, in the very heart of the city. Alta Via 2 trekkers may be able to persuade the driver to let them alight in Bressanone. The coach from Innsbruck takes about two hours to Bressanone, 45 minutes more for Bolzano. Once again, services are more frequent during the high season.

From Milan to Bolzano

Regular trains connect Milan with Bolzano. The journey between Milan and Bolzano takes four hours. Alternatively, and more conveniently, in the high season there is one Autostradale bus every day at 7am from Milan's Piazza Castello to Cortina (6hrs 30 mins; L63,000), calling at Bressanone (4hrs 50 mins; L49,000) and San Candido in the Val di Sesto (6hrs; L58,000) on the way.

BY CAR

Coming from the UK by car may not save you much in terms of money, but the greater freedom and flexibility it allows you once you're in the Dolomites actually makes this a very attractive option. Nor is it a particularly arduous journey. The quickest way is to head for the Brenner Pass that links Austria with Italy. From there, stay on the motorway (which, like all major roads in Italy, has a toll charge) until you come to the exit you want, Bressanone and Bolzano being the most convenient for the Dolomites. There are toll-free roads too, including the winding 182 from Innsbruck via Brennero, and Highway 12 which runs through the Valle Isarco. If you've come via Switzerland, the road from San Moritz through the Münstertal via Mustair will take you to the border with the South Tyrol. A longer but much simpler route is to take the Milan—Venice highway, leaving it at Verona for the Brenner highway.

Be warned, however, that parking facilities in the Dolomites are, in some areas, quite limited; also in many valleys (including the popular Val Gardena) permits are required to drive your own vehicle. See p84 for more information on these permits.

BY COACH

Though there are coaches from the UK to various points in Italy, none as yet travel to the Dolomites. Surprisingly, the fares are not that cheap either and it's often a good deal less expensive to buy a cheap return on a chartered flight than it is to buy a return on a long-distance coach.

Eurolines are the main coach company operating from Britain to Europe. They can be contacted by visiting their offices at 52 Grosvenor Gardens, Victoria, London, SW1; by calling them on ☎ 01582-404511; or by checking their website at www.eurolines.co.uk.

FURTHER INFORMATION

Tourist offices

Italian tourist offices tend to be stuffed with brochures offering very pretty pictures of every region but little in the way of relevant information. Still, some of the staff are very knowledgeable and even if they cannot answer any queries you may have, they should be able to point you in the direction of somebody who can. The following is a list of Italian tourist offices abroad:

● **Australia** (☎ 02-9247 1308), Orient Overseas Building, Suite 202, 32 Bridge St, Sydney
● **Canada** (☎ 514-866 7667), 1 Place Ville Marie, Suite 1914, Montreal, Quebec HB3 3M9
● **UK** (☎ 020-7408 1254), 1 Princes St, London W1R 8AY
● **USA** (☎ 212-245 4822), 630 Fifth Avenue, Suite 1565, New York, NY 10111. Also 124000 Wiltshire Blvd, Suite 530, Los Angeles, CA 90025, ☎ 310-820 2977; and at 401 North Michigan Avenue, Suite 3030, Chicago, Illinois 60611; ☎ 312-644 0990

Compagnia Italiana di Turismo (CIT) offices

Of more use, practically, than the tourist offices, are the offices of CIT, or the Compagnia Italiana di Turismo, Italy's national travel agents. They can help book train tickets, organize walking tours and are packed with information. The addresses of some of their offices abroad are as follows:

● **Australia** (☎ 02-9267 1255), 263 Clarence St, Sydney

● **Canada** (☎ 514-845 4310), 1450 City Councillors St, Suite 750, Montreal, Quebec H3A 2E6. Also at 111 Avenue Rd, Suite 808, Toronto, Ontario M5R 3I8; ☎ 416-927 7712

● **UK** (☎ 020-8686 0326), Marco Polo House, 3-5 Lansdowne Rd, Croydon, Surrey CR9 1LL

● **USA** (☎ 212 697 2497), 342 Madison Ave, Suite 207, New York, NY 10173. Also at 6033 West County Blvd, Suite 980, Los Angeles, CA 90045; ☎ 310-338 8615

Mountaineering clubs

Most countries have an alpine club of some sort. Not only should they have plenty of information about the Dolomites (and the European Alps in general) but, assuming they have some sort of reciprocal agreement with the CAI (see box p19), by joining their society you will be entitled to large discounts at CAI-owned rifugi. The **American Alpine Club** (☎ 303-384-0110) can be contacted at 710 Tenth St, Suite 100, Golden, Colorado, 80401. The **British Mountaineering Council** (☎ 0161-445 4747) resides at 177-179 Burton Rd, Manchester, M20 2BB.

❑ **Websites**

Undoubtedly the most useful website for information on the Dolomites is that belonging to the Lugo di Romagna branch of the Club Alpino Italiano (CAI, see box p19). Well organized and packed with useful information regarding rifugi, prices, trails (with a 'Trail of the month' section), news and pictures, this is definitely one to check before you head off. The address is: **www.racine.ra.it/cailugo/**. Also of some use, though more of a brochure than anything else, is the official website of Cortina d'Ampezzo, **www.sunrise.it/dolomiti/**, which includes brief sections on transport, hotel listings, weather reports and so on. Related websites include **www.provincia.bz.it/**, the homepage of the Südtirol, and **www.unitn.it/trentino**, the website for Trento. Then there's **www.dolomitesholidays.com**, the official webpage for the Dolomites' tourist industry, which reads like a glossy brochure, though it does provide some useful background information about the Dolomites; while **www.initaly.com/travel/in fo/alpine.htm** is the main travel website for the whole of Italy. Other general Italian websites with sections dedicated to the Dolomites include **www.travel.it/** (from which you can reserve hotels) and **www.itwg.com**, which has little on the Dolomites but does provide links to other websites.

Visas and other documents

VISAS

Citizens of countries in the European Union do not need a visa to enter Italy and are entitled to stay indefinitely. American, Canadian, Australian, South African and New Zealand passport holders do not require visas either, though their time in Italy is limited to three months. However, as Italian border guards rarely bother to stamp passports, this means that in effect you're allowed to stay in Italy indefinitely as they have no way of proving that you have stayed longer than your three-month maximum. Should they stamp your passport when you enter and you wish to extend your stay in Italy beyond the three months, the simplest solution is to leave the country and re-enter, making sure, of course, that they stamp your passport when you leave or else it will appear that you haven't left the country at all.

Foreign embassies in Rome
● **Australia** (☎ 06-852721), Via Alessandria 215
● **Austria** (☎ 06-8440141), Via Pergolesi 3
● **Canada** (☎ 06-445981), Via GB de Rossi 27
● **Germany** (☎ 06-884741), Via Po 25c
● **Netherlands** (☎ 06-3221141), Via Michele Mercati 8
● **New Zealand** (☎ 06-4402928), Via Zara 28
● **South Africa** (☎ 06-852541), Via Tanaro 14
● **UK** (☎ 06-4825441), Via XX Settembre 80a
● **USA** (☎ 06-46741), Via Vittorio Veneto 119a-121

OTHER DOCUMENTS AND IDENTIFICATION CARDS

The most useful discount card in the Dolomites is the **CAI membership card**, or a card from one of its affiliated societies. These cards will save you 50 per cent on the price of a bed in all the CAI-run rifugi and give you a discount on their food too. Alas, these savings have to be weighed against the cost of joining the club in the first place: it costs almost £50 to join the British Mountaineering Council, for example, or US$63 (EU63) to join the CAI itself, so you're going to have to spend a long time in the Dolomites to make it worth your while.

Other discount cards you may consider are the **ISIC** (International Student Identification Card), the **Under-26** or **FIYTO card** and the **HI hostelling card**. You'll find these of limited use in the Dolomites, though the ISIC and U26 cards may get you a discount on entry into some museums and other attractions, and on flights back home. The hostelling card, on the other hand, though useless in the Dolomites (where there are no hostels) comes into its own in other parts of the country. Student/youth cards can be picked up from most youth-oriented travel agents, while the HI hostelling card can be bought whilst in Italy: every time you stay in a youth hostel you buy a stamp to put on your card; once you have six you are considered a full member of HI.

If you plan to **rent a car** in Italy, you'll need your driving licence; citizens of non-EU countries may also need an **International Driver's Permit**, obtainable from automobile clubs and valid for twelve months. If bringing your own car you'll also require an **International Insurance Certificate**, or Green Card, which you can obtain from your insurance company back home.

INSURANCE

Insurance is essential. The chances of tumbling down a hillside, losing your rucksack or falling ill are, of course, slim but undoubtedly those chances are dramatically increased if you don't take out any cover.

Remember that if your country is a member of the European Union your health care in Italy should be free, providing you fill out **Form**

□ **Club Alpino Italiano**
The Club Alpino Italiano, founded in 1863 in Turin, is one of the largest alpine societies in the world, with membership well in excess of 300,000 people. Responsible for over 600 rifugi throughout Italy and for maintaining the paths and waymarkings of all the trails, the CAI relies on volunteers drawn from its vast membership pool. The CAI also runs a highly-regarded rescue service, the CNSAS (National Alpine and Speleological Corps) and provides a guide service with 7000 people on call should an emergency arise.

Annual membership of the CAI costs a rather steep US$63, though for this you get significant reductions in rifugi accommodation and food, a number of magazines throughout the year, and rescue insurance. If you don't want the magazines (which are in Italian), the cost is just US$45. Furthermore, if a second member of the same family joins, the cost for him or her is significantly less at just US$18, and there is also a youth membership fee of just US$15.

To find out more about how you can volunteer to partake in some of its activities, or to join the CAI, contact the CAI head office in Milan at Via Ugo Foscolo 3 (☎ 02 7202 3085/2557/3735), or visit the CAI Lugo's website at www.racine.ra.it/cailugo.

E111, available from any post office. Note that this **must** be done before you go. Insurance, however, is still a good idea because, should the worst happen and you have to call out one of the local rescue services, you'll find they aren't included in the coverage provided by E111.

When buying insurance you must make clear to the insurer that you will be trekking in the mountains. If you are going to be climbing and using ropes (*including* vie ferrate) you need to tell them that too. This will probably increase your premium but if you don't make this clear from the start and pay the lower premium you may find, should you have to make a claim, that you aren't actually covered at all.

Remember to read the small print of any insurance policy before buying, and shop around too, for each insurance policy varies slightly from company to company. Other details you may wish to consider include:

● How much is the excess you'll have to pay if you do make a claim?
● Can the insurers pay for your hospital bills etc. immediately, while you are still in Italy, or do you have to wait until you get home?
● How long do you have before making a claim and what evidence do you require (hospital bills, police reports etc.)?
● Does the policy include mountain rescue services, helicopter call-out and so forth? (If it doesn't, don't buy it!)
● What is the insurer's definition of mountain walking? For example, nearly all policies define mountain trekking as any walking done above 2500m. As both of the main trails described in this book climb above 2500m, you'll need to pay the higher premium. However, some of the shorter walks described in this book do not go above 2500m; if you plan on doing these short walks only, you can get away with paying the lower premium.

Budgeting

With the exception of transport and food, Italy is not a cheap country, even by the standards of Western Europe but, if you can stick to a very tight budget, camp out and cook your own food, there's no reason why you can't keep your costs down to no more than a few pounds per day. Most people, however, will prefer to stay and eat in rifugi, enjoy a beer or two now and again, and occasionally spend a night in a hotel or B&B in one of the valley towns. With this kind of lifestyle, you can expect your daily budget to be nearer £15-20.

When to go

The Dolomites have a relatively brief **trekking season** that begins in mid-June and has all but finished by the end of September. It is possible to trek outside this period, in particular October, depending on the weather, though few of the rifugi will be open and the condition of the paths may be close to perilous.

Even during the trekking season the weather can be far from ideal, and some of the routes may close occasionally if the path has become dangerously slippery or unstable. If you try to trek at the beginning of the season you also run the risk of trudging through some late-lying snow. July and August are better, though the latter can sometimes turn out to be a particularly soggy month, with violent storms a common occurrence. This is also the most popular month – a little too popular for many trekkers' tastes – when many Italians take to the mountains during their month-long holiday.

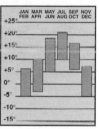

Cortina (1225m)
temperature
(max/min °C)

If I had to pick one month to go trekking in the Dolomites, I wouldn't hesitate to choose **September**. The skies are often clear, the temperature is pleasantly mild and, best of all, the mountains and rifugi tend to be less busy. However, towards the end of the month (from about the 20th) many of the rifugi begin to close down for the winter, so if you're trekking at this time make sure you ring ahead or ask in the local tourist office to find out which ones are still open.

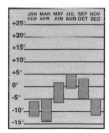

Marmolada (3343m)
temperature
(max/min °C)

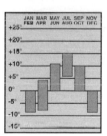

Passo Pordoi (2239m)
temperature
(max/min °C)

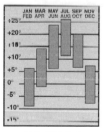

Ortisèi (820m)
temperature
(max/min °C)

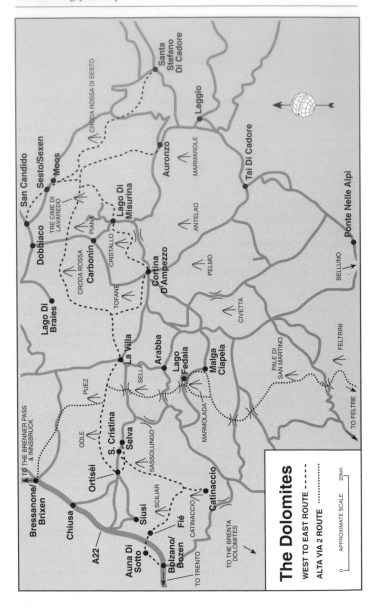

The Dolomites

WEST TO EAST ROUTE -----

ALTA VIA 2 ROUTE ....

0 APPROXIMATE SCALE 20km

Route options

The Dolomites are criss-crossed by a huge and intricate network of trails. Some of these trails have proved to be more popular than others. In particular, there are the high routes, or *alte vie* (*hohenweg* in German). There are currently eight official alte vie, which, approximately at least, increase in difficulty the higher the number.

The first **alta via** was established in the late 1960s. The idea was to establish a high-level trail covering a variety of mountain groups and terrains. Alta Via 1 proved to be so popular that the others followed soon after. The one described in this book, Alta Via 2, is the longest of them all and widely recognized, along with Alta Via 1, as the finest of its kind.

LONG TREKS

This book describes in detail two lengthy trails, each taking anything between 10 days and three weeks to complete. The first trail runs from **west to east** from the regional capital, Bolzano, to Santa Stefano di Cadore in the east. The route runs through the northern Dolomites and passes through such renowned mountain ranges as the Puez group, the Tre Cime di Lavaredo and the Popera. It is a beautiful trail that leads past some magnificent mountain scenery. By the standards of the region it is fairly undemanding, though there are a few exacting stretches here and there. At certain places along the trail we describe a number of alternative paths allowing you to choose the level of difficulty of the trail and which towns and ranges you wish to visit on your trek.

The second trail described in detail in this book is the **Alta Via 2** (AV2), the longest alta via of them all, running north-south all the way from Bressanone in the Val Pusteria to Feltre on the fringes of the Venetian plain. This route has been chosen because of its spectacular views, the variety of the terrain encountered en route, and because it passes over, round and between some of the most spectacular mountain groups in the Dolomites, including the region's highest peak, the Marmolada.

SHORT TREKS

For those who don't have the time, fitness or inclination to complete one of the longer trails, a number of short walks have also been devised which you'll find described (in less detail than the main walks) in Part 5. Remember, too, that both the longer trails can be divided to make a series of shorter treks, and in Part 5 we suggest ways in which this can be done.

❏ VIA FERRATA

Via ferrata (*kletterstieg*) translates, literally, as 'iron way', and refers to the paths, trails and scrambles in the Dolomites where trekkers and climbers are aided by a series of iron handrails, wire cables, ladders and so on. Some of these vie ferrate started out as regular trails, with the ironmongery added later when it became clear that walkers needed a little help to negotiate the path. Most trekkers wouldn't classify these paths as proper vie ferrate, but merely **assisted walks** – the term that we have adopted in this guide. Save for a good head for heights, there are no special skills required on these assisted walks; indeed, they are often a good deal simpler than some normal trails which haven't been furnished with any iron railings. Proper vie ferrate, however, have been deliberately designed to test the nerve and skill of experienced climbers, enabling them to reach heights that would otherwise be out of bounds to all except the best mountaineers.

The history of vie ferrate

The history of vie ferrate is almost as long as the history of mountaineering in the Dolomites. It seems incredible but the first via ferrata was established way back in the nineteenth century with the **Pössnecker Path** on the western face of the Sella massif. Many more were established in the years immediately following WWI, when old military fixtures such as ladders, cables and paths were converted for recreational use.

Then in the 1930s the CAI, in conjunction with a private mountaineers society known as SAT (Societá Alpinistica Trentina) began establishing a more comprehensive network of vie ferrate. Initially, the idea was simply to help mountaineers complete the approaches to a number of popular climbing routes in a less time-consuming and exhausting manner, though without actually helping them reach the summit. Most of these early vie ferrate were built in the isolated Brenta range, and when the work was completed following World War II, the various vie ferrate were linked together to form the **Bochette Way** – a sort of via ferrata 'highway' running through the centre of the range. True to its original idea, the Bochette Way approaches all the major summits in the Brenta, without climbing up to any of them, allowing climbers an easier approach to the various mountains than would otherwise be possible.

Soon non-climbers began to take advantage of these ropes and ladders, and completing vie ferrate became a popular activity in its own right. The CAI recognized this and began designing via ferrata that broke with tradition by leading all the way up to the summit. It is a move that is still the subject of much heated debate today, with many maintaining that this goes against the original spirit of the via ferrata.

Vie ferrate in this book

There are those who think that making a trek in the Dolomites without having a go at a via ferrata is akin to visiting the Tower of London and not bothering to see the Crown Jewels. Certainly a via ferrata provides a fresh and invigorating challenge, and a tremendous sense of achievement at the end of it.

Vie ferrate in this book (cont)

Most of the vie ferrate in this book are little more than assisted walks. On the west-east route, however, we have included detailed descriptions of two vie ferrate trails. The first, the **Sentiero Bonacossa**, is a fairly simple trail and provides a perfect introduction to the world of via ferrate.

The second trail, on the **Croda Rossa di Sesto**, is more challenging but should still be within the capabilities of those with a fair amount of mountain experience and a good head for heights. If you'd rather not try either trail, alternative paths have also been described in detail in this guide. There is also one advanced via ferrata on the AV2, a traverse of the western face of the Marmolada, though again this can be avoided and alternative paths have been described in this book.

Equipment

For assisted trails, some people don't bother with any special equipment and most get by with no more than a **3.5m-length of rope** and a couple of **karabiners**. The rope and karabiners can be bought in any sports shop in the Dolomites, and together should cost you no more than L50,000. This rope is wrapped securely twice round the waist and then knotted at the front. The two karabiners are then attached to the two ends of the rope, which should each be approximately 75cm long (or one arm's length). Once again, make sure the knot is secure. If you are in doubt about what to do, ask the shop assistant to show you. When trekking, these karabiners can be clipped to a metal handrail or the rung of a ladder to ensure that, should you slip, you won't fall off the side of a mountain. This may sound obvious but it is essential to always have at least one karabiner attached to the rail or ladder, especially when moving from one handrail to another.

For proper vie ferrate, as well as the rope and karabiners, you will need a **chest** or **seat harness**, a **helmet** and a **kinetic impact shock absorber**. I also strongly recommend bringing along a pair of tough **leather gloves**, to protect you from frayed wires. For those who wish to tackle the via ferrata on the Marmolada, **crampons** and an **ice pick** are also advisable. Camping shops in the Dolomites sell **complete via ferrata kits** (excluding gloves, ice picks and crampons) for about L150,000-200,000.

Safety

A few simple rules concerning safety when tackling vie ferrate:
● Never tackle a via ferrata without the appropriate safety equipment (harness, ropes etc.).
● If possible, never try to tackle a via ferrata by yourself. Or at the very least always make sure there's somebody within shouting distance when tackling a via ferrata.
● Always test the stability and strength of the cables, pegs etc. before attempting to put your whole weight upon them.
● Only one person should be on a fixed cable at any one time.

ROUTE MARKINGS

Generally speaking, the paths of the Dolomites are very well signposted and the waymarkings are clear and frequent; the responsibility for maintaining the paths falls to the local branch of the CAI and by and large they do a good job. Most trails are marked either with a simple painted **red stripe**, or a **red-white-red 'flag'** painted on nearby trees or rocks. In addition, the alte vie also have triangular markings, with the number of the alta via painted in the middle of the triangle.

Other waymarkings include **wooden stakes** or poles, and **cairns** (piles of stones). Both of these are usually found on higher ground, where the chance of fog is pretty high and normal waymarkings would not be sufficiently visible.

What to take

When packing, you need to strike the right balance between safety and comfort. On the one hand, you'll want to bring a reasonable supply of clothing and other essentials to keep warm and safe; on the other, you'll need to remember that traipsing around the Dolomites with an over-heavy rucksack is no fun whatsoever. Once you've packed, you should practise wearing your full rucksack around the house for a little while to ensure that you're comfortable with it.

As far as **rucksacks** go, everybody has their own preference. Just make sure that yours feels comfortable and is robust. If it's waterproof too, so much the better (though you can buy special waterproof rucksack covers fairly cheaply in camping shops). If you're going to attempt one of the shorter routes only, a 40-litre rucksack or daypack should prove adequate. If you're planning to tackle one of the longer trails, however, a 65- to 75-litre rucksack will be necessary. Those who plan to camp, of course, will need a bigger rucksack still. Try to get a rucksack with external **side pockets**, in which you can store your water bottle, camera and other items that you may need on the trail.

To keep your valuables safe, a waterproof **moneybelt** is essential. In it you can keep your **flight tickets**, **insurance policy**, **cash**, **travellers' cheques**, **credit cards** and any **membership cards** (a CAI card for example) that you may have. A **map holder**, a clear plastic wallet worn around the neck, is also a sensible idea, but bear in mind that you don't want too much hanging from you as there will be occasions when you'll need both hands free for climbing or scrambling; keep the number of luggage items you take to a minimum.

A **sleeping bag** is essential as rifugi owners insist you use one to prevent their sheets from getting dirty. The rifugi do provide blankets, however, so unless you're camping, a simple **sheet sleeping bag** will prove adequate. These can be bought in camping stores or in some of the larger rifugi. Alternatively, you can make one yourself by folding a sheet in half lengthwise and sewing up the bottom and the side.

BOOTS

The condition of your feet will have a direct effect on your enjoyment of the trek. What you need is a pair of boots that will support your **feet** properly and keep them dry and blister-free. If you're buying new boots do so well before you leave to allow time to wear them in. Walking with blisters is no fun and could even become so uncomfortable that you are forced to give up your trek.

Choosing boots

Many people get by in just a pair of trainers but this is not recommended especially if you're carrying a pack. Apart from the risk of twisting your ankle trainers cannot keep your feet dry if it rains. Choose boots that offer **good ankle support**. They needn't be heavy; there's a wide range of modern boots. A top-quality leather boot treated to make it water resistant is often better than a Gore-tex or Sympatex boot. Ensure that there is enough room around the toes for steep descents.

CLOTHING

Items of clothing that you wouldn't be seen dead in on the streets of your home town – knee-length corduroy dungarees, felt hats with feathers in the brim, jackets and trousers of violent hues – are positively de rigueur in the mountains of central Europe. Whatever your dress sense, take at least one lurid item of clothing: should the unthinkable happen, the rescue services will find it easier to spot you if you're wearing something bright.

For most of your time on the trail, you'll need to wear nothing more than a **T-shirt, shorts, boots, socks** and a **sunhat**. Shirts with collars protect your neck; bring several of these and of T-shirts. If it's cold adopt the layered look and peel them off one by one as the temperature rises. Most important is a set of **waterproofs**. Some people opt for a completely waterproof outfit, including trousers, though this isn't absolutely necessary. A healthy supply of socks is essential, however, preferably wool or cotton. Always keep one set of clothes (ideally a pair of long **trousers, socks** and a jumper or **fleece)** dry and separate from your trekking gear, so you can change into them in the evenings; keep them in a plastic bag. A second pair of shoes, **sandals** or **slippers** which aren't too heavy, is also useful for wearing inside the rifugi, where trekking boots are banned.

Toiletries to consider include **soap/shampoo**, **razors**, **tampons**, **toothbrush** and **toothpaste** and a **light towel**. **Lip balm, sun block** or high UV factor **sun cream** are very important; check the UV factor with your pharmacist. **Toilet roll** is usually supplied by the rifugi, but you may wish to carry some of your own just in case. If you're using loo paper on the trail, remember to burn or bury it afterwards.

A basic **medical kit** should contain **plasters**, **antiseptic** and a knee or **ankle stocking** ('tubigrip') to support aching joints. Take a sufficient supply of any prescribed medicines and **paracetamol** for headaches and **aspirin** for inflammation of the joints; both can be used as general painkillers.

Other **essential equipment** includes a **torch**, some **spare batteries** for both your camera and your torch, a **pen knife**, a **watch**, a **compass**, **maps**, **guidebook**, **sunglasses**, some **comfort food** (chocolate or peanuts for example), **tea bags/coffee**, a **sewing kit**, **matches**, a loud **whistle**, a ball of **string** and a **water bottle**. Bin bags are useful too, to keep your clothes dry during a heavy storm and to keep wet clothes separate from the rest of your gear.

Most (European) trekkers also bring a set of **ski poles** or a walking stick, and these will certainly help to alleviate the strain on your knees.

Non-essential items you may wish to consider include a **pack of cards**, a **diary** or **address book**, a **book**, fiction or non-fiction, and a universal **bath plug**.

CAMPING EQUIPMENT

Because camping is illegal in large areas of the Dolomites, camping equipment can be a little hard to come by in the region and you'll probably have to bring most of your gear from home.

Tents should be lightweight but sturdy. If you're travelling by yourself, a bivvy bag may be a better idea. A **three-season sleeping bag** – or, at least, two-season plus **thermal mat** – is essential. See p53 for more information.

You will also have to bring **cooking equipment** (**pans** and a **stove**) with you. Some of the camping shops in the valley towns have **gas cylinders**, and these are indicated in the guide section of this book.

MONEY AND CARDS

In nearly every town and village, large and small, you'll find at least one bank with an **ATM** (also known as a cash dispenser or cashpoint), enabling Visa, MasterCard, Cirrus, Maestro, Eurocard and EuroCheque cardholders to withdraw Italian currency directly from their home bank account. The banks usually charge a small fee for this service but, to compensate, their current exchange rates are often superior to all others. Rather than using a credit card in the ATM, use your bank card (debit/cheque guarantee card) which will probably have one of the electronic money symbols (Cirrus, Maestro etc.) shown on it; with a credit card you'll get a cash advance on your credit card account but may have to pay interest on this money.

You may find one ATM rejects your card, even though it displays the appropriate symbol; try your card at other ATM machines before deciding that it's your card that's faulty. If you have no pin number, you can obtain a cash advance over the counter in many banks; take along your passport, hand over the card and, for a similar fee to an ATM withdrawal, the money is yours.

Carrying a small plastic card around the mountains is also a lot less troublesome than a large wad of travellers' cheques or foreign cash. That said, you should have a small supply of **travellers' cheques** and foreign bills too, in case your card is for some reason unacceptable in the Dolomites. Travellers' cheques in Italian lire or euros attract no commission charges, and most of the big name brands – American Express, Thomas Cook, Visa – are widely accepted. Always keep an up-to-date record of the cheques that you have already cashed, which will come in useful if you should lose your remaining cheques. When purchasing them, buy the majority in large denominations; this will save you commission fees, which are charged per cheque.

The most popular **foreign currencies** are the German mark and the Austrian schilling, which can be changed at the banks and post offices. Note that from January 2002, in Italy, Germany, Austria and eight other European countries not including Britain local currencies such as the lira, deutschmark or Austrian schilling will be replaced by the euro and cease to be legal tender in July 2002. For the rates of exchange at the time of printing, see p56.

Carrying money on the trail
The most important thing to remember about carrying money on the trail is that you should plan ahead and **make sure that you have enough cash**

❏ **Lost cards or travellers' cheques**
Should your travellers' cheques or credit cards become lost or stolen, the phone numbers in Italy of the major companies are as follows:
Visa ☎ 167-82-1001
Amex ☎ 167-87-2000 (toll free)
MasterCard ☎ 167-86-8086
In addition, you can call ☎ 167-82-2056 to have any card blocked.

(lire or euros) for your trek before you set off. On the Alta Via 2, for example, banks, post offices and ATMs can only be found at the beginning and end of the trail in Bressanone and Feltre. Rifugi will accept only local currency, hardly any accept credit cards and few if any will change money for you, so should you run out you'll have to walk down to the nearest pass and catch a bus to the nearest bank or post office.

Remember, too, that smaller bills are better: some of the less frequented rifugi may not have the necessary change to deal with L100,000 notes; if you can break up your big notes in town before setting off you'll make things easier for yourself on the trail.

PHOTOGRAPHIC EQUIPMENT

Film is readily available in the towns and villages of the Dolomites, and even in some of the rifugi. If, however, you have a particular preference for a certain brand or type of film, particularly slide film which is a little harder to come by, bring your own supply from home.

There is plenty of light in the Dolomites, so 100 or 200ASA film should be fine. A **polarizing filter** is also a good investment as it brings out the rich colours of the Dolomite rocks. Bring **spare camera batteries**, too; many of the newer fully-automated cameras pack up completely when the batteries are dead.

RECOMMENDED READING

Guidebooks

The American publishers, Black, produce *The Dolomites of Italy – A Travel Guide*. Written by an American couple, James and Anne Goldsmith, their love of the Dolomites shines through in the writing, and though of dubious practical use, for a general overview of the region this is the best book available in English.

Cicerone Press currently publishes a number of walking guidebooks to the region. Rough Guides and Lonely Planet publish useful general guides to Italy.

Literature

Most of the best books about the region were written in the latter half of the last century, and many, such as mountaineer John Ball's *Guide to the Eastern Alps* (1868), Gilbert and Churchill's *The Dolomite Mountains* (1864) and Amelia Edwards *Untrodden peaks and unfrequented valleys* (1873), are now out of print. You may be lucky enough to track down copies in a secondhand bookstore, but the chances are you'll probably have to go through a book dealer, and pay a vast sum for them too.

MAPS

The Italian cartographers **Tabacco** provide the most extensive coverage of the Dolomites. Maps can be picked up fairly easily in the region for about L10,000 (rising to L13,000 in some of the rifugi). Though the 1:50,000 scale maps provide reasonable coverage of a wide area, the 1:25,000 maps are far more detailed and, for trekking at least, more useful. The trails on Tabacco maps are marked by a red line. If the line is made up of a series of dashes, the trail is not always clear. Similarly, if the trail is marked by a line of red dots, the trail can be uncertain or difficult to follow. I found the distinction between the trails not always accurate. All vie ferrate routes are marked with a series of red crosses, but the cartographers make no distinction between an aided walk (one where a metal handrail has been strung along the path for safety reasons which makes the route completely undemanding) and a proper via ferrata where some expertise is necessary. In my trail maps I have clarified these situations.

Tabacco maps aren't infallible and some are rather out of date but they're very detailed and easy to follow. In this guide you'll find the relevant Tabacco map number for each walk given below the stage heading in the text. Usually I found most trails easy to follow though that may be because I tend to trek towards the end of the season, when all of the trails have been well 'trodden-in' after three months of heavy use by trekkers.

Other map publishers include **Kompass**, who produce the *Wanderkarte* series, and the **Touring Club Alpino's** *Carte delle Zone Turistiche d'Italia*. Both of these are drawn to a 1:50,000 scale.

To find out which Tabacco maps relate to which trail, see p65 for the West-East route, and p153 for Alta Via 2.

Mountain safety

WEATHER AND EQUIPMENT

Your greatest enemy in the mountains is the climate. While you may be walking in searing sunshine during the day, by nightfall the temperature at altitude drops sharply. For this reason, always carry a set of warm clothes, including a **fleece or jumper** and **thermal underwear**. It is imperative that this set of warm clothing is kept dry: when it comes to maintaining body temperature, wet clothes are harmful. Keep this **set of dry clothes** in a plastic bag to protect them from rain while you are out on the trail and change into them in the evenings; don't wear them while trekking. Wet clothes can be dried by knotting them to the outside of your rucksack on a warm day; this will also prevent them from smelling musty.

Before leaving home, it's a good idea to try to conduct a little 'trekking training'. This will not only improve your stamina and fitness but will also allow you gauge your limits before you reach the mountains. Once you've reached the Dolomites, when on the trek, **never go alone**, particularly if you're planning to follow a less-popular path. Other precautions include: check on the **weather forecast** before you set out and adjust your plans accordingly; don't stray from the established trails; carry some **emergency food supplies** with you; wear at least one item of **brightly-coloured clothing**; ensure that your destination **rifugio is open**, particularly if you're trekking at the end of the season when many rifugi begin to close for the winter; before you set out on a section of the trail, check with the nearest rifugio or tourist office that the **path is in good condition**; never attempt a via ferrata without the **proper equipment**; and always carry a **whistle and torch** to summon help should you fall from the trail.

Furthermore, I advise everybody to **begin their trek early** in the morning. Not only are the mountains at their quietest and most beautiful at this time but you are giving yourself more hours of daylight to play with later in the day; this could come in useful if you get into any sort of trouble.

In **bad weather**, should you get caught in a thunderstorm don't stand near anything metal and remove all metallic objects from your person. Don't shelter under trees; just curl up on the ground to minimize the risk of attracting lightning. If instead heavy fog descends and you have the time, don't try to follow the path but stay where you are and wait for it to clear. If time is pressing, summon help by following the procedures outlined below.

EMERGENCY PROCEDURES

There is a standard procedure to be followed should you get into trouble on the trail. Firstly, to summon help, the **international distress signal** is a series of **six short sharp blasts on a whistle**. This should be repeated after a minute's pause. If you don't have a whistle, any audible signal (such as shouting) will suffice. If you are out of earshot, give a visible signal instead e.g. by waving a brightly-coloured garment; again, repeat this signal six times, pause for a minute, then repeat.

(Opposite) Superbly located between the southern slopes of the Alpe di Siusi and the Catinaccio range, the isolated Rifugio Alpe di Tires (see p79) stands at an altitude of 2440m.

Remember that if you hear or see a distress signal, **it is your duty to report it** to the nearest rifugio as soon as possible; prompt action could save lives.

INFORMATION AND RESCUE SERVICES

The local **tourist offices** are a mine of information. They'll be able to tell you the state of the local trails, the rifugi that are open and even the day's weather forecast, which is often printed out and displayed in the window. Most of them speak English too! Up in the mountains, the rifugi perform the same sort of service to a greater or lesser degree.

Rescue services

There are a number of rescue services operating in the Dolomites. Be warned, however, that these services are not free, and the cost of calling out a helicopter runs into many thousands of pounds. You'll need to make sure your insurance policy covers this before you set out (see p19 for further details).

Emergency phone numbers

In Italy, dial ☎ 118 to be put through to the emergency services, including the police, fire, ambulance and helicopter rescue services. For the helicopter rescue service Aiut Alpin Dolomites, dial ☎ 0471-797171. This will be a little quicker and more direct than dialling the general emergency number. There are also several local helicopter services in almost every valley. The local tourist office can supply you with information regarding services and telephone numbers.

Health precautions

POSSIBLE PROBLEMS

Providing you're reasonably fit, the mountains of the Dolomites shouldn't cause many problems health-wise. The region simply isn't high enough actually to cause altitude sickness. Thus your main concern will be the weather: too cold, and you risk hypothermia; too hot, and you may well suffer from dehydration or a touch of sunstroke particularly at high altitudes where the sun can be fierce. Both are easily avoidable: **always**

(Opposite) Cortina d'Ampezzo (see p112), the most glamorous town in the Dolomites, with Monte Cristallo to the north-east.

carry plenty of water with you on the trail, wear a sunhat and sunglasses, use sunblock and you'll prevent all heat-related problems. As to hypothermia, it's simply a case of bringing enough warm clothing and making sure at least one set of clothes remains dry throughout your trek.

The other problems frequently encountered by trekkers tend to be **stomach complaints**. Tap water in Italy is safe to drink, though simply the switch to Italian water from what you're used to may cause you to feel unwell for a day or two. Furthermore, some of the rifugi have their own water source which isn't potable. Signs ('*acqua non potabile*') are usually placed in the bathrooms if this is the case, though it always pays to ask before refilling your water bottle from the rifugio tap.

Even water from a mountain stream, as clear and sparkly as it may look, may be contaminated if there are herds of cows or sheep grazing upstream. Spring water taken directly from source at the side of the mountain should be OK, but otherwise it probably pays to **purify** the water first, either by boiling it, filtering it or adding a few drops of a chlorine- or iodine-based purifier. (Be warned, however, that over-imbibing chemically purified water brings with it a whole raft of other health problems.)

For details on health insurance, and the level of health care offered to EU citizens in Italy, see p19.

PART 2: THE DOLOMITES

Facts about the Dolomites

GEOGRAPHICAL BACKGROUND

As a central part of the 1200km-long alpine crescent sweeping through Europe from the French Côte d'Azur to the Balkans, the Dolomites form the eastern section and the most spectacular part of the Italian Alps. There are 14 major massifs in the Dolomites of 3000m or more, including the **Marmolada**, the highest point in the Dolomites at 3343m, the fortress-like **Sella** and **Pale di San Martino massifs** (whose highest points are 3152m and 3186m respectively), the World War I battlefields of the **Tofane** (3244m), the neighbouring summits of the **Cristallo** (3221m) and **Croda Rossa** (3146m), and the weird rock formations of the **Lavaredo** (whose highest point, officially speaking, actually only reaches 2999m).

With one exception, these mountains all lie within a loose 9000 sq km parallelogram, bounded (even more loosely) by the Valle Isarco in the north-west, the Val Pusteria and Val di Sesto in the north-east, the Piave River to the south-east and the Trento—Feltre road to the south-west. I have concentrated mainly on this area but at the end of the book have included a chapter describing a two-day trek in the isolated 800km-sq **Brenta group**, a via ferrata paradise that lies to the west of the Adige Valley.

The Dolomites are politically divided into three provinces: Bolzano, Trento and Belluno. While the southern provinces of Trento and Belluno are distinctly Italian in flavour, the province of Bolzano, also known as the Alto Adige or South Tyrol (Südtirol) was until 1918 part of the Austro-Hungarian Empire and the majority of the population still speak German rather than Italian (see the People section on p44). It is an autonomous region with special provisions designed to balance the power and influence of German and Italian speakers in proportion to their population.

GEOLOGY

In common with the rest of the European Alps, the Dolomites were formed approximately 60 million years ago during the **Cretaceous Period**, when the continent of Africa slammed into the continent of

Europe. Central and Southern Europe buckled and crumpled under such an impact, and large swathes of land were pushed high into the air: such was the birth of Europe's mountain ranges.

Where the Dolomites differ from the rest of Europe, however, is in the type of rock from which they are formed. Or rather, *rocks*: the Dolomites may share their name with a mineral but it would be wrong to assume that the mountains are made exclusively from dolomitic rock. Much of the rock is **volcanic** rather than dolomitic, and even the mighty Marmolada, the biggest mountain of them all, is composed of plain old **limestone** rather than dolomite rock. Indeed to begin with the entire Dolomite area was limestone, the dolomitization process only occurring much later on.

In order to examine the various rock types in the Dolomites it is necessary first to go back even further in time to the **Middle Triassic Period**, some 230 million years ago. At this time, the area we now call the Dolomites lay largely under a warm tropical sea separating Europe from Africa. And as with all tropical seas, coral and other invertebrate marine life thrived in the warm waters. The evidence for this is scattered all over the western Dolomites in the form of fossils embedded in the rocks and cliffs. There may have been some tiny tropical islands just breaking the surface of this sea as well: islands that would eventually grow to become the mountains of the western Dolomites such the Marmolada, Catinaccio and Pale di San Martino. Many of these 'underwater mountains' were composed largely from the first dolomitic rock, known as the **Sciliar Dolomite**, which began to form at this time, overlaying older rocks such as gypsum, sandstone, limestone and at the very base a series of quartz porphyries.

The other major geological events of the Middle Triassic Period were the **eruption of two huge volcanoes** just to the west of the Dolomites, which filled much of this tropical sea with lava. This lava petrified over the course of time, and the resulting dark brown rock can still be seen on the Alpe di Siusi and in the Val Gardena. The volcanic rock also covered the nascent Marmolada and Latemar peaks, which is possibly one reason why these massifs were not subjected to the dolomitization process, unlike their more-exposed neighbours.

Towards the end of the Triassic era (approximately 200 million years ago) the region, now one huge **tidal-flat**, started to accumulate layer upon layer of a new dolomitic rock. This rock, *Dolomia principale*, is more visible in the central and eastern Dolomites: the Tofane, Cristallo, Marmarole and the Tre Cime di Lavaredo are all largely formed from *Dolomia principale*. This rock also overlaid the existing *Sciliar Dolomite* prevalent in the western Dolomites, and today forms the upper layer of the Sella Massif, the Sciliar Plateau and other groups in the western Dolomites.

For the next 150 million years things remained, geologically speaking, quiescent. With every passing year, however, the continent of Africa was inching towards Europe. When it finally collided, during the Tertiary Period, the marine rocks that lay between them were pushed up and the Dolomites were born.

However, not all of the Dolomite region reacted in the same way. The **Western Dolomites**, or Occidentali, thanks to their underlying strata of tough porphyries, didn't really buckle to a great extent and were lifted up as a single, uncrumpled unit. The **eastern mountains**, or Orientali, however, had no such bumper to protect them and so crumpled and folded, which is why they appear more jagged, with many isolated peaks, whereas the western ranges tend to be more uniform, or 'square' in shape. Since their formation, of course, the mountains have been sculpted by the elements – the wind and rain, the rivers and glaciers and so on – to form the spectacular Dolomite range we see today.

CLIMATE

The Dolomites suffer from a typically **variable** Alpine climate. There are few certainties about the weather here save that the winters will be long and often brutal and the summers short and punctuated by frequent downpours. Very frequent downpours. Locals claim that they receive less precipitation than the alpine regions of Austria, Switzerland and France, though this will be small comfort as you squelch and slip along the muddy Dolomite paths with your boots overflowing, your clothes all heavy and waterlogged, and with little droplets of rain using your nose as a ski-jump. Come prepared for these sorts of conditions, bring adequate wet-weather gear and make sure your boots are sufficiently waterproof.

August is probably the soggiest month of them all, and certainly the one with the most spectacular **thunderstorms**. September and October are more settled, though a little chillier too, and the days are shorter (Italians gain an hour through daylight-saving in September). By November the first snow has often fallen, and by January it's falling fairly regularly, a situation that lasts up until March, which is the main reason why these mountains are so popular with skiers.

Of course with such varied terrain there are regional differences. The southern Dolomites, in particular the **Feltrini**, gets frequent mist and rain sweeping up from the Venetian Plain. Conversely, the northern Dolomites tend to be rather drier because much of the precipitation travelling from the south-west has already fallen by the time it reaches these areas. It is also true that the mornings tend to be a lot drier and clearer than the afternoons, and trekkers who can drag themselves onto the trail by seven o'clock will reap the benefits in terms of quieter trails and better views.

The most important thing to remember about the weather in any mountain range, however, is that there are very few hard-and-fast rules that cover the entire area. Microclimates make the weather picture so much more complex than the over-simplified version given above. It is therefore vitally important that you **check with your rifugio** before heading off on the trail.

For further advice about dealing with the climate in the Dolomites, see p31.

HISTORICAL OUTLINE

Probably the most important and traumatic event in the history of these glorious mountains occurred in the last century. The Great War of 1914-18 not only changed the nationality of much of the region and its inhabitants but it also changed the shape of the very mountains themselves as both sides detonated huge explosives in the futile hope of blasting the opposition out of the area. Certainly when it comes to archaeological evidence, the 'War to end all wars' has no peers in the Dolomites: tunnels, barracks, barbed wire, pathways, supply routes and equipment from the period still lie scattered hereabouts today, as well as a number of monuments to those who perished, many of which stand in isolated, remote locations far from any trails.

The history of the Dolomites, however, doesn't begin and end with WWI. Man first arrived in the region at least 10,000 years ago and has been fighting, negotiating, trading, climbing and exploring in the Dolomites ever since.

Prehistory – the Mesolithic, Neolithic and Bronze Ages

Though the valleys of the Dolomites are today covered with a neat patchwork of cultivated land, the first humans to make the Dolomites their home would have had little idea about farming techniques and animal rearing, surviving instead on the plentiful game found grazing on the lower slopes of the mountains, a diet supplemented with fruit and vegetables foraged from the forests. Scant evidence remains, of course, of this era, though enough has survived – stone tools, simple burial sites and so on – to convince archaeologists of stone age man's presence in these mountains. Much of this evidence now lies behind glass in the local museums, though there is also a set of **Neolithic stone slabs** near Waldrühe in the Val di Sesto which you can visit if you plan to take the west-east route.

Later, from about 5000BC, small settlements began to appear in the valleys surrounding the Dolomites. But as yet no evidence has been unearthed to suggest that villages were also being established within the mountain valleys themselves, at least not until around 1800BC and the advent of the **Bronze Age**. The Dagger of Balest, now housed in the Val Gardena Local Heritage Museum in Ortisèi, is one of the more impressive finds from this era. The **first paths**, such as the Troi Paian in the Val Gardena, also began to appear at this time, linking these settlements together.

The Roman Empire

While things remained relatively peaceful in the mountains during the first half of the first millennium BC, to the south monumental events were occurring. The **Etruscans**, twelfth-century BC migrants to the Italian peninsula from Greece and the Near East, were approaching the peak of their power. Under them a number of large city states were being founded, including Felsina (modern-day Bologna) and Perusia (Perugia).

In the sixth century BC, however, the Etruscans fell as quickly as they had risen. A coalition of Italian city states rebelled against the despotic ruling Etruscan dynasty, the Tarquins, and having failed to develop more modern weapons, the Etruscan Empire quickly succumbed in 505BC. In its stead, the **Roman Republic**, established in 509BC in a city founded, according to tradition, over 200 years previously by the Etruscan brothers Romulus and Remus, began to take charge of the peninsula. Having defeated the Gauls, Carthaginians, and an internal revolt led by a Thracian slave named **Spartacus**, Rome had successfully consolidated the frontiers of its empire by the beginning of the first century BC. One of these frontiers was defined by the Dolomites, which the Romans initially decided to exclude from their empire, stationing border guards along the mountains' southern extremities instead. It is believed that the **Ladin language**, a combination of the colloquial Latin spoken by these border guards, the Celtic language spoken to the north and west of the Dolomites by settlers who had invaded during the Iron Age (c700BC), and the native mountain tongue, was developed at this time. Under **Emperor Augustus**, Rome soon expanded its borders northwards, bringing the Dolomites under Roman control for the first time in 15BC. Two of his stepsons **Drusus**, and **Tiberius** who succeeded Augustus in AD14, led the legions in the conquest.

The Barbarians and Lombards

As the Roman Empire began its slow, inexorable decline following the movement of its main capital to Constantinople (AD324) and its division into two separate halves (AD364), a series of tribes based in central and northern Europe decided that the time was right to invade the Italian peninsula. Beginning with **Attila the Hun** in AD452, Barbarian armies from the north, including the Gothic invaders led by **Odovacar** (who deposed the last Western Roman Emperor in AD476) and the **Ostrogoths**, who in AD488 set up their own empire based in Ravenna, took turns in picking over the carcass of the Roman Empire. The Dolomites, as is so often the case, were largely ignored by these tribes.

Then, around 568, the **Lombards** attacked the peninsula, establishing Trento (just to the east of the Brenta Dolomites) as a duchy and claiming large chunks of the Dolomites as their own. During their reign, large parts of the northern and western Dolomites were being settled by migrants from Bavaria, changing the character of these areas forever by introducing a pervasive Germanic influence. A century later, in 774, the **Franks** under King Pepin and later his son, the charismatic **Charlemagne**, successfully subsumed the entire Italian peninsula, the Dolomites included, under their control as part of the **Carolingian Empire**.

Charlemagne's empire was to last less than 70 years, crumbling soon after his death in 814. To end the internecine squabbling that took place between the pretenders to Charlemagne's throne, the **Treaty of Verdun**, signed between the various factions in 843, split the Dolomites between Italy and Germany. They were to remain divided for almost one thousand years.

Episcopal principalities

By the eleventh century the Dolomites had been further subdivided amongst the Bishoprics of the nearby valleys. The last of the Carolingians, **Ludwig the Child**, donated the Court of Prischna, near Bressanone, to Bishop Zacharias in 901, thereby setting a trend amongst powerful landowners of giving parts of their territory to the church. Emperor Conrad II followed suit a century later, granting to the Bishop of Trento the land around Bolzano, The emperors' reasons for doing so had little to do with piety, however: they were merely interested in securing a safe passage between their capital at Trento and their dominions, and giving the local bishops temporal jurisdiction over large areas of land was a simple, cost-effective way of securing such routes.

Eventually, by the twelfth century, the Bishoprics of Trento and Bressanone had been given jurisdiction over much of the South Tyrol, while those of Feltre and Aquielia had divided the southern and eastern mountains between themselves. Though the **Counts of Tyrol**, rulers of petty counties in northern Tyrol, captured some of this territory for themselves, the bishoprics survived in one form or another and under a number of different rulers for the next 800 years.

The Hapsburg Empire and the Venetian Republic

On the death in 1363 of Margaret Maultasch, the Ugly Duchess, the last of the Tyrolean rulers, the neighbouring Hapsburg dynasty received the bulk of their territory. The County of Tyrol thus became one of the first acquisitions of the then fledgling **Hapsburg Empire**.

The Hapsburgs weren't the only ones with an interest in the Dolomites, however: the glorious **Republic of Venice** was beginning to expand northwards too, and in 1420 took the Piave basin and the Cadore region up to and including the town of Cortina. This absorption of virtually all of the south-eastern quarter of the Dolomites began a prolonged period of hostilities between the two empires.

This internecine battling came to an end with the arrival of a third force in 1796 under **Napoleon Bonaparte**, the future emperor of France. The entire Italian peninsula eventually fell under his sway, and by 1808 Napoleon established the **Kingdom of Italy**, naming himself as king but ruling through his viceroy, his stepson, Eugène de Beauharnais. Napoleon's success in Italy was in part due to his use of disciplined **Bavarian troops** to conquer the mountainous north and so he, negotiating the **Treaty of Pressburg** in 1805, rewarded their country by giving Bavaria the entire Tyrol including all of the Dolomites.

For the first time since Charlemagne the Dolomites were united under a single ruler. It didn't last for long. Though the Tyroleans' efforts at rebelling against Bavarian rule in 1809 under **Andreas Höfer** proved to be in vain, just one year later Napoleon, already disillusioned with his ally, Maximilian I of Bavaria, took the South Tyrol back and attached it to his Kingdom of Italy. The Tyrol remained divided until 1815 and the Battle of Waterloo. In the **Congress of Vienna** that followed, Austria assumed complete control over the entire Tyrol, and maintained it for the next one hundred years, the only blip occurring in 1866 when the Cadore region broke away with Venice to join the newly established independent Kingdom of Italy, formed just five years previously. For the rest of the century the borders remained unchanged.

The beginnings of tourism and the early explorers

Tourism really took off in the nineteenth century. This was the era of the Grand Tour, when it became the fashion among well-to-do travellers from Britain and northern Europe to visit Italy, the home as they saw it of Western Civilization. The Dolomites initially featured in few of their itineraries. After all, much of the northern Dolomites, excluding the Cadore, were still part of Austria at this time. Furthermore, ignorance of the Dolomites was widespread. As **Amelia Edwards**, one of the first travellers to the region, notes:

Even now, the general public is so slightly informed upon the subject that it is by no means uncommon to find educated persons who have never heard of the Dolomites at all, or who take them for a religious sect, like the Mormons or Druses.

Yet those who did venture to this wild alpine region were captivated by what they found, and as these tourists returned home with tales of an untamed and unexplored area, more and more chose to follow in their wake. Among them were a number of mountaineers, amazed that there should be such a concentration of unconquered peaks left in Europe. Thus began the golden age of **climbing** in the Dolomites, a time when many of the loftier peaks, including the Marmolada (conquered in the 1860s by **Paul Grohmann**) were scaled for the first time. The British climber, **John Ball**, explorers Amelia Edwards and FF Tuckett and the travelling geologists, GC Churchill and J Gilbert, all visited the area at this time, recording their experiences in best-selling travelogues. Tourism received a further boost when a **railway** was constructed over the Brenner Pass; the first **ski pistes** were established too, and for the rest of the nineteenth century the Dolomites enjoyed a level of prosperity that it had never known before.

Unfortunately, events and decisions taken in Rome and Vienna in the second decade of the twentieth century soon brought an end to this golden age.

World War I

The war years began peacefully enough for the Dolomites. The Italians initially dithered about whether to join in the fray, and as a result all was quiet on Austria's southern front for the first year or so. Then, on 23 May 1915, Italy decided to join the Allied forces of France, Britain and Russia against the German-Austrian axis.

Suddenly the Dolomites, split by the Italian-Austrian border which ran diagonally from south-west to north-east right through the heart of the mountains, became the focus of extensive military campaigns from both sides. The Italians were keen to push north to sever the Austrian rail links lying to the north of the Dolomites. Having already expended tens of thousands of troops on the Russian campaign, the Austrians decided that an attempt to defend the border as it stood at that time would be futile, indeed tantamount to suicide, for in many places the border ran through highly vulnerable valleys and indefensible mountain passes. But nor were they willing to let the Italians attack the rail links. The Austrians therefore decided a **partial retreat** was in order, and positioned themselves up in the mountains immediately behind the old border.

The map of Europe had changed at a stroke, and Cortina was just one of many towns that found themselves in a different country as the Italians took control of the land the Austrians left behind. From then on the war became one of attrition as each side attempted to manoeuvre itself into superior positions, which often meant climbing to the summit of the nearby mountain and staying there. Ingenious ways of shifting the opposition from these lofty perches were designed and implemented, including the use of **tunnels** as a means of getting near to the enemy in relative safety. Examples of these tunnels can still be seen near the Lagazuoi summit, west of Cortina (see p110), and next to the Locatelli rifugio near the Tre Cime (see p105). Mines and explosives were detonated with gay abandon as each side became more desperate to obtain a breakthrough. The mountains became scarred with the blasts, their features altered forever. The climate became an important and potentially deadly factor too, particularly in the winter of 1916 when the Dolomites suffered its most inclement weather for decades: at least 10,000 men lost their lives to **avalanches** alone in that year.

The fighting was to continue for four years, with neither side emerging victorious. In the end, the destiny of the Dolomites was decided not by bullets and barbed wire but by negotiations: one year after the fighting had ceased, the Dolomites were handed over to Italy following the **Treaty of Germain** in 1919.

Even today, almost 90 years after the fighting has ceased, it isn't hard to find evidence of the battles that were fought here. Apart from the tunnels, caves and barracks still pit the mountainsides, particularly around *Rifugio Auronzo* and on the Croda Rossa di Sesto. A few rifugi have used the WWI debris they have found, lamps, boots, bullets, pistols, as decorations that now hang from their walls. Many of the modern trekking trails are merely old WWI supply paths, and several of these are named after local heroes who fought in the war. Furthermore, the scars left by the huge explosive devices detonated by both sides, such as at Piccolo Lagazuoi (scene of some of the biggest explosions, including one that left a crater on the summit 136m in diameter and over 200m deep), the Croda Rossa di Sesto and the Col di Lana at the southern end of the Val Badia, are still clear for all to see. There's even an **open-air World War I museum** by *Rifugio Bosi* on the flat-topped Monte Piana. The summit of this peak was of crucial importance to both sides as the frontier ran right across its top. The renowned WWI historian, Walther Schaumann, has restored some of the trenches and buildings on the summit, and there are two WWI cannons still in position, as well as plenty of barbed wire. You can visit Monte Piana by taking the short trail described on p196.

Since World War I

By and large, since 1918 things have been pretty prosperous for the Dolomites. Though the fascist government of the 1930s under Mussolini attempted to force the inhabitants to speak Italian rather than their native Ladin/German tongues, they failed miserably, and whilst Germany occupied the entire area during World War II, the mountains mercifully never witnessed the kind of carnage seen 30 years earlier.

After the war, the Dolomites, wholly Italian-owned since 1919, (a fact confirmed by the Treaty of Paris in 1946), enjoyed something of a renaissance. Tourists began to flock back to the region, and the **Winter Olympics of 1956** were held in Cortina. The Ladin culture, for so many years in decline, also enjoyed something of a resurgence and Ladin pride has become the theme of many of their traditional carnivals. With its reputation as a venue for unparalleled skiing firmly established, and a similarly burgeoning reputation for its splendid trekking opportunities, the outlook for the people of the Dolomites remains as rosy as the mountains that surround them.

THE PEOPLE

The demographics of the Dolomites reflect its history, a history in which both the Italians and Austrians have, in one guise or another, taken turns in assuming power.

Though wholly under Italian ownership now, most of the people of the northern Dolomites speak **German** first, and their architecture, culture and cuisine are distinctly Tyrolean. According to a recent census, in the Alto-Adige region (which was part of Austria until 1918) just under 70 per cent of the population have German as their native tongue, as opposed to less than 30 per cent Italian speakers. Also living in this region are around 40,000 **Ladin** speakers (approximately four per cent of the population of Alto Adige) mainly inhabiting the valleys around the Sella Massif. The Ladins are the indigenous people of the Dolomites, and further details on their history, language and culture can be found at the end of this section.

Though Ladin and German speakers have been living side by side for centuries, each has generally kept itself to itself. As a result, the border between the German and Ladin speakers is well defined, and it is quite startling sometimes to find the people of one village speaking Ladin, while the next village just a few hundred metres away has German as its native tongue.

Slightly less clear-cut, however, is the divide between the Italian and German-speakers, for as one approaches the central plains of Italy the Italian tongue unsurprisingly takes over. For those of you planning to do the Alta Via 2, you'll notice the change between the two areas, the border between the two linguistic regions coming somewhere around the tiny **Monte Pradazzo**, which separates the Italian Passo di Valles from the more Teutonic Passo di San Pellegrino.

The Ladin people

The ignorance of these populations is beyond imagination. These good fellows are still in the state of nature described by Jean-Jaques (sic) Rousseau. They have never travelled outside their valleys and have no idea of the rest of the world. The savages of Central Africa are less dumbfounded at the sight of a stranger than these montagnards. **Jules Leclerc, *Le Tyrol et le Pays des Dolomites* (1880)**

With a population approaching just 40,000 and constituting less than five per cent of the population of Alto Adige, the Ladin people of the Dolomites are one of the smallest ethnic minorities in Europe. Famed for their imaginative legends and wood-carving skills, the Ladins live in the

high valleys radiating out from the hub of the **Sella Massif**, valleys such
as Val Gardena, Val Badia, Val di Fassa, Livinallongo and the Val
Ampezzo.

Originally, the Dolomite Ladins formed part of a much larger ethnic
group that also included Ladin speakers of Graubünden in Switzerland
(now known as the **Romansh**, or Swiss Ladins) and the **Friulian Ladins**
(or Furlans) that live in the rugged Austrian/Italian border region to the
east of the Dolomites. But as successive waves of German- and Italian-
speaking migrants passed over the mountains, and as the Ladins themselves migrated to different areas, the language, customs and traditions
evolved separately to the point where the three are now considered separate minorities.

The Grand Tour travellers of the nineteenth century who stopped by
in the Dolomites were on the whole uninterested in the people they found
there, regarding them as uneducated peasants unworthy of their attention.
Only the foreign mountaineers, who relied on the Ladins for their knowledge and skill as guides, had anything to do with them. Indeed, it wasn't
until the next century, as more and more tourists flocked to the region,
that the lifestyle and culture of these mountain folk – who know of the
Dolomites simply as *la crepes* ('the rocks') – were properly studied for
the first time.

Ladin Christianity and festivals

Little is known about the Christianization of the Dolomites, save that in
the early stages the faith struggled to gain a foothold in the mountains,
and many missionaries perished at the hands of the very people whose
souls they were trying to save. What we do know is that by the twelfth
century, all of the valleys had been converted and many churches and
monasteries had been established in the region.

Nevertheless, with Catholic Italy to the south and the Protestants of
the Reformation to the north and west, religious turbulence was never far
away. The continual resurfacing of traditional **pagan beliefs** was also a
problem for the church, and inquisitions against witches were a common
occurrence in the sixteenth century. Indeed, the Catholic church often
regarded the Dolomites as a den of iniquity, as this extract from a report
from 1573 about the region makes clear:

'.... in all classes, higher and lower, clerical and secular, any fear of God, any
Christian love, any honest conscience are almost extinct. Blasphemy, perjury, lux-
ury, drunkenness, gambling, murder, adultery, prostitution, the exploitation of
one's neighbour, envy, hatred and other such horrible vices increase daily as never
before ....' from **Ladins – People of the Dolomite**, Cesare Poppi

Clerical reports also mention that many of the priests serving in the
churches at this time weren't actually ordained, and many were simply
monks who had either deserted or been expelled from their monasteries.

As a result, many were ignorant in matters of religion. To combat the problem, in 1607, a **seminary** was founded in Bressanone to train the local priests, and Jesuit missionaries in the seventeenth and eighteenth centuries reinforced Catholicism's shaky influence in the Dolomites.

Today, the Dolomite Ladins are amongst the most fervent Catholics in Italy. Annual pilgrimages to holy shrines are a popular local activity and Lent is still strictly observed in some valleys, a throwback to previous centuries when self-denial became not only an act of religious piety but also a tactic for staving off famine as stocks dwindled at the end of the winter months.

Nevertheless, the biggest festivals in the Ladin calendar probably have their roots in the pre-Christian era. These are the annual **carnivals**, which celebrate the passing of winter and the coming of spring. During the carnival, men, usually the bachelors of the village, parade through the streets wearing grotesque masks, calling at each house in turn to perform a small pantomime or sketch. Though the carnival declined at the beginning of the twentieth century, it was later revived during the resurgence in Ladin pride that took place after World War II. Today, almost every Ladin town and village holds a carnival of sorts, though most have changed in nature and are now primarily a celebration of Ladin culture. Tourists are welcome to join in the fun in most cases, though in some villages tourists are actually banned from attending.

Ladin land ownership

With all the Dolomite Ladin villages located between 1000 and 1700m, cultivable land is at a premium: in some valleys it can be as low as three per cent of the total surface area. This situation necessitated a clear and well-organized system of land management to stave off the threat of starvation for the entire community, and two such systems developed: the first, the so-called **Latin system**, evolved in around the twelfth century and still prevails in many valleys today. This system is characterized by small-scale intensive farming. Unfortunately, when it comes to agriculture the laws regarding economies of scale teach us that bigger is better: that is to say, this division of arable land into small parcels is actually a very inefficient way of farming that land. Furthermore, under the Latin model it is traditional that, upon the death of a landowner, his estate is split equally between all of the male heirs. Thus as time goes by the land is divided into ever smaller parcels, thereby reducing the quantity of food produced on that land as a whole, with potentially disastrous consequences for the whole community.

To counter this, the villages have organized themselves into **Valley Communities** or *regole*. These Valley Communities control all the land in the valley that isn't in private hands, including the forests and summer pastures, the resources of which they then allocate to the individual households according to the number of its members. This leads to what many people consider to be a fair and sustainable system, but one where, in the words of the Ladins themselves, everybody is 'equally poor'. Nevertheless, the system still exists in various forms to this day and thanks to the prosperity enjoyed by the region as a whole in the last one hundred years, it's fair to say that nowadays everybody is equally rich. The regole have become powerful institutions too, recognized by the Italian government and in charge of far more land than the relevant local authority.

By the seventeenth century a second system, known as the **German model** or *Geschlossenhof* (literally, 'Closed House'), had evolved. Characterized by large estates living in isolation from each other, the German model is a more efficient method of land management, in that landowners are often able to produce a surplus which can then be sold for a profit. Unfortunately, in order that the estates maintain their size, only one heir (in this case, the eldest son) can inherit the land; junior siblings have the option of staying on the farm as farmhands, or migrating to the city to learn a trade. This system still survives in a modified

❏ The Ladin language
Language is the single unifying feature of the Dolomite Ladins. In common with Italian, French, Portuguese and many others, Ladin is a neo-Latin language, that is to say, it is a fusion of the Latin language of the Romans with the native tongue of the people they conquered. This fusion would have begun well before the Romans conquered the Dolomites in 15BC, for prior to this the Ladin people had long been in contact with both traders from the empire and the soldiers charged with guarding the empire's borders. These Latin speakers called the mountain people Rhaeti, possibly after their Goddess of Water and Springs, Reitia.

Whilst contemporary Ladin's Latin roots are only too evident, there is also a large number of words that clearly have not been influenced by Latin. One possible reason for this is that many of these words simply had no equivalent in Latin, referring as they do to specific features of the Dolomites, such as various species of the local fauna and flora which cannot be found outside the mountains. Though all Ladin speakers also have at least one other language and usually two (German and Italian), if you try to speak just a couple of words of Ladin you may find you'll receive a far warmer welcome in the towns and villages of the central Dolomites. Some words and phrases you may wish to try:

Bon di – good morning
Bona sëira – good evening
Assudëi – goodbye
De Gra – thank you

form to this day, and there are over 12,000 Geschlossenhof in the province of Bolzano.

To further relieve the pressure on the land and the often scarce food resources, many Ladin households used to send at least one of their children to work as farmhands and servants in the households of their richer neighbours. Thus the inhabitants of Livinallongo, the poorest valley of all, would send their children to the Val di Fassa, who in turn would send their children to the richer Val Gardena and the Val Badia, while the Ladins of these villages would send their children to the even richer, German-speaking villages to the north.

LANGUAGES

The Dolomites has three lingua franca: German, Italian and the Romansch tongue Ladin (see the box on p47 for details). Most of the people you will meet will be fluent in at least two of these languages. English-speakers, on the other hand, are unusually rare in this part of the world, particularly amongst the older generation, and so a degree of fluency in Italian or especially German would therefore come in very useful. That said, most English-speaking trekkers get by without learning much more than the southern German/Austrian greeting *gusgott*, and the Italian greetings *salve* and *buongiorno*. In Appendix A, p201, you can find a list of basic English words and phrases, along with their Italian counterparts.

ECONOMY

Tourism and **agriculture** are the two biggest industries in the Dolomites today, just as they have been for the last century or so. Fortunately, owing to rigid controls, the rampant development that you'll find in so many other tourist hot-spots in Europe has been kept to a minimum here: while the tourist infrastructure is comprehensive and efficient, there are few high-rise hotels or other blots on the landscape. Thus the Dolomite mountains remain comparatively unspoiled.

Tourism has also benefited other industries. As foreigners arrived in droves in the twentieth century, the reputation and popularity of the locally made **woodcarvings** and furniture spread throughout Europe and beyond. The craft, which has a history stretching back at least as far as the seventeenth century, still flourishes today; visit Santa Cristina in the Val Gardena, which is chock-a-block with woodcarving workshops and their outlets, and you'll appreciate this.

While tourism maintains a discreet but highly profitable presence in the Dolomites, evidence of agriculture and farming is, of course, ubiquitous. The sound of cowbells resonates throughout the valleys and dairy produce – milk, cheese, yoghurt, butter and so on – is the Dolomites primary agricultural export. The cows share their pastures with sheep, of which you'll see many in the Dolomites, and the occasional goat. Even those fields that aren't for summer grazing are reserved for growing grain and hay in order to sustain livestock through the perishing winter months. Other **crops** that you may come across include grapes, particularly on the slopes around Bolzano, apple orchards, near Bressanone, orange trees, strawberries, tomatoes and other fruits, sweetcorn, cabbages and potatoes.

Apart from these industries, a number of companies have set up in the Dolomites that specialize in producing equipment specifically designed for the mountains, such as ski, chairlift and snow-plough manufacturers.

NATIONAL PARKS

In the Dolomites there are seven national parks, or *parco nazionale* in Italian (sometimes referred to as *parco naturale*). However, with no border fences, entrance fees or discernible change in scenery, recognizing which part of the Dolomites lies within the boundaries of a national park and which part doesn't can be a little tricky. Very occasionally, signs mark the limits of some of the parks; other than these, your best sources of information about their extent are the trekking maps, which usually have the park borders marked on them.

The seven national parks include the Parco Nazionale delle Bellunesi Dolomiti, which covers the Vette Feltrine, and the national parks of the Fannes-Sennes-Braies, the Adamello Brenta, the Dolomiti di Sesto, the Puez-Odle, the Alpe di Sciliar and the Pale di San Martino.

Bear in mind that the change in scenery between a national park and neighbouring land is minimal – it's all magnificent – and most trekkers will walk through a park without even realizing they're in one. The main difference between land that's been designated as a national park and land that hasn't is that in the former the **laws** regarding the care of the environment are that much tougher; nevertheless most trekkers will agree that anybody who picks wild flowers or drops litter on their walk deserves to be punished severely.

The other thing to remember about Italy's national parks is that **camping is banned** inside them. Sure, as they are not too well policed, your chances of being caught camping inside a national park are rather slim; but should you be found out, expect draconian punishment. Furthermore, you would be setting a bad example to other trekkers.

For further information about the national parks of the Dolomites, visit the Ufficio Parchi Naturali at Via Cesare Battisti 21, Bolzano (☎ 0471-994300). They have a supply of 1:20,000 maps of all the national parks with walking trails marked on and are the most reliable source of information about the parks themselves.

Practical information for the visitor

LOCAL TRANSPORT

Buses

For most of your time in the Dolomites you'll be relying on the local **buses**. Services travel between major cities and towns through the main valleys, and there is always a bus stop at the main mountain passes, allowing trekkers to alight or join the bus at convenient points on their trail. Free timetables are available at the tourist offices or, if there is no tourist office, at the major hotels. In late summer, outside the main trekking season, buses are less frequent as the services wind down or stop altogether for the winter. There are far more services on weekdays than at weekends too. Where possible, bus details have been included in the trail guides in this book.

For most **inter-city buses** (ie buses travelling between towns and cities rather than within them), the fare is paid on board to the driver – though this isn't always the case, so check first (there's usually an office nearby, or ask a local) before boarding the bus to see if you need to buy a ticket beforehand. Fares are usually cheap (L2000 for a short hop of 10 kilometres or so), though bus drivers rarely have enough change for big notes; make sure you have an adequate supply of small denomination notes.

For **local buses** (ie buses that drive to destinations within town), tickets should be bought in advance from a *tabacchi*, and stamped in the machine on board the bus. Fares are approximately L700 per trip.

The bus schedules given in this guide were taken from the timetables in operation at the time of writing; doubtless some have changed, so always check with the local tourist office for up-to-date information.

Trains

Other transport in the Dolomites includes **trains**, which run through the valleys skirting the Dolomites. These are often very comfortable and cheap too, though the price depends on what class you take and what type of train (most trains serving the Dolomites are of the cheaper, slower variety). The rules concerning train travel are usually printed in English on the reverse of your ticket. The most important thing to remember is that you should always try to **validate your ticket before you join the train**. In larger stations there are validation machines on the platforms. In smaller stations ask around: there may be a validation machine, or you might be able to validate the ticket on the train itself.

ACCOMMODATION

Rifugi

Known as *hütte* in German, many of the mountain refuges, or rifugi, particularly on the more crowded routes, are more like hotels than the simple wooden huts of popular imagination. Usually located at the junctions of a number of different trails, rifugi often enjoy some of the best views in the Dolomites.

Most rifugi are run by the **Club Alpino Italiano** (CAI). Though this is not always the case, they tend to be a little cheaper than the privately-owned ones and there's often a commensurate reduction in the standard of accommodation and food too. Joining the CAI or one of its affiliated societies (see p19) will save you up to 50 per cent on accommodation in CAI rifugi, and usually a reduction in the price of their food as well.

Note that it is essential, particularly during the peak season of August, to **phone the rifugio at least the morning before** to book a bed for the night. The more popular rifugi fill up very quickly, and though some may let you sleep on the floor of their restaurant or bar for a small fee (usually L10,000/5000 non-members/members), many others will send you packing if they decide there is still enough light left in the day for you to reach the next rifugi or town. Except in July and August you should have no trouble finding a bed in a rifugio, though it's still a good idea to phone ahead, if only to ensure that the rifugio hasn't closed for the winter.

In short, rifugi are cheap places to stay but not to eat at, the price of food reflecting the extra transport costs required to bring produce up the mountainside. As a general rule, the more remote the rifugio, the more you can expect to pay for food. Kitchens in the rifugi tend to open only after 7pm, though they'll have cold snacks on sale throughout the day. These snacks can be very expensive (as I write this, whilst enjoying the

❏ **Stamp collecting**
All CAI rifugi and most private rifugi have a rubber **ink stamp** by reception with the rifugio's name and telephone number upon it. Many trekkers like to collect these stamps on a piece of paper; indeed, it used to be the case that, by presenting a full set of stamps from the Alta Via 2 to the tourist office in Feltre, you would be rewarded with a commemorative badge. Although this practice of handing out badges seems to have stopped in the last year or so, the stamps are in themselves a neat (and free!) souvenir of your time in the Dolomites, and provide proof that you completed the route. The inside back cover of this book is as good a place as any to collect your stamps.

❏ **Rifugi etiquette**
Before entering a rifugio, visitors are expected to **remove their walking boots** and leave them on the shelves just inside the door. This applies to everyone who enters a rifugio, regardless of whether they intend to spend the night there or not. You'll often find flip-flops or slippers on these shelves, which you may use indoors instead of your boots. Guests who wish to stay for the night are rarely asked to 'sign in', though if you have a CAI card, or a card belonging to an affiliated society that gives you a discount in the rifugio, it's a good idea to show the staff as soon as you arrive to save any possible misunderstandings later on. Though rifugi supply blankets, you will be expected to have your own **sheet sleeping bag**; though this again can be supplied, either for rent or sale, by the rifugio. A normal sleeping bag is usually acceptable, unless it's become too grubby through excessive camping.

Those trekkers who don't plan to stay the night nor buy any food but have simply come into the rifugi to rest awhile or shelter from the weather, may well find themselves liable to a small **'hospitality' fee** (usually L1000) charged by the rifugio.

sumptuous view from *Rifugio Auronzo's* café, I'm slurping on a Gatorade that set me back L8000), though as with many other establishments in Italy, including bars, it's a little cheaper if you forego a seat and stand instead. By way of compensation, evening meals are usually better value. You often have to pay about L5000 for a hot **shower**. **Accommodation** is usually pretty basic: a few of the larger rifugi may have a couple of private rooms but for the most part you'll be staying in dorms for 10 people or more.

Bivacci
Bivacci are simply unstaffed rifugi, mountain huts situated at various remote locations on the trail, affording life-saving shelter to those who for some reason have no chance of reaching the next rifugio and allowing those without camping gear to enjoy the freedom of a night on the mountains without the beady eye of rifugio staff watching over them. Bivacci are often equipped with **beds and blankets**, as well as a sink, and possibly a kettle, some cutlery and crockery, and even a small dining area. You will, however, need to **bring your own food and fuel**. There may be some food: a few high-energy bars or chocolate lying around, though these are for emergency use only and should be left untouched by those who have their own provisions.

Though there's nobody around to tell bivacci dwellers what to do, there are some essential rules that must be followed by all users to ensure that the huts remain clean and inhabitable. First, **take your boots off** before entering; be careful, when cooking, not to start a fire (more than one rifugio has been razed in this way); **wash up** any cutlery and crockery you use, **always take your rubbish away** with you, and when you finally leave, remember to shut the door behind you to keep out any stray animals!

Camping
If you are going to camp, a **three-season sleeping bag**, or a two-season plus **thermal mat** and clothing, are necessary to keep out that Dolomite chill. The tent or bivouac should also be completely waterproof, to guard against vicious summer storms. In the valleys, the campsites usually are equipped with all sorts of amenities, including shops, swimming pools, restaurants, launderettes and so on. They are, unfortunately, usually located a few kilometres outside the nearest town, though for hardened Dolomite trekkers this distance is but a trifle.

Accommodation in the towns
Though it's possible to trek through the Dolomites without once staying down in a town, for most people a night or two in the valleys is an essential part of their trip, allowing them to have a good night's sleep in a private room with a hot shower, make a phone call or two, stock up on provisions, do some laundry and eat at a proper restaurant. Surprisingly, for most towns in the Dolomites this needn't be too expensive either.

Most towns have some sort of *appartementi* option, (also known as *garni*), which are similar to the bed & breakfast establishments found in Britain and elsewhere. Though prices vary seasonally, outside the peak months of late July/early August you should be able to get a room for as little as L30,000. Furthermore, as is typical in the Dolomites, the tourist offices have a complete list of accommodation in their villages and can book a place for you at no extra charge, so you don't have to traipse around the town looking for accommodation. The tourist offices are very honest too: if you want the cheapest room, they will find you the cheapest room. Be careful, however, to check the details of every appartementi, and in particular its location: an official in the tourist office in Bolzano once booked me into a cheap albergo (mountain inn), without warning me that it happened to be a three-hour walk away!

There are a couple of towns, however, where affordable accommodation is thin on the ground, and appartementi non-existent. (To be fair, both of these towns have camping grounds nearby, so it is only non-camping budget travellers who may find themselves stuck.) One such town is Bolzano, where accommodation is in short supply as it is, and where the cheaper hotels are usually booked by midday. Always try to pre-arrange your accommodation here before you arrive. The same applies to Cortina,

❑ MINIMUM IMPACT TREKKING

The Dolomites is a surprisingly fragile environment, and one that is coming under increasing pressure because of the sheer volume of people who flock to the mountains every year. It is therefore vital that everybody who visits the Dolomites should do their bit to preserve the region. Below is a list of simple but essential rules that, if followed, will help to minimize the damage done to the environment and protect the Dolomites for future generations:

Don't leave litter
Everything you take up to the mountains with you should either be eaten, buried if it's biodegradable, burnt (in the case of toilet paper – see below) or carried back down the mountain to the nearest bin. Many people leave litter for rifugi staff to deal with but this is wrong; you should take all your rubbish with you.

Don't pick the flowers
Many species of alpine flora are already quite rare, including the famous edelweiss. It is very tempting to pick just a few but don't; leave the flowers for others to enjoy.

Stay on the trail
Erosion is a serious problem in parts of the Dolomites. The authorities, however, are able to deal with just one path being eroded. It's when there are many paths, caused by people choosing their own way up or down a mountainside instead of sticking to the main route, that the staff of the national parks have their work cut out. Don't make extra work for them; stick to the main trail.

Burn toilet paper
All loo paper should be burned and faeces buried. Certain trekking routes in Nepal have been nicknamed toilet trails after the vast amount of (used) toilet paper left to hang from trees or on the path itself by thoughtless trekkers. If you have to use toilet paper on the trail, burn it afterwards.

Don't pollute water sources
If you need to relieve yourself on the trail, do so at least 20 metres away from streams, lakes and other water sources.

Similarly, if you are washing clothes or hair in the mountains, take the water from the stream or lake in a bucket to a place at least 20 metres away from the source and do your washing there.

where the cheapest hotel room starts at around L80,000; for this reason, most trekkers prefer to stay in one of the rifugi that overlook the town.

ELECTRICITY

Power points in Italy have the standard European two holes, taking the round two-pin plugs. The electric current is 220V, 50Hz, so North Americans will need to bring an adaptor and voltage converter.

OPENING HOURS

Standard business hours in Italy are Monday to Friday from 8.30am to 5pm, and later in the summer. Most Italian businesses also take a mid-afternoon **siesta**, usually for two or three hours from 1pm. The exceptions to this rule are: **supermarkets**, which open at around 9am and stay open until 7.30pm (with some even opening on Sunday mornings); the **larger post offices**, which also stay open throughout the day (while the smaller ones close altogether by about 2pm); and **cafés**, which do a roaring trade during the siesta.

Banks have unusual working hours, opening early (usually before 9am), closing by about 1pm, then re-opening for an hour or so only at around 3pm.

NATIONAL HOLIDAYS

August is the month when most Italians take their annual holiday. At this time of the year, those living on the scorching plains abandon their homes for cooler retreats on the coast or in the mountains. For this reason, rifugi are often heavily booked for the entire month, so it pays to book your rifugio at least a day in advance at this time. The following are national public holidays in Italy:

Epiphany	6 January
Easter Monday	March or April
Liberation Day	25 April
Labour Day	1 May
Feast of the Assumption	15 August
All Saint's Day	1 November
Feast of the Immaculate Conception	8 December
Christmas Day	25 December
Feast of Santo Stefano	26 December

MONEY

The Dolomites may be trilingual, but the only money that talks in the Dolomites, for the moment at least, speaks Italian. The **lira** (plural *lire*, usually shortened to L, though you'll often see the '£' sign used as well)

❑ **Exchange rates**
To get the latest rates of exchange visit www.oanda.com. At the time of writing they were:

Aus$1	1120
Can$1	1386
DM1	990
Euro	1936
NLG1	877
NZ$1	915
UK£1	3038
US$1	2092

is issued in 1000, 2000, 5000, 10,000, 50,000 and 100,000 notes, as well as 250 and 500 coins. Remember that in Italy, as in most of Europe, the decimal point in a number is written as a comma, and the thousands are separated by full stops rather than commas. So, for example, ten thousand is often written 10.000 in Italy, and two and a half is written as 2,5. Italy is among the first group of European countries committed to using the **euro**, and at the time of writing all shops were being compelled to give the prices of their goods in both Italian lire and euros. In July 2002, the lira will cease to be legal tender. L1000 is approximately Euro 0.5 so a quick way to convert the lira prices in this book into euros without using a calculator is to **divide by 1000 and then divide again by two**.

Receipts

In an attempt to reduce the chronic level of tax avoidance in the country, the Italian government has made it compulsory for all customers to ask for a receipt when buying something. Although highly unlikely, there is the possibility that a member of the fiscal police (Guardia di Finanzia) may grab you when you leave a shop and ask to see your receipt. Failure to produce the necessary slip of paper when requested could leave you with a hefty L250,000 fine to pay.

POST AND TELECOMMUNICATIONS

Don't expect too much from the Italian postal service. Widely recognized as one of the least efficient in the developed world, mail sent from Italy abroad, even to a fellow EU member such as Britain, can take two weeks, and longer if it's non-priority mail such as postcards. One solution is to send all mail express (*espresso*), though an additional fee of around L3500 is charged for this service.

Post offices can be found in all the larger towns and cities. The opening hours of the smaller branches, however, are not always reliable, and many are closed by the early afternoon. For most of the time, therefore, you'll probably be relying on the **tobacconists** (tabacchi), easily identifiable thanks to the large white 'T' sign hanging outside, for purchasing stamps. If it's only postcards or small letters that you wish to send home the tabacchi are fine. For larger items, however, which must be weighed, you'll need to go to the post office.

Post offices in the larger towns are open from 8am-5pm Monday to Friday, and often for a few hours on Saturday morning too.

A **poste restante** *(fermo posta)* service exists in larger towns such as Bolzano and Bressanone. Poste restante mail should be addressed as follows:

> Henry <u>STEDMAN</u>
> Fermo Posta
> L'Ufficio Postale
> 32043 Cortina
> Italy

Telephone

Italy has one of the most expensive telephone services in Europe, with calls to other European countries approximately L1300 per minute depending on the time of day. Calls after 11pm or on Sundays are generally cheaper, depending on the country called.

The easiest way to telephone abroad in Italy is to buy a **phonecard** from a tobacconist, post office, newsagent or vending machine and use it in one of the roadside public phone booths. Cards come in denominations of L5000, L10,000 and L15,000. Some of these telephone booths now accept credit cards too. Alternatively, you can go to one of the telephone offices, many of which are staffed; in this instance, all you have to do is make your international phone call, then pay the cashier at the end of your call. For domestic calls, you can use a phonecard phone or

❏ CALLING ABROAD FROM ITALY

Access codes
To phone overseas from Italy, first dial 00, then the country code, then the area code (minus the first zero), then finally the number itself. Country codes include: Canada and US ☎ +1; UK ☎ +44; Ireland ☎ +353; Germany ☎ +49; Australia ☎ +61; New Zealand ☎ +64.

Making collect/reverse-charges calls
To make a collect or reverse-charges call dial ☎ 170, or ☎ 15 for European countries. A cheaper and easier method is to use the **Country Direct** service. Simply dial the relevant number and request a reverse-charges call through the operator in your country. Some Country Direct numbers include:
- Australia ☎ 172 10 61 (Telstra); ☎ 172 11 61 (Optus)
- Canada ☎ 172 10 01
- New Zealand ☎ 172 10 64
- UK ☎ 172 00 44 (British Telecom); ☎ 172 05 44 (Mercury); ☎ 172 01 44 (Auto BT)
- USA ☎ 172 10 11 (AT&T); ☎ 172 18 77 (Sprint); ☎ 172 10 22 (MCI); ☎ 172 17 77 (IDB)

❏ RIFUGIO MENU

The following is a typical rifugio menu translated into English from both German and Italian. In Appendix B (p207) you will also find a menu guide.

German	English	Italian
speckknödelsuppe	dumpling soup	canerdeli in brodo
backerbsensuppe	noodle soup	pastina in brodo
nudelsuppe	noodle soup	pastina reale
gemüsesuppe	vegetable soup	minestrina di verdura
nudelsuppe mit wurst	noodle soup with sausage	pastina reale con würstel
spaghetti mit fleische	spaghetti with a meat sauce	spaghetti al ragu
hirtenmakkaroni (literally 'shepherd's macaroni'),	macaroni with a tomato sauce	maccheroni al pastore
polenta mit käse	polenta with melted cheese	polenta con formaggio fuso
ei mit schinken und bratkartoffel	egg with ham and baked potatoes	uova con prosciutto e patate
ei mit speck und bratkartoffel	egg with bacon and potatoes	uova con speck e patate
schinkenomlett	ham omelette	omelett con prosciutto
käseomlett	cheese omelette	omelett con formaggio
gulasch	goulash	gulasch
hauswurst mit eine beilage	house sausage with one side dish of choice	
wienerschnitzel	crumbed veal cutlet	cotoletta alla milanese
naturschnitzel	steak or chop	cotoletta
gemischter salat	mixed salad	insalata mista
kaiserschmarren mit preiselbeeren	scrambled omelette batter with bilberries	kaiserschmarren con mirtillo
apfelstrudel mit sahne	apple strudel with cream	strudel di mele con panna

one of the older coin phones, which accept L250 and L500 coins. You may also, occasionally, find one of the old-style phones that work on *gettoni* tokens, with each gettoni worth L200.

Email

Many of the main towns (Cortina, Bolzano, Sesto, San Candido) have some sort of public Internet facility, but not all. A number, particularly on the AV2 route and including Bressanone and Feltre, have no Internet connection available to the public. Where Internet is available, the cost is on

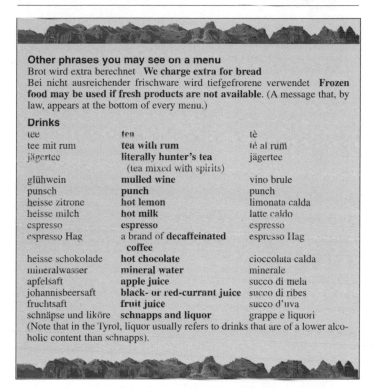

Other phrases you may see on a menu

Brot wird extra berechnet **We charge extra for bread**

Bei nicht ausreichender frischware wird tiefgefrorene verwendet **Frozen food may be used if fresh products are not available**. (A message that, by law, appears at the bottom of every menu.)

Drinks

tee	tea	tè
tee mit rum	**tea with rum**	tè al rum
jägertee	**literally hunter's tea** (tea mixed with spirits)	jägertee
glühwein	**mulled wine**	vino brule
punsch	**punch**	punch
heisse zitrone	**hot lemon**	limonata calda
heisse milch	**hot milk**	latte caldo
espresso	**espresso**	espresso
espresso Hag	a brand of **decaffeinated coffee**	espresso Hag
heisse schokolade	**hot chocolate**	cioccolata calda
mineralwasser	**mineral water**	minerale
apfelsaft	**apple juice**	succo di mela
johannisbeersaft	**black- or red-currant juice**	succo di ribes
fruchtsaft	**fruit juice**	succo d'uva
schnäpse und liköre	**schnapps and liquor**	grappe e liquori

(Note that in the Tyrol, liquor usually refers to drinks that are of a lower alcoholic content than schnapps).

the whole reasonable: usually no more than L7500 for 30 minutes. Where applicable, the town plans in this book have the locations of Internet facilities marked on them.

FOOD AND DRINK

There are two main sorts of cuisine in the Dolomites: Tyrolean food, with its emphasis on fresh breads, soups, dumplings and stews; and Italian food, which is a lot more diverse than the stereotype of pastas and pizzas would have you believe, (though it's fair to say that these do feature heavily on the menus of the southern Dolomites).

For most of your time, however, you'll probably be sampling the delights of **rifugio food**, which is much the same throughout the entire region. Rifugio food is usually healthy and hearty, though sometimes a

❑ Service charges
In Italian cafés it's far cheaper to stand and drink coffee and eat your food at the counter; to be served by a waiter/waitress while seated at a table can treble the price of your food and drinks. A couple of the larger rifugi also apply this rule, so check on this price differential before taking your seat.

little bland. It is also more expensive than corresponding dishes found in the valleys and plains, because of the extra costs of transporting goods up the mountain. As a rule, the more remote the rifugio, the more expensive and less exciting the food is. At a couple of the low-altitude rifugi on the other hand – the *Passo di Valles* and *Passo Cereda* spring to mind – the food approaches cordon bleu standards.

Italians divide their menus into *primo piatto* (first course), *secondo piatto* (second, or main course), *contorni* (vegetables, which you usually order separately from the main course) and dessert. Fixtures on almost all rifugi menus include noodle soup (*pastina in brodo*, *backerbsensuppe*); breaded veal cutlets or *wienerschnitzel*; ham and eggs (*uova con prosciutto*), a common dish often served with potatoes (*patate*); and a few basic pasta dishes.

Tyrolean specialities include *speckknödel*, which are dumplings made of bread pieces and bacon; *Schlutzkrapfen*, a sort of local pasta that resembles noodles; *Tiroler Gerstensuppe*, a Tyrolean soup made from barley and known as *minestra d'orzo Tirolese* in Italian; *kasierschmarren*, another Tyrolean favourite made from scrambled omelette moulded into dough and then fried; and polenta, an inexplicably expensive lump of cooked cornmeal that resembles a yellow bath sponge and tastes little better.

In addition, all rifugi sell chocolates and other **snacks**, which are perfect for maintaining moral and energy levels on the trail, and mineral water, which can either be sparkling (*minerale frizzante*) or still (*minerale naturale*).

Wine and beer
Don't miss the chance to sample the local **wine**, which is quite superb at times and very cheap (usually around L7000 for a carafe). A more refreshing alternative is the local **shandy**, which is beer mixed with lemon juice: delicious.

Self-catering
For those planning to prepare their own food, nearly every town and village has its own supermarket, the location of which is marked on the town plans in this book.

Those attempting the Alta Via 2 will have to carry most of their supplies with them from the beginning, as there are few shops en route. In contrast, if you're attempting the west-east route, you will drop down to a number of valley towns where supplies can be replenished.

Tipping

A service charge is usually included in the price of food in restaurants. Many people leave a small tip on top of this, though you are under no obligation to do so. In bars, Italians often leave the smallest coin in their change as a tip.

THINGS TO BUY

Most of the larger rifugi sell souvenirs – T-shirts, stickers, badges. More substantial items include the renowned **woodcarvings** of the Val Gardena, though these are often too large to carry around the mountains and very expensive to send home. Locally-produced food and drink is another popular choice, particularly **honey**, **wine** and **cheese**, all of which are readily available, cheap and of good quality.

SECURITY

Travelling in the Dolomites is very safe, though it's only common sense to take a few precautions. Never leave your valuables unguarded in your room or dormitory; hand them in to reception if you are making a daytrip from the rifugio and don't want to lug everything around with you. Furthermore, always carry your passport and money with you on the trail, preferably in a moneybelt for extra security.

Fauna and flora

Fauna

For most of the time, the only animals you'll see on your trek are the **livestock** of the local farms that graze on the mountain slopes and sometimes the high plateaux during the summer months. They share their homeland, however, with a wide variety of more interesting creatures which have managed to survive in the region despite the efforts of Italian and Austrian hunters down the years. Hunting, or *la caccia*, remains an extremely popular pastime in Italy, and many of the species of mammals and birds mentioned here have been reintroduced into the Dolomites only fairly recently, having been wiped out in the region during the twentieth century.

The largest of these creatures is the **European brown bear**. Hunted to near extinction in the early part of the twentieth century, a few bears still inhabit the remoter regions of the Brenta range in largely inaccessible areas not crossed by walking trails. Sightings, as you can imagine, are rare. The **lynx** too has made a return to the region, though again they inhabit the remotest regions and it's safe to say you won't encounter one on your trail.

One mammal that you almost definitely will see, however, is the **marmot** (*marmotta*), a 50cm-long, honey-coloured, beaver-like rodent that scurries around the upper reaches of the Dolomites, making high-pitched, bird-like alarm calls whenever danger approaches. Living in groups of 50 or more in burrows three metres deep, the marmot hibernates in winter, living off the fat they have accumulated over the summer months. As a result they are easier to see in August and September, when they tend to be fatter and slower than in their sleek early summer form.

They share the mountains with the **snow** or **alpine hare** (*lepre variabile*), a rare nocturnal animal inhabiting the grassy, high-level plateaux of the Dolomites; and the **chamois** (*camoscio*), small and extremely agile deer that are often found teetering on tiny ledges high up on the cliffs above the trails. They are particularly easy to spot as they live in large groups (approximately 20-30 strong) and tend to scarper when humans approach, dislodging rocks and stones that clatter down the mountainside, thereby alerting everyone to their presence. In the early mornings you'll occasionally find great herds of them grazing on the mountain plateaux and lower slopes. Other deer found in the Dolomites include the protected **roe deer** (*capriolo*) and the much larger red deer or *cervo*, both of which are common in the valley forests (particularly the Val di Sesto). They share these forests with large populations of foxes, martens, squirrels, stoats and badgers.

Inhabiting the same sort of terrain as the chamois, and of a similar colour, the **ibex** (*stambecco*) or mountain goat is, as a result of overhunting, now an endangered species, though small populations flourish in the Fanes-Sennes-Braies National Park and around the Croda del Becco. Ibex are larger than chamois and less shy too, so should you be lucky enough to spot one, the chances are you'll be able to get close enough to take some reasonable photos.

Reptiles and amphibians

The only creature one should be wary of (apart from the bears, of course) is the adder, a two-foot long poisonous snake whose population is small but growing in the Dolomites. Dangerous when disturbed, adders have a distinctive triangular head and a dark line running zig-zag across the length of their grey-green bodies. Far more innocuous are the Dolomites' legions of amphibians, including frogs, tritons and, most unusual of all, the black salamander, a coal-coloured salamander that's slowly disappearing from the region.

Birds

The bird you will encounter most often on your trek is the **alpine chough**. A slightly smaller relative of the crow, alpine choughs have a yellow beak and feet, and jet black plumage. Great (and very noisy) scavengers, they hang around the trails and rifugi in large flocks particularly, for some unknown reason, *Rifugio Bolzano*, in search of scraps.

LAMMERGAIER

More spectacular, though less common, are the raptors. Many of the raptor species were hunted to extinction at the beginning of the last century, only to be reintroduced over the last few decades in an attempt to establish viable populations. The best known of the raptors is the bearded vulture or **lammergaier**, a huge scavenger that can grow up to 1m in length, with a wingspan of three metres or more. Nesting high up in the cliffs, the lammergaier feeds by carrying the bones of its prey up to a huge height, then letting them fall to the ground and dash against the rocks, thus allowing the lammergaier to feast on the marrow. Almost extinct at the beginning of this century, the lammergaier was reintroduced in the late 1980s.

When it comes to grace and power, the lammergaier has only one real rival in the skies: the **golden eagle**. Smaller than the lammergaier yet still very large with a wingspan of over two metres, the golden eagle is in fact dullish brown in colour, though with golden tinges on its head and the tips of its wings. Capable of long periods of flight at great altitude, golden eagles nest on the tops of tall trees or on cliffs, returning year after year to the same eyrie.

GOLDEN EAGLE

Living with these raptors at the top of the mountains is the humble **ptarmigan**, a pigeon-

PTARMIGAN

shaped bird that builds its nests on the ground, there being few predators at the altitudes which they inhabit. Ptarmigans are most famous for their chameleon-like ability to change the colour of their plumage according to the season, swapping their dark brown summer feathers for a plain white outfit at the onset of winter.

Lower down the slopes the variety of birdlife is even greater: **woodpeckers**, **warblers**, **finches**, **nuthatches**, **jays**, **woodlarks**, **crows**, **tits**, **magpies** and many other species make their nests in the forests of the Dolomites. Possibly the most interesting woodland bird, however, is the **capercaillie**, a large, ground-dwelling member of the grouse family that's

CAPERCAILLIE

capable of flying, albeit somewhat less than gracefully: if you hear a lot of flapping, a few twigs and branches snapping and feel the air being stirred around you the chances are it's a capercaillie trying to take off in the near vicinity.

FLORA

One need only look at the terrain of the Dolomites to realize that the region is ideal for the growth of wild flowers. With virtually no permanent snow, plenty of upland plateaux, or *alpe* as they're known locally, and a wide variety of different habitats, the Dolomites are a botanist's dream. Please remember that virtually all wild flowers are protected by law, so don't even think about picking them.

The Dolomites cover all the major **vegetation zones**: lower montane (up to 1400m); upper montane (1400m-1700m); subalpine (1700-1900m), alpine (1900m-2400m) and finally high alpine (above 2400m).

The **lower montane** zone, which covers most of the valley floors in the Dolomites, is characterized by large swathes of pasture interspersed with patches of forest that play host to the beech, easily recognizable by its smooth, grey-silver bark and oval leaves, the red spruce and silver firs. This also the natural home of many wild flowers such as the crocus, the foxglove and trumpet gentian; it is also the habitat of the fungi; **mushrooming** is a very popular pastime in Italy, though it's heavily regulated now, with licences issued to mushroomers who are allowed to pick only on certain days.

As one climbs above 1400m, the beech trees and pastures give way to the larch and scot's pine of the **upper montane** zone. The former is unusual in that it is the only deciduous conifer in Italy, its needles turning a beautiful gold before falling with the onset of winter. On first appearance, the **subalpine** zone is little different from the upper montane region: the larch and red spruce still dominate, though now you may start to see different sorts of conifers appearing such as the arolla pine. This high-altitude tree (arollas never grow below 1300m) has, uniquely, five needles per bunch as opposed to the normal two which you'll find on other pines.

By the time one reaches the **alpine region**, the huge trees of the lower slopes have given way to the dwarf pines, or *pino mugo*, of the higher altitudes, as well as the occasional willow, bilberry bush and rhododendrons. The trees from the upper montane zone that do grow here tend to be twisted and unhealthy in appearance. The *pino mugo*, incidentally, has been deliberately cultivated in some areas as their sturdiness, thick branches and deep roots are considered perfect for preventing avalanches and landslides.

It is, however, the **upper alpine region** that is of most interest to trekkers. Here the dwarf pines vanish and one is left with high-altitude meadows full of unusual grasses.

This is also the domain of wild flowers, of which the Dolomites has over one hundred different species. This is where you'll find the daisy-like alpine aster (*Aster alpinus*), its blue petals and yellow centre sometimes difficult to spot against the cliffs on which it prefers to grow. Here too one finds that most famous of alpine flowers, the edelweiss (*Leontopodium alpinum*), a small, off-white, 'furry' flower that often lies concealed beneath the long grass. Its felt coating covers not only the star-shaped flower but the whole plant, which is rare these days and strictly protected.

Leontopodium alpinum
Edelweiss

Cow parsley

Saxifragia appositfolia
Purple saxifrage

Armeria alpina
Alpine thrift

Aster bellidiastrum michelii
Daisy

Catsear

Papaver alpinum
Alpine poppy

Androsace
Rock jasmine

Aster alpinus
Alpine aster

Linnaea borealis
Twinflower

Gentiana asclepiadia
Willow gentian

Knautia arvensis
Field scabious

Fungus

Senecio
Ragwort

Campanula
Bellflower

Saxifragia caesia
Saxifrage

Fungus

Cow parsley

Scutellaria alpina
Alpine scullcap

Spring crocus

Aconitum volparia
Wolfsbane

Adenostyles glabra
Adenostyles

Pedicularis alpinus
Alpine lousewort

PART 3: WEST TO EAST

Facts about the walk

This walk from the unofficial capital of the Dolomites, Bolzano, to the towns fringing the eastern Dolomites includes some of the most beautiful trails in the whole of Italy. Depending on which route you choose – we give a number of different options at various points along the way as well as three alternative finishes – the entire trek can take anything between 10 and 16 days. Though slightly longer than the AV2 (about 160-200km depending on the trail chosen) the walk is technically a little easier, though this depends on the route you choose. That said, the two most demanding and longest vie ferrate in this book are both found on this route, though both can be avoided by taking one of the other suggested trails. What's more, as the valleys in the Dolomites tend to run from north to south, it follows that this west-east trail rises and falls more often than the AV2, which remains above 1200m for virtually its entire length. So expect a lot of gruelling uphills and tiring descents on the way!

To describe the walk briefly: from Bolzano, the trail climbs the western face of the Sciliar, crosses the southern rim of the delightful Alpe di Siusi, Western Europe's largest high-altitude plateau, before descending to the Val Gardena. Heading east from here via Odle, Puez, the Val Badia and on to the Fanes National Park, the trail then splits into two: the first option is to head up to *Rifugio Biella*, then due east to the glorious **Pratopiazza**; the second, longer and more difficult trail heads south-east towards the **Tofanes** and **Lagazuoi** peaks, then east to the quintessential Dolomite town of **Cortina**, after which it meanders north-east, via the Lago di Misurina and some simple vie ferrate, to the Tre Cime di Lavaredo and a reunion with the first trail. These alternative trails are described in greater detail on pp97-127.

From this point, there are three finishes to the trek. The route you decide to take will depend on how difficult you wish the remainder of your walk to be and how much time you have left. It also depends on

---

❏ **Tabacco Maps**
Tabacco maps 029, 05, 07, 03 and 017 are required for this route, plus 06 for the detour described on p78. If you're planning on finishing in San Candido, you will also need map 010 for the last half of the final stage from Bad Moos.

where you'd like to finish your trek since the three routes lead to three different towns: Santa Stefano di Cadore, San Candido and Auronzo. Full details about each of these three finishes can be found on pp128–150.

BOLZANO/BOZEN

Bolzano is a mountain disguised as a town; as you move around, its appearance changes, you move away and the outline is different, you come back and it has changed. It speaks different languages. It is an actress, like a mountain, fascinating and contradictory, proud and communicative.

Reinhold Messner, climber of all the world's 8000m+ peaks.

Just 80km from the Austrian border and 100km from Switzerland, bilingual Bolzano (285m) is the traditional gateway to the Dolomites and the largest city in the region. Famous for its **markets** (particularly its springtime wine fair, annual flower market in late April and the daily fruit market) and its neat synthesis of Italian and German **architecture**, a pleasant morning can be spent touring its churches, museums and cobbled mediaeval streets. The mighty thirteenth-century Gothic cathedral known as the **Duomo**, on the south-western corner of the neo-Romanesque style main square, Piazza Walther, is the main highlight, and its towering 65m-high sandstone spire is the city's main landmark. A few hundred metres to the north, **Via Dei Portici** is a pretty street lined on both sides with arcades (known locally as *Lauben*) full of expensive shops flogging designer gear.

Services

The city **tourist office** (☎ 0471-307000) is on the eastern side of the Piazza Walther at No 8. They can supply you with a map that includes a suggested walking tour of the city. Open Monday to Friday 9am-6.30pm, Saturday 9am-12.30pm. On the northern corner of the Piazza is a second tourist office, this time devoted to the

Dolomites. Unfortunately, it was closed the last time I visited, though when open they provide quantities of interesting trekking information. There are a number of **sports shops** in town; Sportler at Via dei Portici 37 stocks the widest range of equipment. Opposite the eastern end of the street, on Via Grappoli, is a Despar **supermarket**. The **post** and **telephone** offices are both on Via Isarco, opposite the entrance to the Duomo, while just a few metres further down is Pellini Bistro Veneziano, which has **Internet** facilities.

Accommodation

This is hard to come by in Bolzano, especially when there's a trade fair or convention going on – and there frequently is. Book ahead or turn up fairly early in the morning; otherwise, be prepared to pay top dollar or sleep rough. Or you can camp: *Moosbauer campsite* (☎ 0471-918492) complete with swimming pool, lies to the north-west of town.

Be warned too that room prices are high in Bolzano, and the cheaper hotels recommended by the tourist office are sometimes a two-three hour walk out of town (though the tourist office doesn't always tell you this). *Stazione-Bahnhof* (☎ 0471-973291) at Via Renon 23 is probably the cheapest in the town centre at L50,000 for a single room with breakfast. It's not exactly luxurious, but at least it's central. *Croce Bianca* (☎ 0471-977552) at Piazza del Grano 3, and *Thuille* (☎ 0471-262877) at Via Thuille 5, both charge the same as Stazione-Bahnhof, though neither includes breakfast, while *Adria* at Via Perathoner 17 (☎ 0471-975735) is a good deal classier but a little more expensive, with singles including breakfast starting at

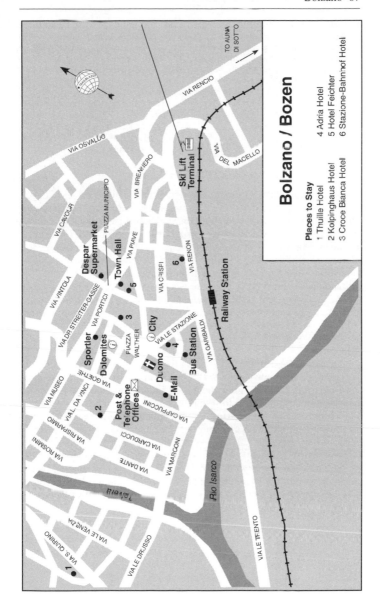

Bolzano / Bozen

Places to Stay

1 Thuille Hotel
2 Kolpinghaus Hotel
3 Croce Bianca Hotel
4 Adria Hotel
5 Hotel Feichter
6 Stazione-Bahnhof Hotel

L65,000. With 75 rooms, the two-star *Kolpinghaus* (☎ 0471-308400), Via Ospedale 3, is the most likely of these 'cheaper' hotels to have some rooms available. Finally, moving up the scale a little, *Hotel Feichter* (☎ 0471-978768) is a charming little two-star place on Via Grappoli. Prices start at L85,000 for a single with breakfast.

Transport

To list all the **buses** from Bolzano would take a book in itself. Destinations within the Dolomites include: Bressanone (9 daily); Cortina (daily at 11.10am); La Villa (2 daily at 8.05am and 9.35am); Ortisèi (16 daily, though a change at Castelrotto is usually required) and San Candido (4 daily).

There are regular **train** services from Bolzano to Bologna (13 daily), Bressanone (24 daily), Innsbruck (18 daily), Munich (9 daily), San Candido (daily) and Verona (24 daily).

BOLZANO → AUNA DI SOTTO/UNTERINN   [MAP 1]

[**Tabacco map 029**] Passing through some picture-perfect villages, farms, vineyards and meadows, the pastoral splendour of this first stage bears little resemblance to the bleak landscapes that you'll encounter further along the trail. Just because it is a fairly low-level walk (Bolzano is less than 300m above sea level, and the path only just shaves the magical altitude of 1000m before falling to 911m at Auna di Sotto), don't be fooled into thinking this is a gentle introduction to the Dolomites. The climb up to Signat is fairly long and wearying, particularly in the humidity that's so prevalent at this altitude; at less than four hours, however, it is also a very short walk, deliberately so to provide you with a gentle introduction to Dolomite-style trekking. The fitter amongst you may wish to continue on to *Pension Steg*, or even the town of Fié (a further 3hrs 35 mins away).

Departing from Bolzano is straightforward enough. Leaving the railway station, turn right down Via Renon (Rittnerstrasse). At the end, by the **Funivia del Renon** cable car, go left (not straight on) and follow the road as it bends around to the south-east. Continue along this road past the **Church of San Laurentius**, a nineteenth-century reconstruction of a twelfth-century building, then turn left onto the road to Renon, just past *Hotel Rentschenhof*.

As the first CAI signpost (at the road junction) on this trail makes clear, you are now heading towards trail 5, which begins a few hundred metres along the road by the *Weine Vini Plattner Waldgries* vineyards; look for the wooden sign carved into the shape of a bunch of grapes. This trail weaves its way up the hill through vineyards and orchards (visit in late

---

❏ **Buses to the Sciliar**

For those who wish to get straight to the mountains, there are buses every 30 minutes from Bolzano bus station to Fié (see p72), on the western slopes of the Sciliar.

Map 1– Bolzano to Auna di Sotto 69

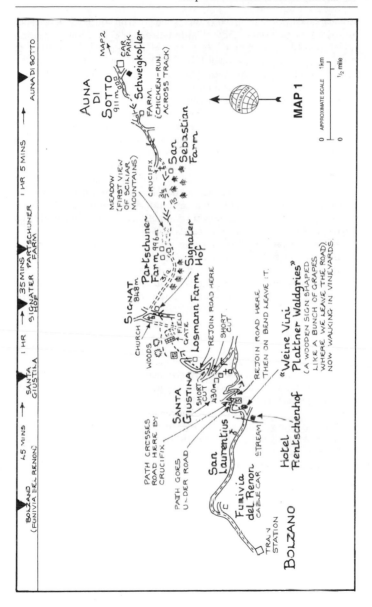

MAP 1

August/September and the vines will be heavy with succulent bunches of grapes) to the tiny settlement of **Santa Giustina** (430m). It is a beautiful if sweaty walk, marred by the fact that you are on occasions required to walk on a very busy, pavement-less road. Take care and follow the map on p69 closely so you don't lose your way; the Tabacco map is also surprisingly accurate for this section.

Leaving Santa Giustuna, which consists of nothing more than two vintners' premises hiding behind an old church, turn left and walk uphill for about 200m, taking the secondary road on your left just past the bend. Immediately before the first hairpin turn right along the first of three short cuts through the woods. A few minutes later, you'll rejoin the road; turn right here and take the second woodland short cut to your left, which again rejoins the road soon after. Turn left here. The third short cut, beginning on yet another sharp turn in the road, is a little overgrown and difficult to negotiate. Go left at the top, then turn right through the woods for a few minutes and you'll emerge two minutes later on an unpaved track leading to **Losmann farm**.

Before reaching the farm, however, look to your left for trail 5 which continues through woods and meadows to the orchards of the tiny village of **Signat** (848m). Walking up to the road and turning left, before long you'll be at *Signater Hof Restaurant and Hotel* (☎ 0479-365353), the perfect place to take a quick break or stop overnight if this first day's walking is proving too taxing. It's L60,000 per person in private rooms.

Behind *Signater Hof*, the trail, now numbered 31a and inexplicably marked with blue and white markings, runs due east and up through the forest. The majestic mountains of the Dolomites – in this case the flat-topped Sciliar Massif looking tall and austere, (though it's actually one of the smaller ranges in the region with the highest point being only 2563m) and to its south the Catinaccio (2981m) – now come into view for the first time on this trail as you pass the idyllic farms of **Partschuner** at 996m (where they keep peacocks) and **San Sebastian** (911m). From here the gently descending path is much easier on the legs as it drifts lazily to the hamlet of **Auna di Sotto/Unterinn** (911m). This is as good a place as any to finish the first day's trekking; should you feel fresh enough to continue, be warned that it's about two hours downhill to the next accommodation.

AUNA DI SOTTO/UNTERINN

An electronic information board in the car park tells you which guest-houses still have rooms available, and enables you to book your accommodation by using the nearby freephone. Behind the information board is one of the better options, *Gasthof Schweigkofler* (☎ 0471-602133) with rooms starting at L30,000 per person including breakfast. Further on towards the church at Huberweg 49, *Neuhuber* (☎ 0471-359082) has rooms for as little as L15,000 per person in the low season, though there are no singles. Should you wish to give up on your trek already, there are 10 **buses** daily back to Bolzano.

Auna di Sotto

TO ERDPYRAMIDEN
& PENSION STEG

VIA PRINCIPALE

Hotel
Neuhuber

Car
Park
ⓘ ● Gasthof
Schweigkofler

TO SIGNAT
& BOLZANO

AUNA DI SOTTO → RIFUGIO BOLZANO [MAPS 2, 3, pp73–75]

[**Tabacco map 029**] This is a very long stage. After an initial descent, the trail climbs steadily from a low of 347m all the way up to *Rifugio Bolzano* at 2450m. Those who wish to break the journey can do so at the pretty hillside town of Fié.

By the church at Auna di Sotto, signs point east through farms and forests to the **Erdpyramiden**, or Earth Pyramids. These are natural stone structures that have been eroded and sculpted by centuries of wind and rain into a series of 5m-high tapered, conical shapes; if you're not observant you can miss them but when you get to a bridge in the woods look up the cliffs on your left and you should see them. You can find similar rock formations in Cappadocia in central Turkey, which, it has to be said, are rather more spectacular.

From the bridge, the path takes you past more farms and into thicker forest. At one point, just beyond **Tasengger farm** (847m), the ruins of **Castelpietra**, one of a number of mediaeval castles and forts that proliferate in these parts, can be clearly seen on the slopes below the path. A few minutes later and you reach a large mountain stream, the **Rio del Passo**. At this point your path, Trail 11, starts to descend steeply southeast to the **Valle Isarco**. Passing a number of farms and the A22 motorway, which you pass under, you'll eventually emerge at the valley floor by Highway 12. *Pension Steg* (☎ 0471-353117; 347m), standing a few metres to the left of the path on the road, has rooms for L40,000 including breakfast. It's a pleasant-enough place, though there are definitely more attractive locations in the Dolomites.

Opposite the *Steg* an old wooden, covered bridge carries you over the stream to some rail tracks. Cross these, turn right and a few metres later take a hard left up round the hill; take a second hard left 100m later, and with any luck you'll be walking on a narrow track by a high wire fence; there's usually somebody around to ask for directions if you have trouble locating the path.

You are now on Trail 1 tracing a series of wide zigzags through the forest to the village of **Fié allo Sciliar/Völs am Schlern** (880m) on the lower slopes of Mt Sciliar. It's a fairly taxing climb but straightforward enough if you bear in mind that after 15 minutes or so, just beyond a small shrine, Trail 1 turns sharply to the right while the main path leads straight on to the hamlet of Novale de Fié. Continue along Trail 1 which you should be able to follow reasonably well, simply because there are no alternative trails to follow; though it has to be said that this path is poorly marked, very overgrown and gradually narrows towards the top of the hill until almost invisible.

An hour or so after leaving *Pension Steg* you'll emerge at the top of the climb by a shed in a field. On the other side of the field is a small rough road; turn left along this road which will lead you round to the centre of Fié by the main road.

FIÉ

Fié is dominated by the steeples and towers of a number of impressive churches, including **Santa Pietro** in the west, the onion-domed **parish church** in the centre of town and the rectangular **Santa Margareth** up the hill off Schlernstrasse.

Ironically, Fié also used to have a reputation for being the home of witches, who would practise their black arts in secret on the Alpe di Siusi and the Monte Pez. This explains why the local tourist board has as its logo a witch on a broomstick. By the parish church there's a small **museum** dedicated to the history of the valley and its many churches.

Fié is the number one village for **hay baths**, a traditional therapeutic treatment that, as its name suggests, involves immersing yourself in a bath full of hay. Hay fever sufferers are advised to forego this particular experience, despite the assurances of the locals that it's pollen free.

Services
On the main road you'll find the **tourist office**, a **trekking shop** next door, and a **pharmacy** and **bank** (including ATM) opposite. **Buses** back to Bolzano leave every 30 minutes.

Accommodation
The tourist office can recommend any number of cosy and comfortable *privatzimmer* (private rooms). *Haselrieder* (☎ 0471-725184), 10 minutes up the hill from the tourist office at Schlernstrasse 29, is good value at only L29,000 per person per night. Just a little further down the hill, *Haus beim Moarhof* (☎ 0471-725401) at No 23, offers huge breakfasts, with prices beginning at L50,000 in the low season, L100,000 in the high. For excellent pizza, visit *Sander Pizzeria*, 10 minutes west of town, which I highly recommend. *Tschaln Pizzeria* on Via Bolzano also has an excellent reputation, though it is closed on Wednesdays.

Map 2 – Auna di Sotto to Fié 73

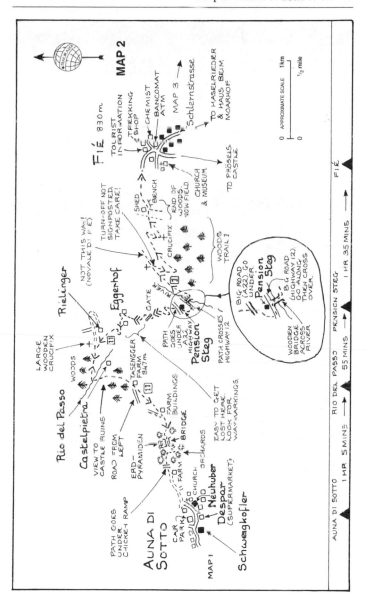

MAP 2

Fié 830m

TOURIST INFORMATION
TREKKING SHOP
CHEMIST
BANCOMAT ATM
MAP 3
Schlernstrasse
TO HASELRIEDER & HAUS BEIM MOARHOF
TO PRÖSELS CASTLE
CHURCH & MUSEUM

APPROXIMATE SCALE
0 — 1km
0 — ½ mile

TURN-OFF NOT SIGNPOSTED. TAKE CARE!

Rielinger

NOT THIS WAY! (NOVALE DI FÉ)

Eggenhof

SHED
BENCH
CRUCIFIX
END OF WOODS/COW FIELD
WOODS TRAIL 1

GATE

RIVER

BIG ROAD (IN22) GO UNDER.
Pension Steg
B.G. ROAD (HIGHWAY 12). GO ALONG, THEN CROSS OVER.
WOODEN BRIDGE ACROSS RIVER

PATH GOES UNDER A.22 / HIGHWAY 12
Pension Steg

PATH CROSSES / HIGHWAY 12

Rio del Passo

LARGE WOODEN CRUCIFIX

Castelpietra

VIEW TO CASTLE RUINS
ROAD FROM LEFT
WOODS

TASENGGER FARM 847m

FARM BUILDINGS

ERD-PYRAMIDEN

BRIDGE

EASY TO GET LOST HERE. LOOK FOR WAYMARKINGS.

PATH GOES UNDER CHICKEN RAMP

Auna di Sotto

CAR PARK
CHURCH
FARM
ORCHARDS

Despar (SUPERMARKET?)
Neuhuber

Schwegkofler

MAP 1

AUNA DI SOTTO — 1 HR 5 MINS — RIO DEL PASSO — 55 MINS — PENSION STEG — 1 HR 35 MINS — FIÉ

❏ **Prösels Castle**

Built on the lower slopes of the Sciliar just a few minutes drive due south from Fié, Prösels Castle is a thirteenth-century mediaeval structure originally built for the Lord of Fié. Abandoned by his descendants in 1804 after the last baron died without any heirs, the castle passed through a number of different hands and eventually fell into disrepair, before finally being restored and opened to the public for the first time in 1981. Today the castle houses the **Batznhäusl Collection of Fine Art**, a **weaponry** and an **art gallery** where local artists can display their work. The castle is one of the most complete mediaeval buildings in the Dolomites, and is open to the public daily except Saturdays.

From Fié you continue to climb, ascending above 2000m for the first time on this trek. Yet the scenery is so gorgeous and the climb so gentle that even though you'll be walking for another four hours or so, it doesn't seem too strenuous. To begin this final stretch: from opposite the tourist office take Schlernstrasse up the hill for 200m, turning off left opposite Hotel Hehlbad onto Trail 1. Continue through **Fié di Sopra/Ober Fié** (970m), or Upper Fié, and pass that plush woodland retreat, *Hotel Waldsee* (☎ 0471-725041; rooms start at L70,000 per person). Trail 1 then leaves the main track a few hundred metres past **Lake Huber**, heading to the right through the forest. Twenty minutes along this path and you'll find yourself in a large meadow in the heart of the forest, in the middle of which is *Rifugio Tuff Alm* (☎ 0471-726090; 1274m). Your trail passes just south of the rifugio, plunging into forest a few minutes later. Through the trees the path affords intermittent views of by-now faraway Fié as it winds its way south then west, climbing ever higher all the time.

Just past the 1800m mark an alternative path to *Rifugio Bolzano*, Trail 3, becomes available. I suggest you stick to the more scenic and gentle Trail 1, however, for this will take you through a narrow, damp, and cool gully on wooden walkways, unique in the Dolomites, as far as I'm aware, past an *oratorio*, or wayside shrine, set in the side of the cliffs and on to **Malga Seggiola** farmhouse (1940m), where they have fresh milk for sale. From here, the path heads north-east up the southern slopes of the Sciliar with the Catinaccio mountains appearing for the first time to the south-east. At the summit, the CAI-owned *Rifugio Bolzano* or *Schlernhaus* (☎ 0471-612024), built in 1885, stands 2457m above sea level on the southern slopes of the Monte Pez. Its austere exterior belies its cosy pinewood interior. The food is excellent, with good healthy portions of well-cooked staple meals, and the tap water is potable. Standard CAI prices (L32,000/

Map 3 – Fié to Rifugio Bolzano 75

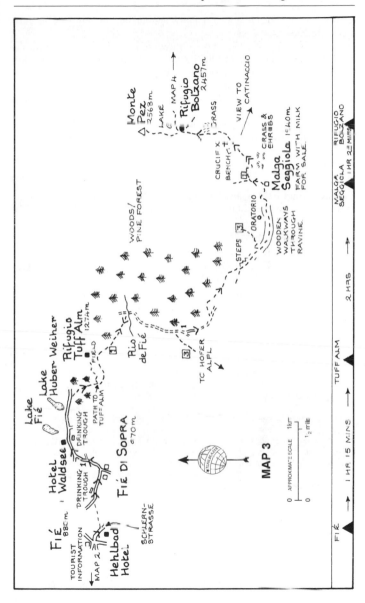

Monte
△ Pez
2563m

Lake ← MAP 4 →

Rifugio
Bolzano
2457m

LAKE

VIEW TO
CATINACCIO

GRASS

CRUCIF X
BENCH ↑

GRASS &
EHRUBS

Malga
Seggiola 1540m
FARM WITH MILK
FOR SALE.

WOODS/
PINE FOREST

ORATORIO

STEPS 4

WOODEN
WALKWAYS
THROUGH
RAVINE.

Lake
Fié

Lake Huber Weiher

Rifugio
Tuff Alm
1274m

Rio
de Fié

FIE-D

PATH TO
TUFF ALM

TC HOFER
ALPL

Fié
880m

TOURIST
INFORMATION

MAP 2

Hehlbad
Hotel

Hotel
Waldsee

DRINKING
TROUGH

DRINKING
TROUGH

Fié di Sopra
880m

SCHLERN-
STRASSE

MAP 3

0 APPROXIMATE SCALE 1km
0   ½ mile

FIÉ ◀── 1 HR 15 MINS ──▶ TUFF ALM ◀── 2 HRS ──▶ MALGA
SEGGIOLA ◀── 1 HR 25 MINS ──▶ RIFUGIO
BOLZANO

16,000 non-members/members) apply, and the hut is open from 1st June to the middle of October.

Impressively just 106m above *Rifugio Bolzano* is the peak of Monte Pez, the highest point in the Sciliar range and the supposed site of pre-historic ritual sacrifices and mediaeval pagan ceremonies. From the summit, a wonderful 360° panorama takes in the Catinaccio and Latemar range to the south-east, the Sassolungo and Sella groups to the east and the Puez-Odle to the north of these. Furthermore, behind you to the west beyond Bolzano are the Venoste and Brenta peaks. To walk to the top of Pez, head due north from the rifugio; it takes only 20 minutes or so.

RIFUGIO BOLZANO → RIFUGIO ALPE DI TIRES AND THE CATINACCIO LOOP   [MAPS 4–5]

[**Tabacco map 029**] Our adherence to Trail 1, which began at the Valle Isarco, ends a couple of hundred metres beyond *Rifugio Bolzano*; while it continues north to the village of Siusi/Seis which you can see in the distance below the northern end of the plateau, you should take Trail 3-4

❑ The Alpe di Siusi/Seiser Alm

The Alpe di Siusi is the largest alpine plateau in Western Europe, encompassing a total area of some 55 square kilometres. Formerly a deep oblong basin lying at the bottom of the ocean, the plateau was created about 100 million years ago when the continents of Europe and Africa collided, pushing the Alpe di Siusi upwards to its present altitude some 500m above sea level. Framed by the Sassolungo and Sciliar to the east and west respectively—mountains made up largely of ancient coral reefs which once formed the sides of this underwater basin – and by the Val Gardena and the Catinaccio group to the north and south, the upper strata of the Alpe di Siusi plateau is formed from a dark brown rock which has its genesis in the Triassic period (200-250 million years ago) when the lava from now-extinct volcanoes near Monzoni poured into the underwater basin. Today much of this rock is covered in a soft, water-retaining, russet-red **clay**. It is a fertile earth, ideal for agriculture and grazing, and the plateau is dotted with small farmsteads and *fienili* (wooden huts used for storing hay). The plateau is also renowned for its **wild flowers**, including the alpine poppy, monk's hood, crocus, snowbell and the armeria, also known as the 'Witch of the Sciliar'. Unfortunately, the arrival of tourism has had a devastating effect on this local flora, and many of these plants are close to disappearing from the Alpe di Siusi. For this reason, the plateau and the neighbouring Sciliar massif have together been designated as a national park, and vehicular access is now limited almost solely to public transport.

Map 4 – Rifugio Bolzano to Rifugio Alpe di Tires 77

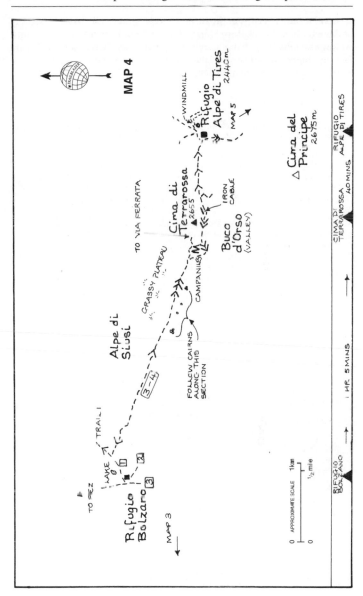

straight ahead. Initially undulating, after 15 minutes it begins its inex-orable climb up the western slopes of the **Cima di Terrarossa** (2655m). Alpine choughs are prevalent around this part, their harsh caw-cawing by far the loudest sound on the plateau. The path is fairly easy to follow thanks to a large number of small cairns placed at intervals along the route; that and the passing of thousands of boots that have stained the once-grey path a dirty burgundy.

❏ **A detour from Passo Principe to Rifugio Passo Santner**
[**Tabacco map 06**] This trail begins at the Passo Principe (see pp79–80 for details of the trail up to the passo) and necessitates an overnight stay at the *Rifugio Passo Santner*. The first part of this walk along Trail 584 involves a gentle descent into the Val dal Vajolet and the large old CAI **rifugio** (☎ 0462-763292) of the same name. From here, path 542s heads right and up the hill towards a second hut, the privately-owned *Rifugio Re Alberto 1/Gartlhütte* (☎ 0462-763428; 2621m). This two-hour trail, squeezed between the mighty Torri di Vajolet to the north and Cima Catinaccio to the south, is particularly steep and precarious and non-climbers may well find the going a little too tough. Some cables have been added for safety, but it's still a very demanding ascent.

Incidentally, the name Catinaccio contains elements of both Ladin and German and is related to the German word *Rosengarten*, or 'Rose Garden'. According to legend, this garden was the home of a number of dwarves who lived under the benevolent rule of their king, Laurino. Cut off by the steep slopes of the Catinaccio from the outside world, all was peaceful in Laurino's kingdom. Unfortunately, this idyllic state did not last. One day, a party of local villagers, intrigued by the red roses that grew on the outer slopes of the Catinaccio all year long, decided to explore the mountain and discovered the dwarves' kingdom. The king was kidnapped during the subsequent attack and many of his treasures stolen. In the fullness of time King Laurino managed to escape, but on returning to his kingdom placed a curse upon the roses that had led his capturers to his realm, turning them to stone and forbidding them from being seen in their vivid glory by anyone during the day or night. Fortunately for us, the king forgot to mention those few minutes that belong to neither day nor night; thus, for a few brief moments at dawn and dusk, we can see these petrified roses glowing a deep red. And this, according to Ladin legend, is why the Dolomite mountains sometimes glow an unnaturally vivid red, a phe-nomenon that we now call alpenglow.

Continuing with the trail, from *Alberto 1*, Trail 542s now bends south and up to the tiny privately-run *Rifugio Passo Santner/Santnerpass Hütte* (☎ 0471-642230; 2734m), nestling precariously on a ledge above a sheer drop. As it is so small, with only eight beds in total, and because of its popu-larity with climbers, trekkers are advised to ring ahead if they wish to stay here.

To return to the main trail, head back the same way as you came.

Map 5 – Rifugio Alpe di Tires to Rifugio Passo Santner 79

At the end of the climb a signpost points right, past several *campaniles* (literally 'steeple' in Italian though these are actually naturally sculpted limestone pinnacles) on your left and on down to an assisted section of the trail, where metal cables have been fixed by a particularly narrow part of the path. The **Cime del Principe/Grasleiten** (2675m), part of the Catinaccio range, looms to the south. Though just a few hundred metres to your right, the peaks are separated from your trail by the narrowest of valleys, the **Buco d'Orso** ('Bear Hole').

Rifugio Alpe di Tires/Tierser Alpi-Hütte (☎ 0471-727958; 2440m), in view since virtually the beginning of your descent, lies an easy 15-minute uphill stroll from the assisted section of the trail. Though privately owned, this rifugio is great value (L17,000 for a bed in a dorm), particularly if you choose the excellent set menu in the evening. Be careful

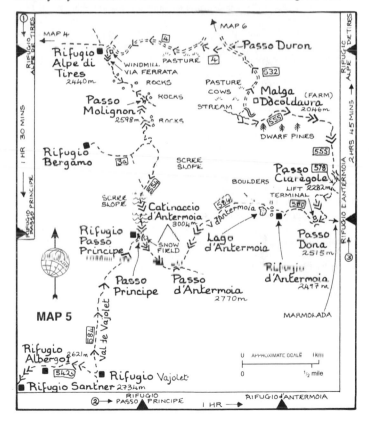

when paying, however: the rifugio likes you to settle the night before and automatically charges L10,000 for breakfast the next morning; if you don't want the breakfast, make sure that this is deducted from your bill.

The path now heads south towards the Cima Catinaccio before looping back to *Rifugio Alpe di Tires* via the Val d'Antermoia. Those wishing to forego the walk to *Rifugio Santner* as described in the box on p78 may wish to check into *Rifugio Alpe di Tires* now, so you can leave some of your non-essential luggage behind.

From the signpost by the *Alpe di Tires* windmill take path 554 to the south. An iron cable has been fixed to the rock to help you tackle the first few minutes of the climb towards the **Passo Molignon** (2598m), which should take you less than 20 minutes. From the pass, the path all the way down and up to the **Passo Principe** (2599m) is clearly visible, etched into the scree on the north-western slopes of the towering Antermoia peak ahead (3004m).

On the way, in the distance to your right, you'll notice the CAI's *Rifugio Bergamo/Grasleiten Hütte* (☎ 0471-642103), a handy escape option should the weather take a turn for the worse, which it frequently does around these parts. At the pass itself is the minuscule *Rifugio Passo Principe/Grasleitenpasse Hütte* (☎ 0462-64244; 2599m), tucked away in the shadow of the Valbona peak. Basic in the extreme, this privately-run place is way overpriced at L28,000 per night and should really be considered only in an emergency.

From the Passo Principe, Trail 584 continues east up and over the Antermoia Pass, a stiff but short 15-minute climb. At 2770m you have reached the highest point on the trail, save for the via ferrata finish at the Croda Rossa di Sesto (see p131). At the top, ignore the two more-obvious passes that appear on your right, and instead follow the waymarkings as they drop down into the **Val d'Antermoia** to your left. A walk along the rocky valley floor will bring you to the valley's sombre cobalt blue lake, **Lago d'Antermoia**, above which, in the distance to the east, you can see the ice-capped summit of the Marmolada. The CAI's *Rifugio d'Antermoia* (☎ 0462-802272; 2497m), with beds for 44 people, sits close by. Standard CAI prices (L32,000/16,000 non-members/members) apply.

Continuing east along path 580 to the **Passo Dona** (2515m), the view suddenly opens up to reveal the nearby Sasso Piatto and Lungo to the north-east with the Sella Massif beyond.

The route now descends north to the **Pian dele Gialine** (2331m) where you switch to Trail 578, then change again five minutes later at the **Passo Ciarègole** (2282m) to Trail 555. This steep dirt track through moorland and, towards the end, dwarf pines which seem very reluctant to let trekkers pass, will take you down to the small valley farm of **Malga Dòcoldaura** (2046m). Joining the gravel track (Trail 532) and turning

Map 6 – Rifugio Alpe di Tires to Saltria 81

left, after a quick march uphill through the verdant pastures of the **Val Duron** you find yourself at the junction with Trail 4 which heads back towards *Rifugio Alpe di Tires*.

RIFUGIO ALPE DI TIRES → VAL GARDENA   [MAPS 6–7]

[Tabacco maps 029 and 05] This stage takes you round the eastern edge of the Alpe di Siusi and on to the resort valley of Val Gardena. After the previous day's exertions, this is a simple stage. There are in fact many trails that cut north across the Alpe di Siusi to the Val Gardena but the one we have chosen is particularly short and gentle, following mountain roads for almost the entire way. At the end you arrive at the village of Santa Cristina, from where you have a number of options, as described on p82.

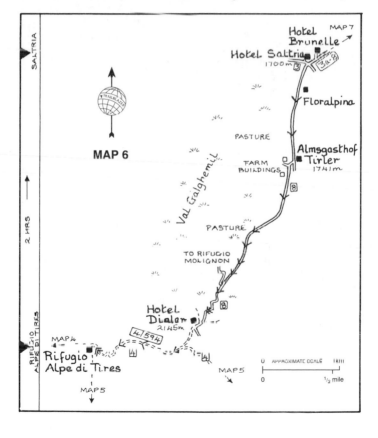

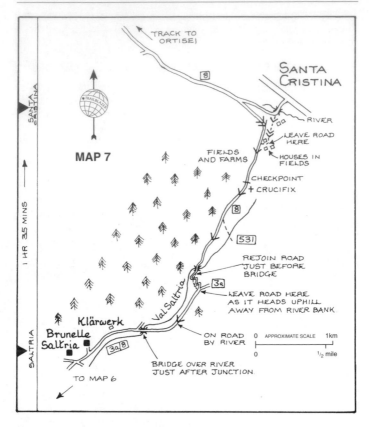

MAP 7

TRACK TO ORTISEI

SANTA CRISTINA

SANTA CRISTINA

1 HR 35 MINS

SALTRIA

RIVER

LEAVE ROAD HERE

FIELDS AND FARMS

HOUSES IN FIELDS

CHECKPOINT

CRUCIFIX

REJOIN ROAD JUST BEFORE BRIDGE

LEAVE ROAD HERE AS IT HEADS UPHILL AWAY FROM RIVER BANK

Val Saltria

ON ROAD BY RIVER

Klärwerk

Brunelle

Saltria

BRIDGE OVER RIVER JUST AFTER JUNCTION

TO MAP 6

0 APPROXIMATE SCALE 1km

0 1/2 mile

From *Rifugio Alpe di Tires* head due east on Trail 4-594, taking the left-hand fork where the path splits into two to bring you out at **Hotel Dialer** (☎ 0471-727898; 2145m; L75,000 per person with breakfast, rising to L95,000 in August). From here, continue north on the rather dull Trail 8, ignoring the left-hand detour to *Rifugio Molignon* but continuing instead down the **Galghemil Valley** to *Almsgasthof Tirler* (1741m) and the Saltria junction (1700m) where a number of large hotels huddle together; here go right, past the bus stop and the driveway of *Hotel Brunelle* and follow Trail 3a/8 as it wends its way along the banks of the **Ruf da Jënder**. At one point, at the very moment where the road climbs away from the river, it is possible to take a short cut through the forest, rejoining the path a few minutes later (see Map 7 for details). After they join the tarmac road leading

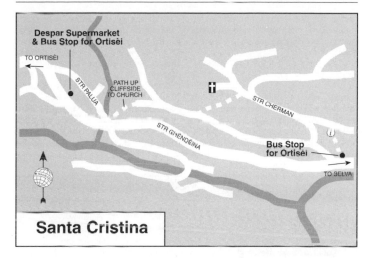

Santa Cristina

into **Santa Cristina**, paths branch off west and east to Ortisèi/St Ulrich and Selva/Wolkenstein respectively. You can go to both these villages on one of the local buses that run frequently up and down the valley. From Selva there is a 'short cut' up to *Rifugio Puez*, a walk of three hours. In this book, however, we recommend and have described the walk east from Ortisèi because not only is Ortisèi the largest and most interesting village in the valley with a greater variety of services and facilities for trekkers but it is also the gateway to the Odle range, a range that you'll miss if you take the Selva short cut.

To reach Ortisèi, you can continue on Route 8, though this is an unexciting walk past an interminable series of farms and pensions. If I were you, I'd take the bus (L2000, pay on board) which leaves from below Santa Cristina's **tourist office** (☎ 0471-793046) and also near the Despar **supermarket**. Interestingly, the **Church of Santa Cristina** that dominates the town dates back to the fourteenth century, though of the building you see today only the bell tower wall is original. The path leading up to the church from the highway is punctuated by five **Stations of the Cross**.

ORTISÈI

The ridge-turreted **Church of San Antonio**, built in 1673, marks the centre of Ortisèi (1265m) and sits in the square of the same name. Above the square you'll find the **Val Gardena Local Heritage Museum**, one of the better museums in the Dolomites. The exhibits date back to the Stone Age, and include some impressive Bronze Age artefacts such as the fourth century BC dagger of Balest and an entire gallery dedicated to the work by local artist Josef Moroder-Lusenberg. He also contributed the altarpiece, *Adoration of the*

Magi, for the parish church which stands above the western end of Streda Rezia, immediately behind the tourist office.

Services

Just below the parish church is the **tourist office** (☎ 0471-796328) at Streda Rezia 1. In the same building is the **telephone office**, while immediately below them is the **post office**, round the back of which you'll find the entrance to the Grupa Hëus Jeuni on the third floor,

a youth society with **Internet** facilities. Continuing down the hill on Streda Rezia, at No 28C on the bend is Sport Moroder, one of the better **trekking shops** in the village, while the local **pharmacy** is next door. Further on, on the other side of the road at No 31, is the Planinschek Foto **camera shop**, while Bazar Rusina opposite has **maps, postcards** and English-language **newspapers**. For food supplies, the local Despar **supermarket** lies 150m east of the square .

❏ Val Gardena/Gröden

Flanked by the Valle Isarco to the west and the passos Gardena and Sella to the east, the Val Gardena is one of the most popular holiday resorts in the Dolomites. Tourists flock year-round to enjoy both the trekking and skiing opportunities available in the nearby mountains (the valley holds one of the **World Cup** races in December), and to savour the scenic, pastoral splendour of the valley itself, with its rolling hills and quaint Tyrolean villages.

Though first settled by farmers in the Middle Ages, the Val Gardena has a history stretching back many thousands of years. The **Troi Paian path** linking Passo Gardena with the village of Laion, at the western entrance of the valley, is said to be a prehistoric trading trail and one of the oldest walking routes in the Dolomites. (Parts of the original route can be seen above Ortisèi). A number of bronze age items have also been unearthed in the valley, most of which now reside in the Val Gardena Local Heritage Museum in Ortisèi. Today there are four major villages in the Val Gardena. Ortisèi with its population of 5200 is the largest, followed by Selva (2700), Castelrotto (2400) at the western end of the valley, and finally Santa Cristina (1700). Each of these villages is trilingual, as you can tell from the road signs. Apart from tourism, the major industries in the valley are agriculture and woodcarving using the locally-grown cemblan pines. Said to have started in the 16th century, the woodcarving industry now employs about 3500 people in the valley, particularly in Santa Cristina which today is full of shops selling the sculptors' work.

In an effort to minimize the traffic choking the valley, the local authorities have introduced the **Gardena Card**, a seven-day pass allowing unlimited, free use of all lifts in the valley, free use of the local buses anywhere between Ortisèi and Passo Gardena and reduced rates on certain tour companies operating in the Gardena. The card currently costs L65,000 and is available from the local tourist offices.

Please note that there are no campsites anywhere in the Val Gardena.

Accommodation

Ortisèi's private accommodation is good value, much of it in the L30,000-40,000 range including *Santifaller Gerlinde* (☎ 0471-796716) at Streda Stufan 40, a friendly, family-run place with large rooms (L35,000 per person) and hearty breakfasts, and the nearby *Santifaller Raimund* (☎ 0471-796337) at No 31 a smaller, simpler but equally friendly place. Other private houses recommended in this range include *Aurelia* (☎ 0471-796258) at Streda Rezia 240, and *Sayonara* (☎ 0471-796611) at Streda Vidalong 17 on the southern side of the river.

Transport from the Val Gardena

There are 10 direct **buses** every day (and 11 from Ortisèi) to Bolzano (No 120; 55 mins from Ortisèi, 1hr 10 mins from Santa Cristina, 1hr 25 mins from Selva) and five to Bressanone (No 122; 53 mins from Ortisèi).

For most other destinations to the west it is usually quicker to travel first to Castelrotto at the western end of the valley and change there. There are also four buses running daily through the valley to Castelrotto (at 8.25am, 9.25am, 4.20pm and 5.35pm from Ortisèi). The journey from Ortisèi takes 32 minutes.

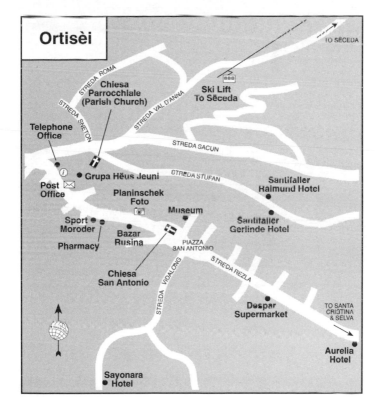

ORTISÈI → RIFUGIO PUEZ   [MAP 8–9]

[**Tabacco map 05**] From Ortisèi, the route now leads up the western face of Le Odle to Sëceda. This can be walked by following Trail 2, though most people prefer to take the cable car up to Sëceda. This isn't such a bad idea, for the ascent is almost 1200m (from 1265m to 2456m), and the scenery and views are not very exciting. Unfortunately, the car was temporarily closed for renovations when I visited, though it should have opened again by the time you read this. The cost is usually about L12,000 one way and it should follow roughly the same operating times as before, namely 08.30 to 17.40 every day in the summer season.

However, to satisfy those fundamentalist trekkers who view any sort of transportation during a trek as an anathema, the walk from Ortisèi to Sëceda is described in the box below.

❏ Ortisèi to Sëceda

From the parish church above the tourist office, head up the hill on Streda Sneton, taking a right turn onto Streda Roma. After a few metres, you'll see a bridge over a stream on your left, followed by a second wooden bridge a little further on. Walking by the stream along the path, before long you'll come to the **Café Val d'Anna** on your left-hand side. Keep on the track as it bends left up a fairly steep grassy hill, then turns left again over a tiny waterfall, before finally bearing right towards the road. Currently at the very top of this path, which is marked with black dashes on the Tabacco maps, there appears to be some sort of engineering project going on, so the route may have altered slightly by the time you read this.

Across the road at the top and a few metres to your left is a signpost for Trail 2, beginning behind the **Costamula de Sot** farmhouse (1536m). After 10 minutes or so you'll find yourself walking by a pretty stream, which you cross by an old farmhouse. Continuing up the hill through the gate, go left at the junction onto Trail 8, then, two minutes later, turn right back on Trail 2 as it heads off into the forest. Be careful here, for after no more than a minute a smaller trail branches off left from the wide track; this is the trail you should take.

From now on until the Sëceda the going is fairly steep. After 30 minutes walking through thin forest with the cable car visible to your left you come to a ski piste and, turning right, you follow it up the hill; there are no markers along this piste. Fifteen minutes further on, you'll see on your left a sign nailed to a wooden farm building. Take path 6 to the left, and follow it as it wends its way up through the grassy **Alpe Mastlè** to Sëceda, the terminus for the zigzag from Ortisèi. Here, you can try to continue on to the *Rifugio Puez*, though this makes for a very long stage. You may therefore wish to break it up by staying in one of the rifugi on the plateau.

Map 8 – Ortisèi to Sëceda 87

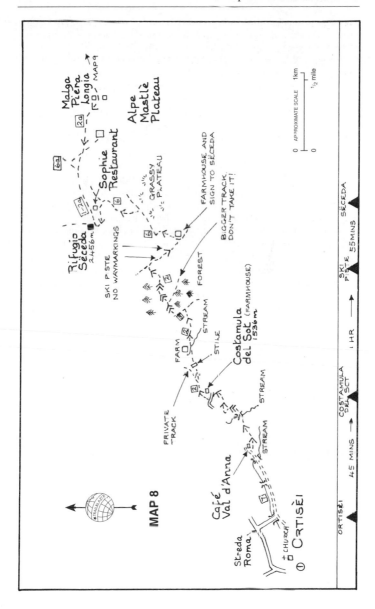

Those of you who do decide to take the cable-car option may wish to press on beyond *Rifugio Puez* to *Rifugio Gardenaccia* or even the town of La Villa, thus completing two stages in one day.

Your walk begins by **Rifugio Sëceda** (2456m), where an easy path, Trail 2a, heads off east beneath the brow of the hill above the pleasantly undulating **Alpe Mastlè plateau** billowing out below you to your right like a giant green blanket. Selva/Wolkenstein is visible in the valley beyond the plateau with the sheer face of the Sella and Sassolungo groups forming a stupendous backdrop further south.

Ignoring Trails 6 and 1, paths that lead off to the left and right respectively, continue straight on Trail 2a as it descends to the **Malga Piera Longia** (2297m), a farmhouse in the midst of some massive grey limestone boulders. This is followed by the grassy **Plan Ciautier**, a section of the trail that, if anything, is *over-filled* with signposts; don't be distracted, however, but keep to Trail 2a as it emerges from the shadow of the giant Odle pinnacles and descends to a dry rocky river bed.

At this point, a few people get lost. To avoid this you must be very careful not to cross the bed immediately but walk on down to the large fir tree, the only tree of any size, growing on the riverbank on your side. From here, cross over to the path on the opposite bank, a path that points you towards the next waymarking painted on a large boulder 30m away. The next signpost lies 150m beyond this, pointing left up towards the **Forcella Forces de Sieles** (2505m) on Trail 2, a steady climb that grows ever more steep as you near the top.

Nor is the climbing finished once the forcella has been reached, for a series of three short iron cables strung along to your left lead you up the cliffside to the north. The magnificent vista from the small grassy plateau at the top encompasses the Fanes group to the east, Sella to the south-east and the Odle peaks and Sëceda to the west.

Sitting on the grass, you'll be relieved to know that the hard work for the day is now over: from here the path continues east over a small stretch of scree (with one short section aided), before descending to the more verdant slopes of the **Pian dal Ciaval** where walking becomes easier. The *pian*, in the early morning at least, is often teeming with herds of chamois that dash off as you approach, before tentatively closing in again behind you as you move off. By 9am, however, the herd has usually been usurped by a dozy flock of sheep that merely grazes and gazes as you walk on by.

About an hour after leaving the Forcella Forces de Sieles you'll reach the junction with path 4 (which has come up from Selva via the deep, narrow chasm of the **Val Lunga/Langental**, to the right of your trail), and after that the pink and grey striations of the **Col De Puez** (2725m) appear immediately to your left, a sure sign that you are just a few minutes away from the rifugio which shares its name.

Map 9 – Sëceda to Puez 89

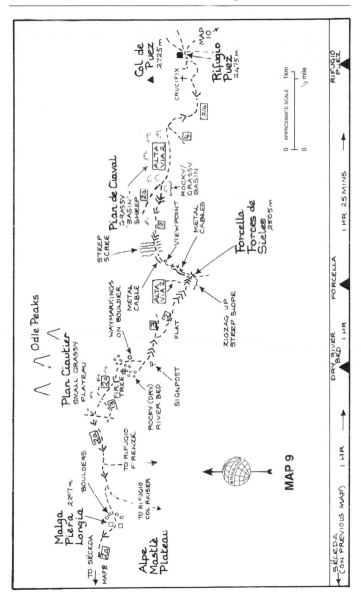

Another hugely popular rifugio, the large and chilly but homely CAI-owned *Puez* (☎ 0471-795365; 2475m) is a friendly place, though ask for a bed in one of the smaller rooms downstairs rather than in the noisy but capacious attic where they'll doubtless try to put you. Beds cost L13,000 for members, double for non-members.

Those who wish to avoid spending a night in the valley town of La Villa tomorrow may wish to extend their journey by continuing on to *Rifugio Gardenaccia*, a couple of hours to the east of *Rifugio Puez*. See the beginning of the next stage for a description of the walk to the Gardenaccia.

RIFUGIO PUEZ → LA VILLA/STERN   [MAP 10]

[Tabacco map 07] In this stage you leave the Puez range, heading east to the Ladin-speaking Val Badia. This is a very short and easy downhill stage, almost a rest day in fact; although you may feel that you don't need one, I'm afraid you have little choice because the next accommodation after La Villa, *Rifugio Fanes,* lies about six hours away. Assuming, therefore, that a walk in one day from *Rifugio Puez* to *Rifugio Fanes* is out of the question, you have two options: walk for only a couple of hours today, spend the night in La Villa, and begin the climb up to *Fanes* in the morning; or, if you walked on from *Puez* to *Rifugio Gardenaccia* as suggested in the last stage, then you can walk all the way from *Gardenaccia* to *Fanes* in this stage, an exhausting but by no means unfeasible trek.

To begin, from *Puez* take Trail 2/4/15 eastwards, opting for Route 15 only at the junction some 20 minutes later. Follow the waymarkings which alternate between 5 and 15 and continuing east along the rocky and largely flat plateau, taking care not to twist your ankle in the fissures that scar the karstic ground of this eerie plateau. The waymarkings are frequent, as they need to be in this often misty area.

Before long the path starts to descend by stages down towards the Val Badia. It's almost as if you're walking down some giant staircase, with a steep descent being followed by a piece of level ground, followed by another descent to another level area, and so on and so on. In this manner you'll reach the junction with Route 11 at the top of a steep gully; descending to the foot of the gully, continue following Route 11/15 as it heads due east over the grass and on down to *Rifugio Gardenaccia/Gardenazza* (☎ 0471-849282; 2050m). This privately-owned, summer-only rifugio (it's usually closed by the end of September) has rooms with two or three beds and charges L29,000 per person, L38,000 with breakfast. The descent to La Villa begins to the south of the rifugio with another steep gully. Having negotiated this, you will now find the path bending to the left, with a superfluous iron cable strung along a narrow section of it at the beginning.

Map 10 – Puez to La Villa 91

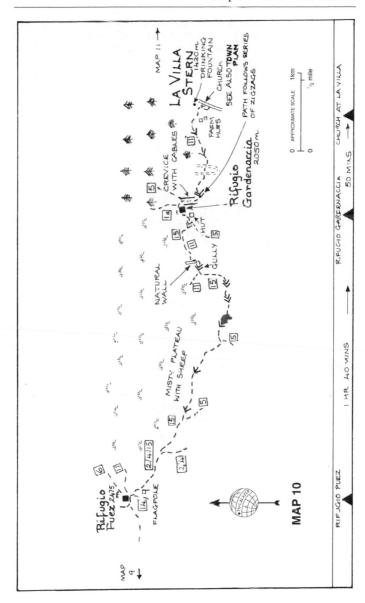

MAP 10

MAP 9 ↓

MAP 11 →

Rifugio Puez 2475 m
FLAGPOLE

MISTY PLATEAU WITH SHEEP

NATURAL WALK

GULLY

HUT

Rifugio Gardenaccia 2050 m

CREVICE WITH CABLES

LA VILLA STERN
1420 m
DRINKING FOUNTAIN
CHURCH
SEE ALSO TOWN PLAN
FARM HUTS
PATH FOLLOWS SERIES OF ZIGZAGS

APPROXIMATE SCALE
0 .... 1km
0 .... ½ mile

RIFUGIO PUEZ → 1 HR. 40 MINS → RIFUGIO GARDENACCIA → 50 MINS → CHURCH AT LA VILLA

La Villa is already in view below you, though the descent to town is a long one. But after traipsing through the *pineta* (pine forest) for the best part of an hour – and assuming you've been following Route 11 and ignored the turn-offs to *Sponatahütte*, Fontanaccia and *Hotel Dolomiti* – you emerge at the top of town by a wonderful old tumbledown farmhouse, followed soon after by the old **church** of La Villa and the nearby **drinking fountain**. The **tourist office** lies 10 minutes beyond the church, further down the hill.

❏ **Val Badia/Gadertal**
The village of La Villa lies in the heart of the **Val Badia/Gadertal**, a north-south oriented valley stretching north from Arabba and including the triangular, high-level plateau of **Pralongia** that sits in its centre. This is Ladin country, with well over 90 per cent of the valley's inhabitants claiming the Rhaetian language as their mother tongue. The valley is of particular interest to geologists, as it marks the border between the Eastern (*Orientali*) and Western (*Occidentali*) Dolomites (see p37), the division line running along the **Gadera River**.

The villages in this area are all rather small. The largest, **Pedraces/Pedratsches**, can boast of just 1300 inhabitants, while the six villages of Alta Badia, 'High Badia', which lies immediately to the south of the village of La Val, have fewer than 5000 residents between them, a figure supplemented by a fluctuating population of up to 16,000 tourists at any one time, most of whom stay in one of the hundred-plus hotels, pensions and B&B's that exist in this valley. These tourists flock here for the sporting possibilities – the Gran Risa ski-slope is said to be the favourite piste of skier Patrick Tomba – while in summer the valley's cycling marathon continues to grow, with over 6400 riders from 29 nations competing in 1998.

LA VILLA/STERN

La Villa (1420m), lying in the heart of Val Badia, has a population of just under one thousand and is the third largest village in the entire valley. It's a lovely little place (show me a village around here that isn't!) and a pleasant-enough place to spend a night. It lacks any major attractions, the **church** at the top of the village is typically alpine, while the small **castle** nearby is privately-owned and only opens to the public for concerts.

Services

The **tourist office** (Monday to Saturday 8am-noon, 3-7pm; Sunday 10am-noon, 4-6pm; ☎ 0471-847037) lies in the centre of town, across the road from the Despar **supermarket** and **telecom office**. The Alimentari Giornal shop, just a little way down the road on the opposite side, has a basic **trekking department** at the back and also sells **maps**. There are at least three **banks** on this street too, each with its own ATM.

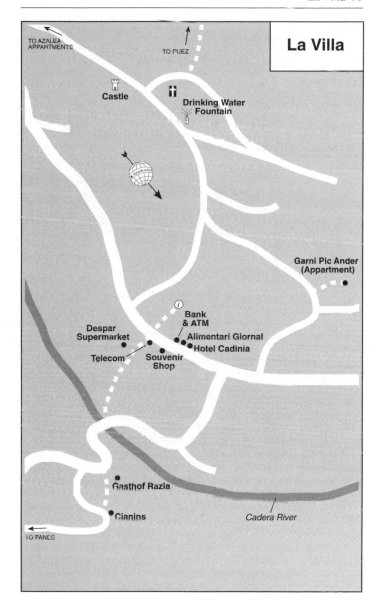

TO AZALEA APPARTMENTS

TO PUEZ

Castle

Drinking Water Fountain

TRAILBLAZER

Garni Pic Ander (Appartment)

Despar Supermarket

(i)

Bank & ATM

Alimentari Giornal

Telecom

Hotel Cadinia

Souvenir Shop

Gasthof Razla

Cianins

Cadera River

TO FANES

La Villa

Accommodation
It's possible to get a private room with breakfast for around L30,000. Recommendations include *Garni Pic Ander* (☎ 0471-847280) with rooms for L35,000 including a huge breakfast; and the slightly cheaper but equally cosy *Azalea* (☎ 0471-847232), though it's about 300m out of town: when you reach the church, turn right up the road rather than into La Villa itself.

Transport
From La Villa there are **buses** to Bresssanone (11 daily; change in San Lorenzo), Ortisèi (4 daily), Arabba and the Passo Pordoi (4 daily) and Bolzano (2 daily).

LA VILLA → RIFUGIO FANES   [MAPS 11–12]

[Tabacco map 07 and 03] If you stayed overnight in La Villa, luxuriating in the comforts of town life (such as hot showers and good food), this stage will be something of a rude awakening as you reintroduce yourself to the rigours of high altitude walking. From La Villa, the climb to the weird and wonderful **Parco Naturale Fanes** is nothing short of horrendous, a four-hour uphill slog where the summit never seems to get any nearer. But then, as an Italian trekker said to me as we were doing this climb, Non dura, non bella – 'if it ain't hard, it ain't beautiful' – a philosophy that can be applied to all sorts of situations. And besides, this walk is not without its merits, especially the early stages through the forest bearding the lower slopes of the **Piz di Lavareda**, which is rich in bird- and plant-life.

Beginning at La Villa's Despar supermarket, head down the hill to the river, cross over the bridge, then go up the opposite slope past the tiny settlement of **Cianins** just above the *Gasthof Rezia*. Waymarkings now begin to appear, so follow the signs for Trail 12 to the **Val Medesc**. Bisecting the larger Trail 15, Trail 12 then hugs both banks of a delightful mountain stream as you follow eastwards and upwards. The forest soon shrinks in size as dwarf pines and alpine shrubs take over, and eventually even these disappear as you begin to make your way over shattered rocks towards the **Forcella de Medesc** (2533m). Crossing to the northern side of the Val Medes, the last 200m are the hardest.

Route 12 continues its progress north-east down into the **Alpe di Fanes** (Fanes plateau). The path rises and falls over the plateau's natural undulations, meandering eastwards over rocks and wild grass to a junction with trail 7.

Turn right here but after just a few minutes go left on route 7 (the turn-off is not signposted) and follow the trail as it climbs up and over a lip into a large, eerie basin. It doesn't matter if you miss the turn-off: both 7 and 12 head to Rifugio Fanes, though the former is definitely the more interesting.

There's definitely something strange about this basin, though what it is exactly is hard to define. Certainly it is a very atmospheric place,

Map 11 – La Villa to Forcella de Medesc 95

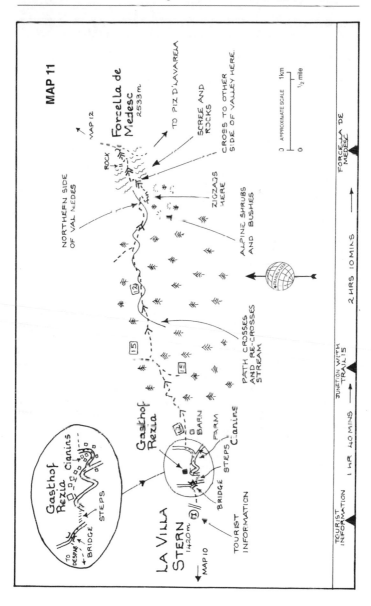

MAP 11

Forcella de
Medesc
2533m.

TO PIZ D'LAVARELA

MAP 12

ROCK

NORTHERN SIDE
OF VAL MEDES

SCREE AND
ROCKS

CROSS TO OTHER
SIDE OF VALLEY HERE.

ZIGZAGS
HERE

ALPINE SHRUBS
AND BUSHES

PATH CROSSES
AND RE-CROSSES
STREAM

0   APPROXIMATE SCALE   1km

0   ½ mile

Gasthof
Rezia   Cianins

TO DESPAR

BRIDGE
STEPS

Gasthof
Rezia

BARN
FARM

Cianins

BRIDGE
STEPS

La Villa
Stern
1420m.

MAP 10

TOURIST
INFORMATION

TOURIST
INFORMATION

JUNCTION WITH
TRAIL 15

FORCELLA DE
MEDESC

1 HR 40 MINS   2 HRS 10 MINS

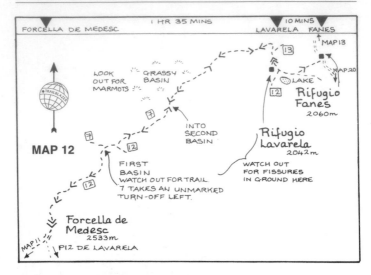

spooky even, particularly when there's a little mist around, as there nearly always is! Only the shrill warning of the local marmots and the
alarmed twittering of birds disturb the unnatural silence of this strange
land. It's easy to see why this small clump of mountains has inspired
more legends and fairytales than any other part of the Dolomites.
Remember to be careful when walking on this land. Ensure your boots are
firmly laced for the karstic terrain is sliced with natural fissures that could
easily cause twisted ankles. Up here, nobody can hear you scream.

Cutting straight across the centre of the basin, route 7 then begins its
descent to **Rifugio Lavarela** (or **Lavarella** as it's sometimes spelt) and its
near neighbour, **Rifugio Fanes**. Of the two, *Fanes* (☎ 0474-501097;
2060m) is the larger and busier and feels more like a hotel; in my opin-
ion their dormitory beds (L32,000 in the summer) are overpriced. The
Lavarella (☎ 0474-501079; 2042m) is, on the other hand, more cosy and
intimate and for this reason wins my vote. The bar seems pretty well
stocked too. Rooms here start at around L40,000 per person including
breakfast.

The dark-green lake between the two rifugi, incidentally, is said to
have turned that colour after a magic mirror, which reflected a person's
darkest secrets, was flung into it.

(Opposite) The crucifix behind the Casera Cavallo di Sopra, with the Remeda
Rossa peak in the background.

Map 13 – Rifugio Fanes to Rifugio Fodara Vedla 97

RIFUGIO FANES → TRE CIME DI LAVAREDO/DREI ZINNEN

From *Rifugio Fanes* the trail divides into two. **Route A** heads north-east up to *Rifugio Biella* and the Croda Del Becco, before heading east to the Tre Cime on one of the most attractive paths described in this book. **Route B** on the other hand is a tad more taxing but takes in such mountain groups as the Tofane and Cristallo, as well as the fashionable town of Cortina. Both routes are described below.

ROUTE A: VIA THE CRODA DEL BECCO

Rifugio Fanes → Rifugio Biella   [MAPS 13–14]

[Tabacco map 03] This is a relatively easy and short stage. Indeed, those who are into sprint-trekking may wish to combine it with the one after. I advise you not to: the next leg is one of the most beautiful walks in the entire Dolomites, best appreciated at a gentle, strolling pace rather than a sweaty rush, so stop overnight in *Rifugio Biella*. This rifugio lies on Alta Via 1, and as a result is extremely popular; try to book a place in advance.

From *Rifugio Fanes*, head north along Alta Via 1 (Trail 7), a gravel road hugging the western and northern banks of the **Rio San Viglio**. Various little short cuts, some just a few metres long, are marked on the Tabacco maps; follow these or stick to the road – it doesn't really matter,

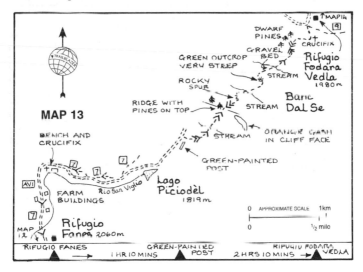

MAP 13

(Opposite) Top: The village of Auna di Sotto with the Sciliar massif in the background. **Bottom:** The Rifugio Biella.

for either way you'll end up eventually at the **Lago Piciodèl** (1819m) lying to the right of the road.

The next section of the trail is difficult to follow. You can if you prefer simply continue on the road, as this also leads (via *Rifugio Pederu*) to *Fodara Vedla*. It's a tedious hike, however. Far quicker and more scenic is the short cut marked with black dashes on the Tabacco maps. Unfortunately this trail is also difficult to find for the beginning is marked only by an old wooden post by the side of the road with a splash of green paint on top of it. The best advice I can offer for finding the trail is as follows: while standing by the Lago Piciodèl, cast your eyes along the line of cliffs to your right and you will notice that, ahead of you at the northeastern limits of these cliffs, there's a vivid orange gash in the top of the cliff-face. Immediately below it to the left is a low ridge topped with trees. It is this ridge that you will be aiming for on the short cut.

As you walk along the road, a path etched into the cliffs leading up towards the ridge becomes visible on the cliff-face. Follow this path with your eyes and you'll discover that it eventually joins the road by the old green-painted post referred to above. The path itself is steep and slippery, so take care. At the top, you'll notice that the ridge actually stands at the southern end of a small north-facing valley. You now head east along the

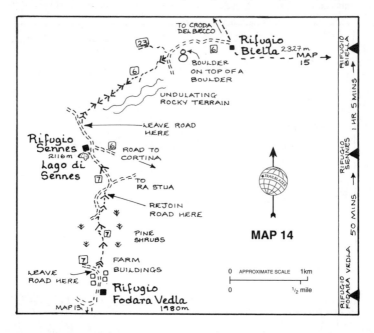

southern extremity of this valley, hugging the northern face of the **Banc dal Se**. It's a narrow and occasionally precarious trail, with the path a little too crumbling and dilapidated in some places. Concentrate hard.

Eventually, after skipping over a few small mountain streams and round a couple of rocky outcrops, you'll reach the other side of the valley. Passing over the lip, you descend into a much greener, verdant stretch of landscape and head towards *Rifugio Fodara Vedla* (☎ 0474-501093; 1980m) by a jeep track. Nestling amongst a cluster of old wooden farm buildings in the heart of the Fannes-Sennes-Braies National park, this is a very comfortable privately-run rifugio with both en suite private rooms (L40,000 per person) and dormitories (L27,000).

From the rifugio, go north along the road, leaving it after 150m or so for Trail 7 heading right through pine shrubs and rejoining the main road a few hundred metres further on. Follow the road for a few hundred metres, then turn left onto a minor track and eventually you'll arrive at *Rifugio Sennes* (☎ 0474-501092; 2116m) by the lake of the same name. If you can afford the extra cost and don't mind cutting short your trek today, you'll get more for your money here than at the *Biella*. The family who run it are excellent hosts, the rooms are comfortable and clean, and it's usually a little quieter here too. Prices start at L37,000 for a bed, with an extra L8000 for breakfast.

Should you decide to carry on, the walk from the *Sennes* to *Biella* along Trail 6, which leaves the road to the right a few hundred metres above the *Sennes*, is an interesting one. This initially steep trail takes you across some curiously undulating ground, as if you're walking on a petrified bowl of baked beans covered with grass. After about 30 minutes you'll be able to see the CAI-owned *Biella* (☎ 0436-866991; 2327m). This ramshackle little place is hugely popular, though it owes its success to its location; it's the first rifugio on Alta Via 1 and lies just below the Croda del Becco summit. Otherwise it's unremarkable. A spot on the giant bunk bed (it sleeps 24; 12 up, 12 down) in the attic costs L32,000, or half-price for members. Alpine ibex, introduced into the Fanes-Sennes-Braies park 30 years ago, often linger in the gully below the rifugio.

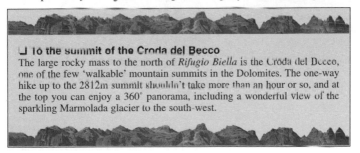

❏ To the summit of the Croda del Becco
The large rocky mass to the north of *Rifugio Biella* is the Croda del Becco, one of the few 'walkable' mountain summits in the Dolomites. The one-way hike up to the 2812m summit shouldn't take more than an hour or so, and at the top you can enjoy a 360° panorama, including a wonderful view of the sparkling Marmolada glacier to the south-west.

RIFUGIO BIELLA → RIFUGIO VALLANDRO   [Map 15–16]

[Tabacco map 03] For many people, this is the best walk in the
Dolomites. It's understandable, for this stage involves some unstrenuous
walking through glorious sun-kissed fields where sheep, horses, goats
and cattle graze and almost from the moment you leave the rifugio you
see fantastic views of distant peaks. *Vallandro*, too, is a worthy destination, being one of the best privately-run rifugi in the Dolomites.

From *Rifugio Biella*, take route 28 eastwards. After 10 minutes you'll
be walking along a chilly, windswept spine towards the **Forcella
Cocodain** (2332m), with views to the south beyond **Lago de Fosses**
towards the **Gruppe di Lavinores** and the **Tofane** peaks (and on a very
clear day even the **Marmolada**), and north to the snow-capped peaks of
Austria. Thirty minutes later, Route 28 takes a sharp turn to the left
(north) and begins to head down to the level pasture of the **Campo
Latino**. Such is the 'layered' rock formation of the **Remeda
Rossa/Rotewand**, the summit of which lies to the south, that making this
descent feels like walking down a giant, uneven staircase. The path is not
clear, so stick closely to the waymarkings throughout.

At the end of the descent, signs point right (east) along Trail 3 to a
ridge (ignore the turn-offs left for Lago di Braies), where you'll often see
horses and sheep drinking from a trough. The path continues down to a
small farmhouse, *Casera Cavallo di Sopra* (2164m) that's been converted into a café. It has a distinctly Australian feel to it with kangaroo signs
abounding; the children were playing with a boomerang when I called in.

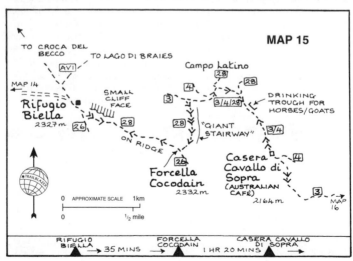

Map 16 – Casera Cavallo di Sopra to Rifugio Vallandro 101

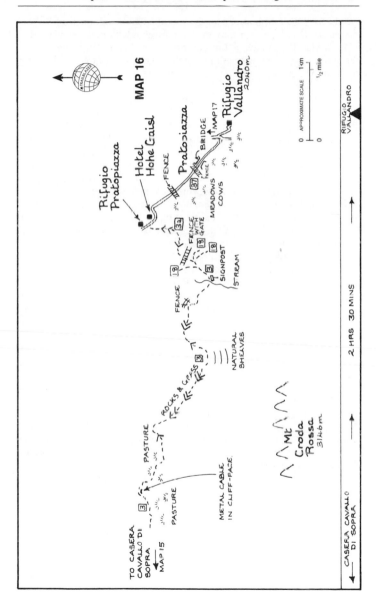

Just beyond the farmhouse, a signpost points up the hill on Trail 3. After the initial ascent the path through fields strewn with rocks and boulders is fairly flat. If you have a Tabacco map, you'll notice that there's a via ferrata coming up but it's nothing challenging: just an iron cable fixed to the cliff to help you negotiate a section of the trail where the path narrows slightly. The views over into Austria are amazing.

The path hugs the northern slopes of the **Croda Rossa/Hohe Gaisl** (3146m) for much of the next half hour before the descent to the Pratopiazza begins. According to Ladin legend, the Croda Rossa owes its vivid pinkish hue to a young princess by the name of Moltina. Newly wed and still very timid, Moltina was subjected to great ridicule when her darkest secret – that she had actually been brought up by marmots – was revealed to the public by a jealous love rival. Embarrassed by her antecedents, Moltina blushed crimson. In sympathy, and to express solidarity with the unfortunate maiden, the mountain, too, blushed. Typically, scientists have rejected this explanation as to why the mountain is coloured the way it is, preferring to believe instead that it has something to do with the presence of large amounts of iron oxide in the rock.

The path, sometimes fairly steep, wends its way through the rocks and grass down the slope to a stream, which you ford. Soon after, a signpost points the way to the **Pratopiazza/Plätzweisensattel** on Route 3a, and just two minutes later, after negotiating a couple of fences, you find yourself on the rolling hills of this picturesque plateau with the red face of the Croda Rossa to the west. The plateau is prime grazing land and undoubtedly one of the most beautiful in the Dolomites.

The path cuts through the plateau to *Rifugio Pratopiazza* (☎ 0474-748650; L35,000 with breakfast, L50,000 for a room) now dwarfed by the three-star *Hotel Hohe Gaisl* next door (☎ 0474-748606; per person prices start at L65,000 half-board). Both offer perfectly acceptable accommodation, but I advise you to persevere on to *Rifugio Vallandro/ Dürrensteinhütte* (☎ 0471-972505; 2040m) at the end of the rough road. Situated near the ruins of an old Austrian fort from WWI, this is one of the best-value, privately-run rifugio in the Dolomites, with beds in an eight-bed dorm just L18,000. The food is similarly reasonably priced: ask for a coffee in the morning and you'll get a jug of it. Furthermore the view south towards the sheer wall of the Cristallo isn't bad either!

RIFUGIO VALLANDRO → RIFUGIO LOCATELLI   [MAPS 17–18]

[Tabacco maps 03 and 010] From the *Vallandro*, head north (back the way you came) through the cow pastures, then take a sharpish right turn going round the hillside on Trail 34, part of Alta Via 3. A sign by a ruined hut points up to the summit of the cutely-named **Strudelkopf** (Monte Specie in Italian; 2307m), and down to the less endearingly-titled **Helltal**

Map 17 – Vallandro to Hotel Tre Cime 103

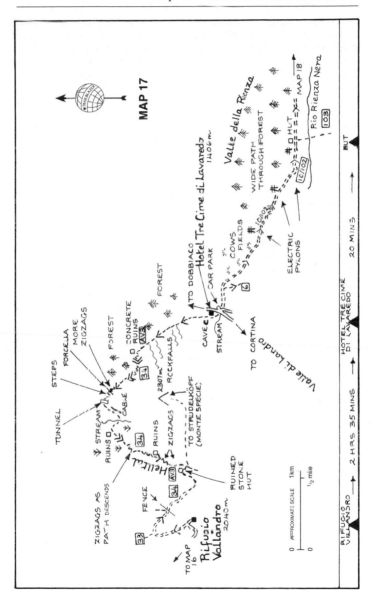

MAP 17

TO MAP 16

Rifugio Vallandro 2040m

ZIGZAGS AS PATH DESCENDS

FENCE

RUINED STONE HUT

33

34

AV3

34

TUNNEL

STEPS

FORCELLA

MORE ZIGZAGS

FOREST

CABLE

STREAM

RUINS

RUINS

ZIGZAGS

2307m

TO STRUDELKOPF (MONTE SPECIE)

ROCKFALLS

CONCRETE RUINS

AV3

3+

FOREST

FOREST

TO DOBBIACO

Hotel Tre Cime di Lavaredo 1406m

CAR PARK

CAVE

STREAM

TO CORTINA

Valle di Landro

Valle della Rienza

COWS FIELDS

6

ELECTRIC PYLONS

WIDE PATH THROUGH FOREST

HUT

C/102

HUT

103

TO MAP 18

Rio Rienza Nera

APPROXIMATE SCALE

0   1km
0   ½ mile

RIFUGIO VALLANDRO   ◀   2 HRS 35 MINS   ▶   HOTEL TRE CIME DI LAVAREDO   ◀   20 MINS   ▶   HUT

(Val Chiara). Passing along the left-hand side of this valley, notice how the meadows gradually yield to the dwarf pines, which in slow sequence give place to their fully-grown cousins further down. The route zigzags down to a stream, crosses it, and then hugs the northern slopes of the Strudelkopf overlooking the Val Chiara. After a gentle climb to a precipice (ropes and chains have been provided for your security), a wooden staircase preceded by a short tunnel leads you to a forcella through which you gain access to the **Valle di Landro/Hohlensteintal**. The main road between Cortina and Dobbiaco rumbles beneath you as you pick your way through the alpine forest along a simple stone path. Note that the current edition of the Tabacco maps demarcates the path around the forcella with red dots, though the path is clear and well-marked the whole way.

Following a lengthy zigzag section, the narrow forest path then makes a bee-line for *Hotel Tre Cime* (☎ 0474-972633; 1406m) at the foot of the hill by the main road. This old hotel is the only surviving building of what used to be the village of Landro. Run, seemingly without help, by an eccentric old woman, the two-star *Tre Cime* charges between L80,000 and 110,000 for a double or L75,000-110,000 per person half-board, the price depending on the season.

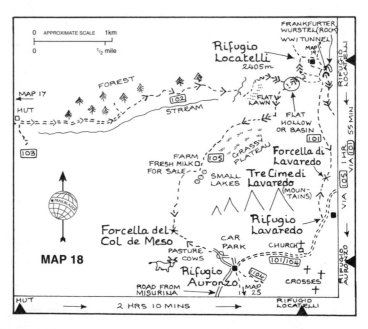

Enjoy the hotel's outdoor café and bask in the sun (assuming, of course, that there's sun to bask in), for from now until *Rifugio Locatelli*, 999m above you to the east, it's uphill all the way, the trail describing an exponential curve up the **Valle Della Rienza/Rienztal**. (If you've had enough walking, bus No 112 from the main road drives between Cortina and Dobbiaco and on to San Candido.)

The first section, beginning in the car park over the road from the hotel, initially stalks the shadow of the overhead electricity pylons, (ignore the turn-off for Trail 6) before joining the **Rio Rienza Nera** by a hut. The path forks nearby; take the left-hand track, Trail 102, as it follows the course of the river along the northern wall of the valley. The path almost imperceptibly distances itself from the river at one stage, only to rejoin it later on by a small verdant patch of grass, a good place to rest awhile.

Thus far the slope has been insignificant, but after this grassy 'lawn' the path now climbs much more steeply, crossing from the northern to the southern valley walls until it reaches a small plateau and the junction with Route 105. The climb up continues for another 20 minutes or so; though you may be exhausted, look out for the wild flowers that grow in abundance around this area. Marmots, too, live in the valley. Eventually, the massive rocky 'molars' of the **Tre Cime** ('Three summits', though there

❏ **The Galleria Locatelli**
Just to the south of the Locatelli, past the curious but aptly-named **Frankfurter Wurstel** or **Salsiccia** ('sausage') rock, a sign points the way to the 'Galleria e vie di gerra del paterno', a World War I tunnel running virtually parallel to Route 101 from *Rifugio Locatelli*. Built by the Austrians, the tunnel burrows its way up the cliff towards the summit of **Monte Paterno**, which at the time was held by Italian forces. It was near the summit of this mountain that **Sepp Innerkofler**, a renowned alpine guide who was helping the Austrians, fell to his death, probably after being mistakenly shot by his own side.

It doesn't take long to explore the tunnel: 10 minutes to the entrance from the *Locatelli*, a further 10 minutes through the first stage, and a final 20 to 30 minutes through the steep second stage. A torch is essential for exploring some of the darker passages, though the tunnel walls are regularly punctured by 'windows' – originally gun emplacements – which give marvellous views to the west and east. At the end of the tunnel a via ferrata heads east towards *Rifugio Pian de Cengia*, though most people are content to explore the tunnel only, a mute tribute to the ingenuity and dedication of humanity when it comes to maiming and killing each other.

are actually four different peaks) appear ahead of you on your right. Just below the junction with Route 101, a signpost instructs you to turn left. You can ignore it and scramble up the hill directly to the rifugio – it will save you five minutes. *Locatelli/Drei Zinnen Hütte* (☎ 0474-972002; 2405m), located just outside the shadow of the Tre Cime peaks, is another busy, cosmopolitan establishment, like so many rifugi around here, though its more remote location ensures that it's at least a little more exclusive. Beds are L32,000/16,000 for non-members/members in one of their large 24-bed dorms (the *Locatelli*, incidentally, has room for 160 people). There are also more expensive doubles/family rooms (with four beds). Note that while food is served throughout the day, in contrast to most other rifugi the kitchen **closes** at 7pm.

Moving on from the Locatelli From the *Locatelli* you have a number of different choices. Read pp128–150 to help you decide which path to take. Those who wish to continue trekking for a few days should head south on 101 and join Route 104 (see map 26 on p127). But if you're in hurry to finish the trail, take the simpler option on Trail 102 down to *Rifugio Fondo Valle* (see map 19 below). On this path you head north-east through the fields around the **Laghi dei Piani/Bödenseen** then south-east past a waterfall; five minutes later you're rewarded with a fine view over the **Val Sassavecchio/Altensteintal**, which you'll be walking through for the next hour or so, the white stone path cutting a swathe through the alpine shrubs all the way to *Rifugio Fondo Valle* (☎ 0474-710606; 1548m). Don't be put off by the masses of people, particularly families, that swamp this rifugio during the daytime: they've largely disappeared by 5pm, allowing you to enjoy in relative peace some of the best food and biggest portions on your walk. Beds at this privately-owned rifugio cost L23,000 (dorms only), with showers another L5000. Watch out for the

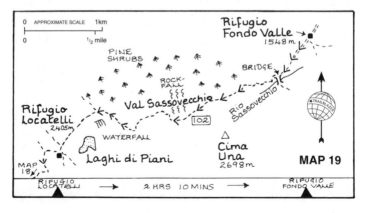

low roof beams in the bedrooms. The water is potable here. If you wish to end your trekking now, there are five **buses** from *Hotel Dolomitenhöf* (a 20-minute downhill walk away) to Sesto and San Candido.

RIFUGIO FANES → TRE CIME DI LAVAREDO/DREI ZINNEN ROUTE B: VIA TOFANE, CORTINA AND MISURINA

Rifugio Fanes → Cortina d'Ampezzo   [MAPS 20–22]

[Tabacco map 03] This particular leg of the trail takes approximately eight hours altogether, and involves some rather difficult stretches. The landscape around here is dramatic: scenes from the Sylvester Stallone movie *Cliffhanger* were filmed near Lagazuoi, and with its sheer vertical drops and rough, jagged peaks, you can understand why they chose this location. Once again, however, there are plenty of rifugi along the way, should you decide to break it up into stages.

The first half of this trail follows Alta Via 1 along a rough and dusty track leading south from *Rifugio Fanes* past the **Passo di Limo** (2174m) to the *lago* of the same name (2157m). From there, head south on Trail 11 to the high altitude farmhouse, the **Malga Fanes Grande** (2102m). Fording a tributary of the Rio di Fanes, continue on Trail 11 as it climbs very gently up to the **Passo Tadéga** (2143m). Just before the pass is a turn-off to the right to **Cunturines**, the legendary location of the castle of the mythical Fanes people. Not so long ago, archaeologists discovered the skeleton of a prehistoric bear, *Ursus spelaeus*, who lived in a cave on the Cunturines 14,000 years ago. Incidentally the valley you are currently walking through was once an extremely important supply route for the Austrian troops stationed on the southern front during World War I.

Fifteen minutes beyond the Passo Tadéga you have a choice of paths: if you don't have a good head for heights, or if the going is slippery, you are best advised to stick to Trail 11, taking a sharp left turn further on through the **Vallone di Lagazuoi** on Trail 20, which begins by *Rifugio Alpina* (1726m). Allow an extra hour for this detour. Otherwise, leave Trail 11 for AV1 as the latter climbs up the western slopes of the **Punte di Fanes**. The two paths reunite on the Alpe di Lagazuoi.

Almost three hours after setting off from *Rifugio Fanes* you'll reach the **Forcella del Lago** (2486m), a small saddle squeezed between the Cime del Lago and the Cime Scottoni. From here the trail becomes a little tricky, and a steady nerve is required as you descend into the **Alpe di Lagazuoi** across loose and slippery stones and boulders. You have now joined Trail 20 with the unbroken line of the **Lagazuoi Grande** to the south on your left. Assuming conditions are clear and visibility is good (a dubious assumption to make in this part of the world) *Rifugio Monte Lagazuoi* (☎ 0436-867303), at 2752m the highest point on this stage, should be visible ahead of you at the end of a 250m uninspiring trudge up

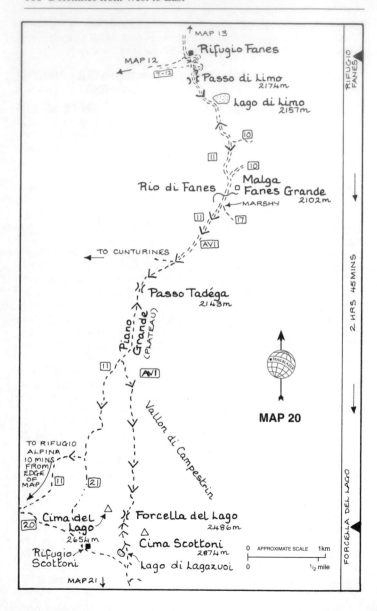

MAP 13

Rifugio Fanes

MAP 12

7-12

Passo di Limo
2174m

Lago di Limo
2157m

10

11

10

Rio di Fanes

Malga
Fanes Grande
2102m

MARSHY

11

17

AVI

TO CUNTURINES

Passo Tadéga
2143m

Piano Grande (PLATEAU)

11

AVI

Vallon di Campestrin

TO RIFUGIO
ALPINA
10 MINS
FROM
EDGE
OF
MAP

11

21

20

Cima del Lago
2654m

Forcella del Lago
2486m

Rifugio
Scottoni

Cima Scottoni
2874m

Lago di Lagazuoi

MAP 21

TRAILBLAZER

MAP 20

0   APPROXIMATE SCALE   1km

0   1/2 mile

RIFUGIO FANES

2 HRS 45 MINS

FORCELLA DEL LAGO

Map 21 – Lagazuoi to Passo Falzarego 109

a ski-slope. The privately-owned rifugio, with its comfortable beds and superb sunset views, is ample compensation for all the effort expended. And I haven't even mentioned the stunning panorama yet, which many consider to be the finest in the Dolomites. Moving clockwise from the Sorapiss peaks: the Antelao summits are just to their right, followed by the Civetta range to the south, the glacier-capped Marmolada with the Pale di San Martino peeking around from behind it, and finally the Sella range to the west. If that panorama doesn't persuade you to stay overnight, nothing will; beds start at L30,000, with breakfast L12,000 and showers L6000. If you plan to catch a bus from the pass below, be warned that, while there are four **buses** daily from Passo Falzarego to La Villa and five to Cortina in the high season, these have ceased running by mid-September.

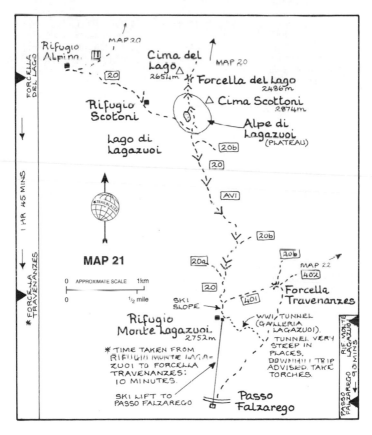

❏ The Galleria Lagazuoi

All around *Rifugio Lagazuoi* lies the rusting, twisted detritus of World War I. The fighting was particularly heavy here, for the main front between Italy and Austria passed precisely through the Passo Falzarego, the mountain pass below the rifugio. Though the Austrians held the pass before the war, they found it expedient to retreat up to the mountains to the north, which were far easier to defend, following the Italians' decision to join the hostilities in 1915. To give you an indication of just how close the two opposing forces were along this border, the summit of the Piccolo Lagazuoi on which the rifugio now stands was held by the Austrians, while the Italians held the ledge below the rifugio, known as the Cengia Martini, for over two years until an Austrian bomb in 1917 put a huge hole in its centre.

The 1100m-tunnel, the Galleria Lagazuoi, that leads all the way up to the summit from the ledge, was built by the Italians in an attempt to reach the Austrian forces assembled above them. For their part, the Austrians tried to remove the Italians by mining the mountain, producing the ugly pits and two huge landslips that still disfigure the mountainside today. The tunnel proved to be a failure, however: the Austrians, hearing the work going on inside the mountain, withdrew their troops to a place of relative safety.

A failure though it may be, the tunnel is an impressive piece of engineering and, following its restoration a few years ago, it is now possible to walk along the entire length. However, it is extremely steep in places (iron cables have been attached to the walls at intervals) and you're best advised to walk *down* it rather than trying to head uphill; the downhill trip all the way to the Passo Falzarego (2105m) should take no more than 90 minutes. Torches are essential and are available for rent from the rifugio.

The battle-scarred scenery that is visible round *Rifugio Lagazuoi* continues as you head due east towards Cortina d'Ampezzo, beginning along Trail 401, then continuing straight ahead on 402 at the **Forcella Travenanzes** (2383m). Stick to 402 as it aims south at the **Forcella Col dei Bos** (2331m – the peak after which it is named lies to your right), then change to path 404 a few hundred metres further on. You are now walking along the southern perimeter of the Tofane range beneath the sheer walls of the **Tofana di Rozes**. Exhilarating, isn't it? Especially with the Cinque Torri and the Croda da Lago in the distance to the south. The path that heads off left leads to another World War I tunnel known as the **Galleria del Castelletto**. Features of the 800m tunnel include ammunition stores and gun emplacements, though to scramble up it, indeed to reach it in the first place, requires some climbing and vie ferrate skills.

The **Castelletto spur** itself was a perfect observation post during World War I, and was used as such by the Austrians until the entire spur

Map 22 – Forcella Travenanzes to Ristorante Pietofana 111

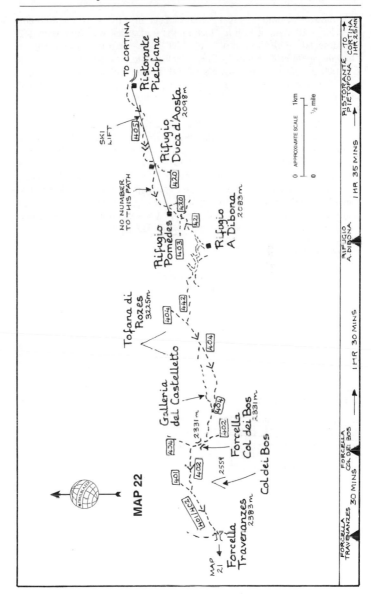

was blown to smithereens by the Italians in July 1916, with many Austrians still stationed on it. Back on the trail, branching right onto 442 you descend rapidly to a dirt road which leads down to *Rifugio Angelo Dibona* (☎ 0436-860294; 2083m), a smart rifugio with beds starting at L26,000 per night, with showers L6000. Because of the lack of budget accommodation in Cortina, most trekkers prefer to spend a night here and visit Cortina in the morning before making their way to the next rifugio later on in the day.

For those who decide to continue to Cortina, there are three options. Most trekkers prefer to go to the nearby *Rifugio Pomedes* to the north along Trail 421, from where you can catch a chairlift down to the road to Cortina. If, however, you decide to walk, I should warn you that the final descent into Cortina is long and, save for the views over Cortina itself, unexciting. Indeed, for large stretches you will be following Trail 405, which lies in the shadow of the chairlift anyway. The third and least popular option is to try to hitch to Cortina d'Ampezzo from outside *Rifugio Dibona*, though lifts can be hard to come by late in the day.

CORTINA D'AMPEZZO

'For the present, however, every inn, homestead, and public building bespeaks prosperity. The inhabitants are well-fed and well-dressed. Their fairs and festivals are the most considerable in the whole of the South Eastern Tyrol; their principal church is the largest this side of St Ulrich; and their new gothic Campanile, 250 feet high, might suitably adorn the piazza of such a city as Bergamo or Belluno.'
Amelia Edwards, *Untrodden peaks and unfrequented valleys*

The oh-so fashionable resort of Cortina d'Ampezzo (Cortina for short; 1225m), right in the middle of the Dolomites, has a population of just 7000, a figure that swells by a factor of four or five with shoals of tourists during the hiking and biking summer months and the winter ski-season. The town is engaging enough but the real charm of Cortina lies in its surroundings. Hemmed in on all sides by verdant pastured slopes, Cortina lies in the centre of a huge and breathtaking amphitheatre of mountains. Beginning with the distinctive three-pyramid shape of the Tofane (3244m) in the west, a clockwise inspection of the mountains will take in the appropriately-named Croda Rossa ('Red Rock'; 3146m) due north, the Cristallo (3221m) and its neighbour, the Pomagagnon, to the north-east, and, confronting them across the Tre Croci valley, the Sorapiss (3205m) and Marmarole (2961m) ranges to the south-east of town. To complete the picture, beyond these last two in the far distance to the south is the symmetrical summit of the Antelao (3264m) and the Becco di Mezzodi, standing all by itself (like a 'carious tooth of Dolomite' according to the nineteenth-century explorer, Dr Gilbert), then the spiny ridge of the Croda da Lago (2751m), the flat-topped Lastoni di Formin and finally, opposite the Tofane, the teeth of the Cinque Torri.

Quaint, affluent and peaceful, the face of the modern town belies its turbulent past. Cortina has had more than its fair share of excitement: crushed by the Lombards, fought over by the Venetians and the Hapsburgs under

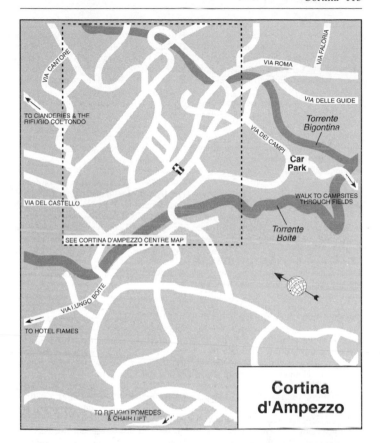

Cortina d'Ampezzo

Maximilian 1 who led them to victory in 1511, the town was the battleground for some of the heaviest fighting during World War I changing sides at the beginning of the encounter, and passing from Austrian to Italian control in 1915.

Today, the foreign invaders tend to come dressed in Gore-Tex and lurid jackets. The tourist industry in Cortina began at the end of the last century when climbers, skiers and scientists flocked to the town and the mountains

that surround it. Its reputation as a premier location for winter sports grew steadily, and in 1956 the town hosted the Seventh Winter Olympic Games. Even James Bond paid a visit in the film *For Your Eyes Only*, pausing just long enough to win the heart of a young Russian skater before being chased out of town by a gang of skiers with machine guns.

Sights within Cortina are few, though if you have the time do visit the local **museum** (9am-12.30pm, 4-6pm) on the town's main street, the Corso Italia. Both sections of the museum, the Pioneers, Guides and Rock Climbers Museum and the Fossils Museum, hold many items of interest to trekkers (L3000 for each section).

A little way further up the Corso, the eighteenth-century Baroque **church** is rather humdrum compared to some around here, though the tower measures a lofty 75m, making it one of the tallest in the Dolomites, and its chimes are said to be identical to those of London's Westminster Abbey.

Services

The centre of town is the **Piazza Roma**, a two-minute walk downhill from the rusty-roofed **bus station**, where you'll find one of Cortina's three **tourist offices** (☎ 0436-3231, 📄 0436-3235, 🖥 apt1@sunrise.it) – the others being at the bus station, dealing solely with bus enquiries and luggage storage, and at the Agienda Soggiorno Turismo, 200m downhill from the Piazza Roma on Via Mercato. All have approximately the same opening hours (daily during the trekking and skiing season, 9am-12.30pm, 4-7pm), though their knowledge of local trekking possibilities is limited; for the latest on **trekking information**, you're better off visiting the **Guide Alpine Scuola D'Alpinismo** (☎/📄 0436-868505; 🖥 guidecortina@mnet-climb.com; www.mnet-climb.com/guidecortina), next to the museum at Curso Italia 69a. They arrange vie ferrate trips for beginners and can also organize guides for special excursions.

You can find any number of **banks** in town, most with ATMs. The **post office** (open Monday to Friday 8.10am-2.30pm, Saturday 8.10am-1.30pm), through the tunnel next to *Café Royal*, also has exchange facilities, and they tend to charge less commission than the banks in Cortina.

A little further east along Via Largo Poste in the arcade on the northern side is Dolomiti Multimedia, which offers **Internet** facilities (L7500 per half-hour; Monday to Friday 8.30am-12.30pm, 3-7.30pm). For **supplies**, the Cooperativa, opposite the municipality at Corso Italia 40, has a camping section on the third floor, a supermarket on the first, and they sell a number of books and maps on the Dolomites too. For a more complete collection of **maps**, however, visit the Libreria Lutteri, next to *Café Royal*. They also stock day-old **English newspapers**. Finally, of the many **camera shops**, Foto Roma at Corso Italia 189 seems the most expert and reasonably priced – though as with everything else in Cortina, don't expect to come across any bargains.

Accommodation

To give you an indication of the scale of the tourist boom enjoyed by Cortina over the last hundred years, when Amelia Edwards visited there were just three hotels: now there are over seventy, not to mention four campsites in the immediate vicinity; not bad, considering the town suffered two world wars during this time too.

Three of these campsites, *Rochetta* (☎ 0436-5063, 📄 0436-2852), *Cortina* (☎ 0436-867575) and *Dolomiti* (☎ 0436-2485), lie in the same area 2km to the south of town, reachable by bus No2 from Piazza Roma; the fourth, *International Camping Olimpia*, lies 4km to the west (bus No 1 from the Piazza Roma). All offer roughly the same services, including hot water showers, power points and washing machines, (the *Cortina* also has a pool, while the *Rochetta* has mini-golf). They charge approximately the same too, namely L7000 per person and L17,000 per tent, though this is usually negotiable, depending on the season. The *Rochetta* and *Cortina* are open in the

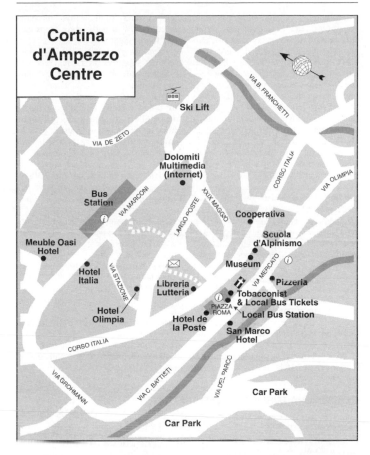

Cortina d'Ampezzo Centre

VIA B. FRANCHETTI

Ski Lift

VIA DE ZETO

Dolomiti Multimedia (Internet)

CORSC ITALIF

VIA OLIMPIA

Bus Station

VIA MARCONI

LARGO POSTE

XXIX MAGGIO

Cooperativa

Meuble Oasi Hotel

Scuola d'Alpinismo

Museum

VIA MERCATO

Pizzeria

Hotel Italia

VIA STAZIONE

Libreria Lutteria

Tobacconist & Local Bus Tickets

PIAZZA ROMA

Hotel Olimpia

Hotel de la Poste

Local Bus Station

San Marco Hotel

CORSO ITALIA

VIA GROHMANN

VIA C. BATTISTI

VIA DEL PARCO

Car Park

Car Park

summer only. Of the hotels and guest-houses, the clean, basic one-star *Fiames* (☎ 0436-2366) at Località Fiames 13, is the cheapest, though it's a way out of town near the *Olympia* campsite. The room-only tariff starts at L45,000 per person, but you're probably better off paying a little more, moving up a star and into town to the family-run *Italia* (☎ 0436-5646; minimum L60,000 per

person) opposite the bus station, where the hosts speak good English and the breakfasts are huge.

Moving up another notch in quality, the three-star *Hotel Olimpia* (☎ 0436-3256) is a little soulless, though it does boast its own sauna, Jacuzzi and gym. Room prices start at L65,000-85,000. The stately *Hotel De La Poste* (☎ 0436-4271, 🖃 0436-868435) has become something of a landmark since its inception in 1835, and the same family still runs it. It's all very sophisticated and the sgl/dbl prices reflect this: L210,000/360,000–390,000/780,000 half board, prices depending on the season. For my money you're better off nipping over the road to the homely *San Marco* (☎ 0436-866941, 🖹 0436-866940), another nineteenth-century establishment, with prices beginning at about L220,000 in the high season.

Thankfully, the cost of eating out in Cortina is not as painful as the cost of sleeping there, and there are a number of cheap pizzerias dotted around town. Mention, too, must be made of *Pasticeria Alvera* at Curso Italia 191: try their *fiamma & cioccolato* – little chocolate mountains that provide the perfect luxury antidote to all the rifugio stodge you've been munching on for the past week.

Transport

For long haul destinations to the north, such as Bressanone, Vienna, Munich, Innsbruck etc, you will need to travel to Dobbiaco and catch a train or bus from there.

For southerly destinations, (Venice, Rome etc) catch the trains from Calalzo. The 'high season' as mentioned below usually runs from late June to mid-September.

You can go by bus to the following:
Belluno: 10 daily, 1hr 55 mins.
Bologna: daily in high season, 3.30pm, 4hrs 40 mins.
Calalzo: hourly, 55 mins.
Dobbiaco: 6 daily, 45 mins.
Milan: daily in high season, 1.30pm, 6hrs 30 mins. Also Saturdays and Sundays at 8.20am in high season.
Misurina: 4 daily in high season, 35 mins.
Padova: daily in high season, 3.30pm, 3hrs 10 mins.
Parma: daily in high season, 3.30pm, 6hrs 40 mins.
Passo Falzarego: 7 daily in high season, 35 mins.
Passo Tre Croci: at least 4 daily in the high season, 20 mins.
Rifugio Auronzo: 3 daily in high season, 1 hour.
San Candido: 4 daily, 55 mins.
Treviso: 1 daily in high season, 3.15pm, 2hrs 25 mins.
Venice (airport/centre): daily in high season, 3.15pm, 3hrs/3hrs 15 mins. Also on Sundays (8.20am) and Thursdays (3.30pm) in the high season only.

CORTINA → MISURINA AND RIFUGIO COL DE VARDA
[MAPS 23–24]

[**Tabacco map 03**] This is an extremely long stage, involving three climbs of varying degrees of difficulty and a similar number of knee-quaking downhills. En route you pass through both the Val Granda, also known as the Val Padeòn, and the eerie Val Popena with its herds of grazing chamois, and unless you're in a big hurry you may wish to break your hike between the two at either *Rifugio Son Forca* or the four-star *Hotel Passo Tre Croci*.

From Cortina, take the road going uphill behind the bus station by the *Meuble Oasi*. On your right there's a sign for **Cianderies**, one of Cortina's many tiny suburbs and the terminal for two chairlifts. Going left at the end of the road towards the swimming baths (*piscina comunale*), you follow the road until you come to the charming little **Church of**

Map 23 – Cortina to Tre Croci 117

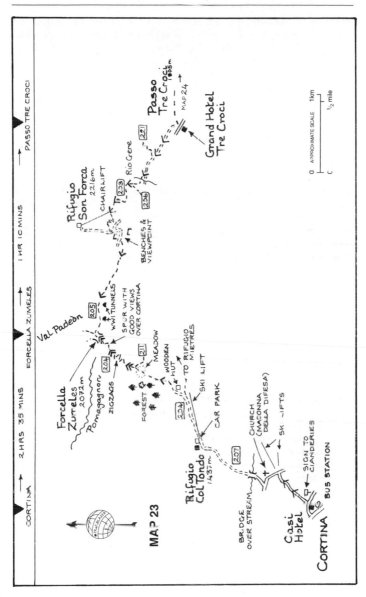

CORTINA → 2 HRS 35 MINS → FORCELLA ZUMELES → 1 HR 10 MINS → PASSO TRE CROCI

Passo Tre Croci 1805m

MAP 24

Grand Hotel Tre Croci

221

Rio Gere

Tr 223

256

Rifugio Son Forca 2216m

CHAIRLIFT

BENCHES & VIEWPOINT

205

Val Padeon

WWI TUNNELS

SPUR WITH GOOD VIEWS OVER CORTINA

Forcella Zureles 2072m

Pomagagnon

ZIGZAGS

204

211

MEADOW

WOODEN HUT

TO RIFUGIO MIETRES

SKI LIFT

FOREST

TO RIFUGIO

CAR PARK

204

Rifugio Col Tondo 1437m

207

CHURCH (MADONNA DELLA DIFESA)

SKI LIFTS

SIGN TO CIANDERIES

BUS STATION

BRIDGE OVER STREAM

Casi Hotel

CORTINA

MAP 23

APPROXIMATE SCALE

0   1km
C   ½ mile

Madonna Della Difesa; just past it, a wide and muddy track (Trail 207) heads up the hill through woods to **Rifugio Col Tondo** (1437m), which isn't actually a proper rifugio but merely a chairlift terminal with no accommodation or dining facilities.

From the car-park on the other side of the rifugio, Trail 204 goes up the hill in the shadow of the chairlift. Twenty minutes later a secondary path cuts left towards and then around behind a wooden hut, where Trail 204 branches off left. The path is narrow and muddy and traverses a number of summer streams but it's clearly marked and this uphill stroll through a forest of oak and pine is very pleasant.

On the far side of a small forest glade, where Route 204 joins 211, look up through the trees to the east and you'll see the sheer walls of the rocky spine known as the **Pomagagnon**, behind which you'll find the Val Padeòn. The **Forcella Zumeles** (2072m), invisible from where you're standing now, though it's your entrance into the Val Padeòn, lies at the end of Trail 204. This trail leaves the tall trees of the forest for the smaller, stunted shrubs and wild flowers of the upland slopes. It's a white-stone path, secured by lengths of timber, that zigzags up the hill for the next 45 mins, passing above a rocky spur on the way from where you can enjoy a sweeping view of Cortina and the valley below, including the old Olympic ski-jump to the south of town. Amazingly even at this height and distance you can still hear Cortina's church bells. The forcella lies directly behind the outcrop, a further 30 minutes away. As a reward for your exertions thus far, take time to enjoy the view over the Val Padeòn, with the Croda Rossa d'Ampezzo straight ahead and the Cristallo to the right.

From the forcella, you now take Trail 205, a largely flat path heading east (right) towards *Rifugio Son Forca*. The path passes by two World War I tunnels on your right, through which you can see back towards Cortina. Trail 205 merges with 203, then bends right through a designated viewpoint towards **Rifugio Son Forca Barone Franchetti** (☎ 0436-5273; 2216m). Open from July to September only, this family-run rifugio is well located, with superb views north-west and south-east and a deserved reputation for good food. Prices start at L23,000 per person, with breakfast an extra L8000. Between the rifugio and the viewpoint, two paths lead south-east from the same starting point by the chairlift, near a blush-pink gash in the rockface. The smaller footpath is a slightly more interesting route than the four-wheel drive track, though the latter provides a more direct and quicker route to your next destination, the **Passo Tre Croci** (1805m).

PASSO TRE CROCI

To call this settlement a 'village' would be to exaggerate the size of this place. Passo Tre Croci is nothing more than a four-star hotel with a church next door and a few houses over the road. *Grand Hotel Tre Croci* (☎ 0436-867141) is lovely despite the ugly concrete exterior, and the summertime prices which

Map 24 – Tre Croci to Misurina 119

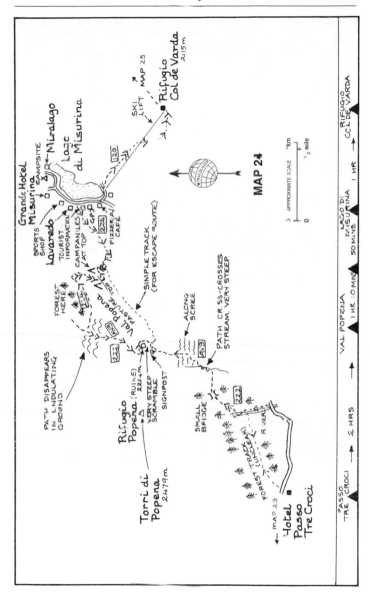

climb up to L200,000 per person in the August holidays are reasonable. All 84 rooms have private bathrooms, a TV, mini-bar, and a balcony, and there's always the chance that you'll end up staying in the same room as that once used by Elizabeth Taylor and Richard Burton.

In the high season there are usually four **buses** daily from Cortina to Misurina that stop in Tre Croci (8.55am, 10.10am, 3.15pm and 5.05pm), and four travelling in the opposite direction (10.05am, 12.10pm, 1.10pm and 5.30pm). The 10.05am and 1.10pm to Cortina continue on to Passo Falzarego, and likewise all except the last bus to Misurina carries on to the large and popular *Rifugio Auronzo* (see p124) , in the shadows of the Tre Cime.

There now follows a very laborious stretch along the main road. You can try to follow the path leading through the woods, where chamois can often be seen grazing, but take care: few people come this way, the ground is very uneven and though there appears to be a path, it peters out after 10 minutes or so.

Eventually, whichever route you've taken, you'll arrive at a wide mountain stream, a stream that flows down from the Lago Cristallo and under the main road. Trail 222, part of the Alta Via 3, begins immediately after the bridge, heading upwards and northwards through pine forest and meadow before eventually arriving on more exposed slopes beneath the **Torri di Popena**. The path now becomes much steeper as it crosses and re-crosses a small stream; looking across the valley, note the three **Sorapiss glaciers** across the valley to the south.

Ninety minutes after leaving the forest, you come to a signpost. Though it isn't clear from the directions on it, the pass into the Val Popena is immediately above you, a 70-metre scramble away. The waymarkings try to plot a safe and simple path to the summit; they fail miserably simply because the stones are loose and constantly moving. I'm afraid you'll just have to pray your footholds are secure as you ascend. If it feels unsafe, or if the weather looks like taking a turn for the worse, consider taking the trail straight ahead along the **Pale di Misurina** instead, from where you can rejoin the path as it heads down to the Lago di Misurina. Unfortunately you'll miss out on the wonderful Val Popena if you take this route but it's better to be safe than stranded.

If you successfully manage to scale the slope to the forcella, at the top you'll find the ruins of **Rifugio Popena** (2214m). Part of the inscription etched into marble on the side of the hut reads: 'The Street of the Skies in the mountains embraces me with its silence.' And the silence here is truly deafening. You're probably feeling pretty ruined yourself by this stage, so rest in quiet contemplation of the valley before you and examine the cliffs carefully for the agile chamois. This area is officially known as the **Val Popena Alta** and is more of a mini plateau than a valley; the larger Val Popena Bassa lies to the north at the far end of this valley. The path from here through the valley is not clearly marked, with only infrequent red splashes and the occasional cairn plotting the way. But no matter, for the route is straightforward enough: down along the grassy floor of the valley, stopping at the fossil observation point to check out the petrified creatures patterning the rocks, then right, up and out of the valley along the well-marked Route 224. You must take care not to miss the turn-off for 224, which isn't signposted. As you complete your climb out of the Val Popena, a mild ascent by the standards of this stage, you'll be confronted by a series of impressive campaniles. From here, the trail zigzags monotonously down to **Lake Misurina** (1752m).

MISURINA

There's no doubting Misurina's beauty, though to me it always feels lacking in soul, probably because every building bar the post office is dedicated to the tourist trade. Stretched along virtually the entire western bank of this dark green, twelve-hectare tarn is one long line of hotels, pizzerias, cafés and souvenir shops. There's a **tourist office** too (☎ 0435-39016), with some handy photocopies of bus timetables and information on nearby rifugi; and a well-run *campsite* (☎ 0435-39039) at the northern end of the lake (L6000 per person plus L4000 per tent in the low season).

Of the hotels, *Sport Hotel* (☎ 0435-39125) is the least expensive, with rooms beginning at around L30,000 per person, though *Miralago* (☎ 0435-39171), by the campsite, is better value, offering more comfortable rooms

and a more efficient service for just a little more money (L35,000 per person). *Lavaredo* (☎ 0435-39227), by the post office, is a three-star place where all rooms are en suite and come complete with telephone and TV. Prices start at L50,000 per person, room only.

The oldest hotel in the village is the 100-room *Grande Hotel Misurina* (☎ 0435-39191), at the northern end of the lake above the Despar supermarket. Built in 1899 at the (then) exorbitant cost of L500,000, the rooms today have TV and mini-bar and vary between L98,000 and L150,000 per person in the summer.

From Misurina there are seven **buses** daily to Cortina, five directly to *Rifugio Auronzo*, two (at midday and 5.20pm) to Auronzo and one (at 5.27pm) to Dobbiaco and San Candido.

The final leg of this stage for those hoping to stay at *Rifugio Col de Varda* is a hike up the hill along Route 120, which begins by the southern end of the lake. It really is a monotonous 50-minute amble and if you've come all the way from Cortina today you'd be forgiven for taking the chairlift up (the last one usually leaves around 6pm). *Col de Varda* (☎ 0435-39041; 2115m) itself is a pleasant little privately-run place that charges a very reasonable L25,000 for a bed, though I found the staff not very friendly and the beds too soft.

RIFUGIO COL DE VARDA ➤ RIFUGIO AURONZO
[MAPS 25, p123]

[Tabacco map 03] Another hard stage, again involving multiple climbs and descents. There are also short stretches of via ferrata, particularly on the last section between the *Fonda Savio* and *Auronzo* rifugi, though it's nothing particularly strenuous or technically demanding. Indeed, this last section is a popular day out for Italian families, and you'll never be short of people laughing at your inexpert technique as you progress along the path; as such, this trail provides the perfect introduction to the world of vie ferrate. The path that you will be following for the entire stage is Trail 117, known as the **Sentiero Bonacossa** after a famous local alpinist, Alberto Bonacossa. Originally established during World War I by the Alpine Troops, you'll still find caves and barracks used by the two sides dotted along the route. Restored by the CAI in 1955, it's a fabulous walk through the heart of the **Cadini di Misurina**, the small range of mountains east of the lake.

In contrast to the crowded second part, the first section of this walk from *Rifugio Col de Varda* to the *Fonda Savio* can be a lonely experience, though it should pose few problems for the sure-footed. These cliffs saw some of the heaviest fighting and the cliffs are riddled with tunnels; bullets, cartridges and water bottles are still often unearthed near the path.

From the *Col de Varda*, a stone pillar marks the beginning of the Sentiero Bonacossa to the **Forcella di Misurina** (2395m) – and an awkward beginning it is too: while the slope of the path up the side of the mountain, known as the **Grave di Misurina**, is gentle, the path itself is formed of loose stones that, particularly near the top, like to hurl themselves down the cliffside as soon as you put your foot on them. This can be quite unnerving. Nor is the path for the whole of this first section to the rifugio clearly marked, though that isn't too much of a problem: just aim towards the gap in the cliff-face that you can see from the rifugio; this is the forcella so you can't go too far off course.

Approaching the summit, wire cables have been attached to the wall to help you gain the top. More cables and a small ladder lie on the other side too, providing a safe passage to trekkers as they descend into the valley. This part of the path that hugs the northern slopes of the **Cima Cadin di Misurina** (2674m) is steep, as your knees will soon tell you, but it's only half an hour or so before you reach the bottom. Here a signpost points out Route 118 down the valley to Misurina (for quitters) and a second one points up to Route 117 along the southern extension of the **Torre del Diavolo**. Waymarkings are few but once again just follow your nose uphill and you'll soon run into the path.

This really is a painful 50-minute ascent: 30 minutes of zigzagging up the slope, followed by a ladder or two, and then, just when you think you've done the hard part, the path gets difficult to follow and you have to scramble over very loose rocks. Do try to keep to the path on this final bit: scrambling at this altitude with a steep drop below can seriously fray the nerves. Reach the top (2603m), and suddenly you're in tourist land, with sometimes hundreds of trekkers dotting the valley floor below you – though you may not see them just yet.

Map 25 – Rifugio Col de Varda to Rifugio Auronzo 123

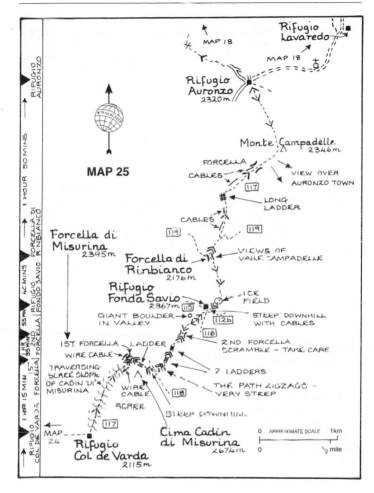

The descent into the valley is straightforward enough, especially when one considers what's gone before, though the trail is particularly badly marked. Actually, I think that's a good thing: if you do find some red markings and follow them, they'll lead you down to the giant rock on the valley floor, whereas if you follow one of the horizontal trails hugging the slopes of the **Cima Cadin N.O.** east (to your right), you'll save yourself some time and a bit of a climb up to the rifugio too.

The *Rifugio Fonda Savio* (☎ 0436-39036; 2367m) is a well-situated little place built just below the Passo dei Tocci and dedicated to the three Fonda Savio brothers of Trieste, all of whom perished during World War II. It's quite expensive, especially considering it's little more than a draughty shack, but then you pay a premium for location: and with the fantastic views towards Monte Piana and Cristallino, with the Val Popena Bassa between them, it is a location worth paying for. Open July to September, beds at the hut start at L16,000 for CAI members, L32,000 otherwise.

The 'thrill' of the final part of this stage begins at once with a sharp descent east, luckily aided by an iron cable. At the bottom, continue north over snow patches and boulders. Look ahead now and, slightly to your left in the distance you'll see a huge beige horizontal scar on the eastern face of the Cima Ciadin di Rinbianco. This scar is your path, the continuation of Route 117. Before you reach that section, however, take a little time to enjoy the views over the **Valle Campadelle** to your east from the **Forcella di Rinbianco** (2176m), where Routes 117 and 119 meet.

Almost immediately after this forcella, the main stretch of the via ferrata begins, a rather scary little shuffle with the aid of a wire cable around an obstructive boulder. The vie ferrate sections continue off and on for most of the next kilometre or so, the cables appearing when the path is too narrow to walk without them. Many people don't even bother with karabiners but if you've got them, use them. It's true that there may be one or two others on the trail who think you look a bit silly, being all strapped up to the cliff-face while they amble past; but think how much more of a fool you'd look if you fell, and the emergency services charged with scraping up your shattered body from the valley floor discovered a perfectly good set of ropes and karabiners in your rucksack.

As well as iron cables, this particular via ferrata also includes a ladder about 45 minutes on from the forcella. The ladder is attached to a crevice in the side of the cliff-face, and though slippery from the water dripping onto it from the neighbouring cavern, it's not difficult to negotiate.

The path continues north-east between the spires and towers to the **Monte Campadelle** (2345m). Ahead of you the Tre Cime rise up like four giant prehistoric teeth, a most dramatic backdrop for *Rifugio Auronzo* and its inevitable tail of parked cars that snake down the hill along the road. Your via ferrata experience is over, at least for today, and the rest of the walk is plain sailing as you amble along the gently undulating spine of hills towards the rifugio, with glimpses of the Lago Auronzo to the south-east.

A lot of people don't care for **Rifugio Auronzo** (☎ 0435-39002; 2320m), probably because it looks like a big flash hotel and is always chock-a-block with day-trippers who've driven up here from Misurina and beyond. But I personally quite like the place: the staff were helpful when I visited, and the views down to the two lakes, Auronzo and

Misurina, can't be beaten. It's cheap enough too, at L25,000 per bed (L20,000 with card), or L50,000/45,000 per person in a double. The water is unsafe to drink here.

RIFUGIO AURONZO → RIFUGIO FONDO VALLE
[MAP 18: p104, MAP 26: p127]

[Tabacco map 017] You now have three options to get to *Rifugio Fondo Valle,* described as routes (i), (ii) and (iii) below. Whichever way you choose this stage is simple, though Route (i) is slightly harder than either (ii) or (iii). Route (i) also provides a short cut for those wishing to finish their trek in the village of Auronzo on Route Z. See p144 for details.

Route (i)

This is the perfect stroll to revive you after the previous stage's exertions and prepare you for the next, another tough one. During this walk, from the *Auronzo* to *Rifugio Fondo Valle,* you will descend almost 800 metres, and apart from a brief uphill section to the second of the three rifugi you'll pass en route, it's downhill all the way.

The first of these rifugi lies just 20 minutes away from the *Auronzo* on a flat, uncovered road that's closed to traffic. The rifugio in question, the tiny **Lavaredo** (2341m), is privately owned and charges an extortionate L40,000 per person (17 beds in total; no phone). Really, it should only be considered if the *Auronzo* is full.

The road continues for a short distance behind the *Lavaredo* before ending by a ruined hut and a painted direction-board at the junction with Route 104. Your path leads off to the right where, by a large and permanent puddle known as the **Lago di Lavaredo**, it divides into innumerable smaller tracks most of which rejoin Route 104 soon after. Stick to the marked path to be on the safe side.

The path descends gently as it passes between the southern slopes of the **Croda del Passaporto** (2701m) and the pretty, grassy plateau sloping down towards the Val di Cengia. Route 104 rises, then drops into a windless basin in the centre of which is a small, blue *laghetto,* the **Laghi di Cengia** (2324m). The next stretch of Route 104 is clearly visible ahead as it zigzags up the hill like stitches in cloth. (The path on the upper level is Route 107 to the Bivacco Toni, and doesn't concern us here). At the end of the zigzags the trail heads north, passing a ruined hut and signposts, before coinciding with Route 101 at the brow of the hill opposite. The views north towards *Rifugio Locatelli* and south towards the Cengia peaks are splendid. Just a little further to the east, round the rock wall, is *Rifugio Pian di Cengia* (☎ 0337-451517; 2528m). Privately-owned, this isolated, red-shuttered rifugio charges L25,000 for a bed for the night. The tap water is drinkable here. Just by the rifugio are the remains of World War I barracks and trenches.

Route 101 continues east round the ridge, past the 'No mountain-biking' signs (!), through the **Passo Fiscalino** and down steeply towards the beginning of the **Val Fiscalina/Fischleintal**, on the northern slopes of the **Croda dei Toni**. Half an hour of walking down past suffering trekkers heading the other way, you arrive at the penultimate rifugio on this stage, *Zsigmondy Comici Hütte* (☎ 0474-710358; 2224m). Often surrounded by a morass of shirtless sunbathers, their sweat-soaked tops drying in the breeze on their walking poles, this is a CAI-run rifugio, and a night here costs L32,000/16,000 in the dorm; there are also some double rooms. A stein of lager here is only L6000 – which goes some way towards explaining the *Comici's* enduring popularity, in spite of the fact that it's miles from the nearest village or town.

> ❏ **The trail to Auronzo**
> Those planning to finish their trek in the village of Auronzo should stop for a night in the *Zsigmondy-Comici*. From here, you can follow Route Z as described on p144.

The relentless trek downwards continues as you head north through the **Val Fiscalina** along the eastern slopes of the **Cima Una** on Route 103, part of Alta Via 5. Once again the descent is sharp initially, but gentle for most of the way thereafter; benches dot the route here and there for those who wish to give their knees a temporary rest. The uneven peaks to the right (east) are the **Cima Undici** (3092m), jagged and broken like the teeth of a child force-fed sherbet lemons since birth. Trees begin to appear about half way along, and the *Hotel Dolomitenhöf* appears in the distance soon after. About 20 minutes from the end the path turns sharp left, crosses a bridge and slopes down to *Rifugio Fondo Valle* (see p106 for details).

Route (ii)   [MAP 18: p104]
From the *Auronzo*, bear west across the road to the far end of the car park. From here, Route 105 heads off round the mountainside through fields of pasture and cow pats to the **Forcella del Col de Mezo** (2315m); to the left the path leads off to the Forcella Deli Argena, but you should head right and after five minutes of walking on a shallow scree round the base of the Tre Cime, *Rifugio Locatelli* appears in the far distance ahead of you, in the shadow of the **Tobin Tower**.

It's over an hour's walk away, however, an hour in which you'll pass a huddle of three small lakes and a nearby small farm selling fresh milk. You will also have to negotiate a quite short but inconvenient descent to a little grassy depression, from where it's a sharpish 25-minute climb to the rifugio.

For details on the *Locatelli*, the nearby World War I tunnel and the walk down to the *Fondo Valle*, see pp105–106.

Map 26 –Rifugio Locatelli to Rifugio Fondo Valle 127

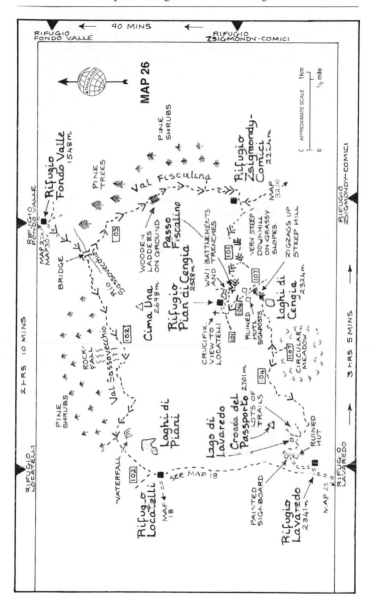

Route (iii)

For those who just want to get their hiking over and done with as soon as possible but don't just want to catch the bus back from the *Auronzo*, Route 101, heading off north from the road, 300m past the church and behind the *Rifugio Lavaredo*, is a convenient short cut to the *Locatelli*.

Rising up to the **Forcella Lavaredo** (2454m), the path traverses the western scree of the Croda Passaporto and the Paterno, parallel to the WW1 tunnel (see p105). The entire walk shouldn't take more than an hour. For details of the trail from the *Locatelli* to the *Fondo Valle*, see p106.

THE FINALE

Having made it as far as *Rifugio Fondo Valle* (or the *Zsigmondy Comici* if you're heading to Auronzo), you now have to decide which direction you wish your trek to take now, how difficult you want your final stage to be and, just as importantly, which town you wish to have as your final destination. We have described three possible trails below, each leading to a different final destination. The first and longest, **Route X**, is the two-day trek to the town of Santa Stefano di Cadore, situated at the southern end of the Val Padola. If you choose this option you will have the satisfaction of knowing that you have walked through the Central Dolomites from west to east since Santa Stefano di Cadore is widely regarded as the easternmost extremity of the Dolomites. However, the trek as described below involves some lengthy stretches of vie ferrate including a sheer drop down the southern face of the Croda Rossa di Sesto with only a wire cable for security. Attempt this walk only if you have had some experience of tackling vie ferrate, have the proper equipment, and if the weather looks favourable. Furthermore, it has to be said that Santa Stefano is probably the least interesting town of the three options given here.

Route Y by contrast is possibly the simplest of the three, a leisurely promenade west along the Val di Sesto to the gorgeous historical town of San Candido. It's a fascinating trail that's also to be recommended as a day-trip for those trekkers who've reached *Rifugio Fondo Valle* and who wish to continue to Santa Stefano but are waiting for the weather to improve.

Finally, **Route Z** takes you to the lakeside town of Auronzo di Cadore from *Rifugio Zsigmondy-Comici*. This route involves a hike down the Val Giralba from *Rifugio Carducci*, and again it's fairly straightforward. If you previously took Route B to Cortina, you should already be at *Rifugio Zsigmondy-Comici*. If you took Route A, on the other hand, and are now

---

(Opposite) Top: The Tre Cime di Lavaredo. **Bottom:** First World War caves near the summit of the Croda Rossa di Sesto.

at *Rifugio Locatelli*, walk south on Route 101 to *Rifugio Lavaredo*, then follow Route (i) as described on p125.

ROUTE X (Stage 1): RIFUGIO FONDO VALLE → SANTA STEFANO DI CADORE   [MAPS 27–29]

[**Tabacco map 017**] This two-part trek begins with a leisurely stroll down to *Hotel Dolomitenhöf*, some 25 minutes north of the *Fondo Valle*. Just after the *Dolomitenhöf*, on the same side of the road, Trails 124 and 153 head off by a signpost (right) into the forest. A second signpost, seven minutes later, splits these two routes, the way to *Rifugio Prati Di Crossa Rossa* on Trail 124 leading off right. It's a reasonably steep walk over mud and tree roots, past innumerable Scots pines, mushrooms, purple trumpet gentians and other Dolomitic vegetation. You'll see few trekkers en route since most prefer to take the chairlift from Bad Moos.

Forty minutes later another signpost appears right in the middle of the forest. As you face the sign with the valley and the Sexten Dolomites in the background, turn right (north); if you don't pass a small wooden fienili after about two minutes, you've taken the wrong path. The proper trail wends its merry way to the privately-run **Rifugio Prati di Croda Rossa**, aka **Rotwandwiesenhütte** (☎ 0474-710651; 1900m), beautifully appointed and set on a lush green lawn dotted with deckchairs and wooden huts. There's a volleyball court and a small zoo of goats and rabbits. The Rudi Hütte chairlift and restaurant are just 200m away. The *Prati* has a reputation for being one of the liveliest in the Dolomites and it is reasonably good value with beds beginning at L30,000, or L40,000 for a double.

This *prati*, or plateau, is something of a trekkers' junction, with day-trippers taking the chairlift up before setting off along one of the myriad of trails that pass through here. To begin the second part of this stage, follow the hordes as they cross the lawn along the fenced-off path leading up the hill from the chairlift. At the end of this path, ignore the turn-off for Route 18 to the left and Route 100 to the right. Instead, take the path signposted '15a and 15b' which snakes along the northern side of the **Croda Rossa di Sesto**. After 20 minutes, the two trails separate; you should take Trail 15b, the higher of the two, and continue tramping up the slopes at an oblique angle until you get to the signpost at the top. The view back over the village of Sesto from here is a good one, especially with the accompaniment of cowbells echoing up from the valley below.

Having lost most of the day-trippers at the turn-off from 15a, in all probability you'll now shake off the last few at this signpost: for where they head straight on and continue along 15b, you should take the only

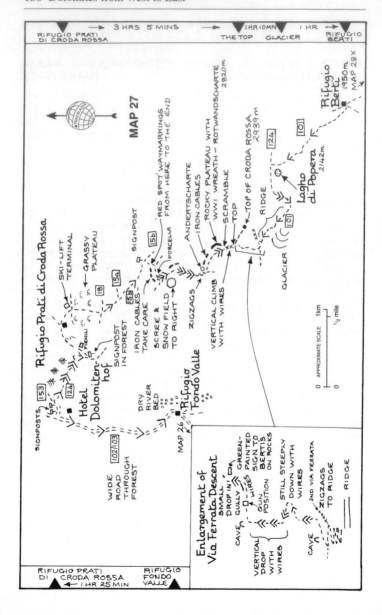

MAP 27

RIFUGIO PRATI DI CRODA ROSSA → 3 HRS 5 MINS → THE TOP 1HR10MN GLACIER 1 HR → RIFUGIO BERTI

RIFUGIO PRATI DI CRODA ROSSA ← 1 HR 25 MIN   RIFUGIO FONDO VALLE

Rifugio Prati di Croda Rossa

SKI-LIFT TERMINAL
GRASSY PLATEAU
18
15a
15b
SIGNPOST
IRON CABLES TAKE CARE
RED SPOT WAYMARKINGS FROM HERE TO THE END
FORCELLA
SCREE & SNOW FIELD TO RIGHT
ZIGZAGS
VERTICAL CLIMB WITH WIRES
ANDERTSCHARTE
IRON CABLES
ROCKY PLATEAU WITH WWI WREATH – ROTWANDSCHARTE 2820m.
SCRAMBLE
TOP
TOP OF CRODA ROSSA 2939m
RIDGE
124
GLACIER
101
Lago di Popera 2142m.
Rifugio Berti 1950m. MAP 28 X

PIENILI
SIGNPOST IN FOREST
153
124
Hotel Dolomitenhof
SIGNPOSTS
102/103
WIDE ROAD THROUGH FOREST
DRY RIVER BED
Rifugio Fondo Valle
MAP 26

0 APPROXIMATE SCALE 1km
0 ½ mile

Enlargement of Via Ferrata Descent

SMALL DROP IN GULLY
GREEN-PAINTED WIRES
CAVE
GUN POSITION
SIGN TO BERTI'S ON ROCKS
VERTICAL DROP WITH WIRES
STILL STEEPLY DOWN WITH WIRES
2nd VIA FERRATA
CAVE
ZIGZAGS TO RIDGE
RIDGE

other path possible, going sharp right *away* from 15b and almost doubling back on yourself. Seconds later, you're scrambling over loose rock as you head west, then south, along the rocky path. You'll soon encounter this stage's first **via ferrata**, a wire rope positioned to help you scramble round and over some difficult stretches of the path. You may not think so now but this is probably the easiest via ferrata of the entire stage.

After half an hour or so you'll reach a small forcella where you should go left and follow the red spots and triangles (as, indeed, you should do for the entire ascent) as they lead you past frozen ice and scree (part of a small snowfield) to the next via ferrata. This is another simple test, this time with vertical ropes leading you up towards the **Anderterscharte** (2698m), which you'll gain after a stiff climb some 30 minutes later . The splintered planks and stone walls of the Anderterscharte were once part of an Austrian army barracks and are amongst the most extensive World War I fortifications remaining in this area. If you're having trouble scrambling to the top, think how much harder it would have been for the soldiers who not only had to do this in winter but who had to dodge snipers' bullets at the same time!

The path continues *around* the small peak to your left; don't follow the path that goes over it. A wire cable has been fixed to the path to ensure you negotiate it safely. You are now heading south at an altitude of over 2700m, with views west as far as *Rifugio Locatelli* and beyond. Another cable-assisted scramble to another forcella brings you out into a small stony plateau, the **Rotwandscharte** (2820m), with a black iron wreath on your left commemorating those who fell fighting on the mountain in WWI. Still the path climbs, and after a zigzag scramble over stones and rubble – mind your step – a final vertical cable leads you out onto the summit ridge

❏ The Croda Rossa di Sesto

The Croda Rossa di Sesto is one of five summits that together form the so-called **Sextener sundial** – a semicircle of peaks surrounding the Val Fiscalina. While **Neuner** (2936m), **Elfer** (3092m), **Zwölfer** (3091m) and **Einser** (2698m) – nine o'clock, eleven o'clock, twelve o'clock and one o'clock – have kept their original names, the **Zehner** peak (ten o'clock) was renamed the **Croda Rossa di Sesto**, or **Sextener Rotwand** ('Sextener Red Wall'; 2965m) to give its German name. This mountain was, like so many in the Dolomites, the scene of some fierce fighting between the Austrians who were stationed on the northern side of the summit and the Italians who held the south. During this stage you will pass by gun positions and barracks from both sides, the distance between them near the summit being less than 100m.

of the **Croda Rossa di Sesto/Sextener Rotwand**, with the actual summit to your left. You are now at an altitude of over 2900m, (the cross is at 2939m) and if the climb didn't leave you breathless, the view from here on both sides certainly will. Splashed in green paint on one of the rocks, an arrow points the way up through a narrow crack in the rock to your final destination on this stage: *Rifugio Berti*. Pause for a second by that sign: this, after all, is the highest point of the entire west-east trail.

Immediately after the crack, the descent (one could almost call it the plummet) begins. The initial via ferrata descent of 20m or so is a good trial. If you come through safely and without too many difficulties, you should be able to proceed. If on the other hand this vertical climb down proves too taxing or terrifying, turn back: it's always better to lose your self-esteem than your sanity (or worse). And besides, the mountains will still be here next year, so you can always have another crack at it then!

The path hugs the cliff-face for the next 100m or so, most but not all of it protected by wire cable. After climbing over the three-foot high wall of a gun position blocking the way, the trail passes the cement-fronted cave, complete with ornate window frames, of a former Italian military post.

The real via ferrata descent begins now. Right in front of the cave you'll notice a **wire cable** draped down and attached to a vertical cliff-face. This is your way down from the mountain. If it's any comfort, the first few steps are the trickiest. Everybody has their own method of tackling such a descent. Some lean out and scurry down the cliff-face in a technique similar to abseiling, letting the rope slide through their hands as they go. Others barely hold onto the rope at all, but clamber down by finding finger and footholds in the rock. Either way, it's a difficult descent and should only be attempted by those with the right equipment – a full vie ferrata kit including karabiners, rope, harness, helmet and gloves – and it should not be tackled alone: two memorial plaques near the bottom are a lasting reminder of those who failed to take adequate safety precautions. Apart from a couple of **ladders** (the easiest parts of this clamber down), the wire cable is the only man-made assistance afforded to you. The entire descent takes about 1hr 10 mins,(less for experienced climbers), with only one 10m stretch where you don't need to hang on to any wires.

At the bottom, past a large dank cave and a plaque inscribed with Italian verse, the path splits again: the right branch goes up along the Sentinella Scharte, but you must turn left on Trail 101 and after an initial downhill scramble in which you must be careful not to miss the red-spot waymarkings, you continue on a rocky ridge alongside the grumbling glacier. If there's no mist around you can see the rifugio ahead of you to the east and, compared to what you've gone through before on this stage, this final stretch is relatively uncomplicated. Rare **yellow alpine poppies** grow by this glacier. At the end of the ridge, the red spots continue to guide you down through the rocky passage to **Lago Popera** (2142m).

Turn right immediately after the lake (still on Trail 101) and go round the hill; the rifugio and its bar is less than 30 minutes away. Owned by the CAI, *Rifugio Berti* (☎ 0435-67155; 1950m) charges the standard L13,000 per night for members, double for non-members. Those arriving late in the afternoon when it is growing dark and the rooms are full can sleep on mattresses in the bar, where the wall are lined with the detritus of WW1, including old bottles, tin cans and lamps, for just L10,000/5000. There's not much difference between this and sleeping in a room, for the cabins are cramped and the beds small. CAI members also receive discounts on all food and drink here. The tap water is not drinkable.

ROUTE X (Stage 2): RIFUGIO BERTI →SANTA STEFANO DI CADORE   [MAPS 28–29]

[Tabacco map 017] The second part of this, the most difficult finale, is relatively painless with no steep climbs, no vie ferrate and only a couple of stiff downhills. Nevertheless, it's a long and drawn out descent that takes you from *Rifugio Berti* to the easternmost point of the Dolomites, Santa Stefano di Cadore, with most of it conducted through alpine forests.

The initial walk along the white stone path to the *Rifugio Lunelli* (☎ 0435-67171; 1570m) is probably the steepest part of this stage as you descend some 400m down the eastern slopes of the Monte Popera, fording a number of small streams as you go. The rifugio itself, which you should reach in just under an hour, is privately-run and good value at 18,000 per bed (L25,000 with hire of sheet sleeping bag). The family who owns it will go out of their way to help though little English is spoken.

Continuing east, just before the tarmac begins take a path to the right (signed on a nearby boulder as Trail 164, though it's marked as 151 on Tabacco maps), and continue south towards the river which you'll have to cross. The path on the opposite bank is difficult to find so don't attempt to ford the river immediately; instead, walk downstream along the north bank for a few minutes until you see a signpost on the far side pointing out the continuation of Trail 164 towards *Bivacco Piovan* and Casera Aiarnola. For the next 15 minutes follow the steadily uphill path through the forest (chamois live in the area) all the way up to a segment of exposed cliff-face. Turning left and continuing through the forest, after a few minutes you'll come to a wide, dry water course. A mudslide on the far side has swept away all the signposts, though when I last visited a temporary metal waymarking hung from a bush showed the direction.

Passing above the (s)lime-green **Lago Cadia**, this uphill stretch turns south after 20 minutes or so, and a few minutes later you'll reach the signposted **La Sapada junction** (1743m). Two wide tracks now present themselves, both reduced to muddy, puddle-spotted 'slipways' by four-wheel drives. Take the right-hand fork (Trail 164) to the small clearing in the forest known as the **Busa dal Pintar** (1743m).

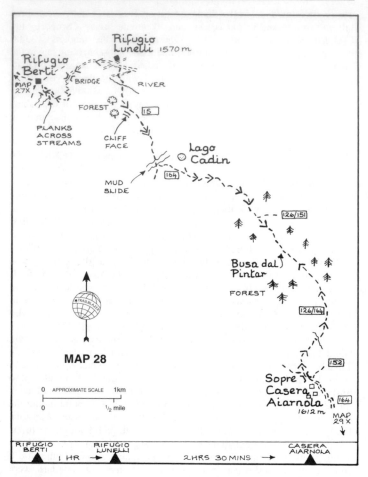

Rifugio Lunelli 1570m

Rifugio Berti

MAP 27X

BRIDGE

RIVER

FOREST

15

PLANKS ACROSS STREAMS

CLIFF FACE

Lago Cadin

MUD SLIDE

164

126/151

Busa dal Pintar

FOREST

126/164

152

Sopre Casera Aiarnola 1612m

164

MAP 29 X

TRAILBLAZER

MAP 28

0   APPROXIMATE SCALE   1km

0   ¹/₂ mile

RIFUGIO BERTI   RIFUGIO LUNELLI   CASERA AIARNOLA

1 HR ➤   2 HRS 30 MINS ➤

And so Trail 164, now a level forest path carpeted with pine needles, continues its progress south-east. The red-painted waymarkings disappear for a little while but no matter for the path is always obvious.

Fifty minutes after leaving the Busa dal Pintar you'll arrive at the Sopre Casera Aiarnola junction (1650m) with Trail 152, followed a few minutes later by the **Sopre Casera Aiarnola** itself (1612m), a huddle of three old farm buildings in a clearing in the forest that have fallen into disrepair.

Map 29 – Sopra Casera Aiarnola to Danta di Cadore 135

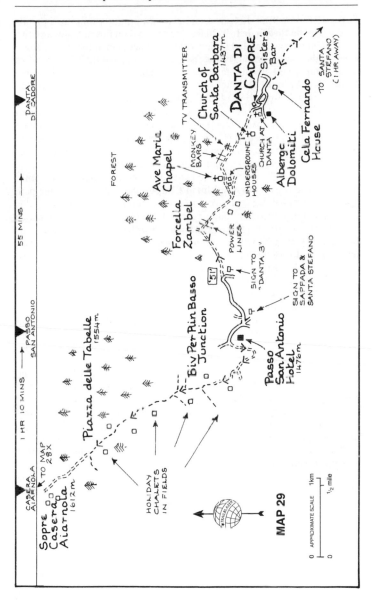

MAP 29

Sopra Casera Aiarnola 1612m.

Piazza delle Tabelle 1554m.

Biv Per Rin Basso Junction

Passo San Antonio Hotel 1476m.

HOLIDAY CHALETS IN FIELDS

SIGN TO "DANTA 3'"

SIGN TO SAPPADA & SANTA STEFANO

POWER LINES

Forcella Zambel

Ave Maria Chapel

MONKEY BARS

FOREST

TV TRANSMITTER

Church of Santa Barbara 1437m.

DANTA DI CADORE

Sisters Bar

UNDERGROUND HOUSES

CHURCH AT DANTA

Albergo Dolomiti

Cela Fernando House

TO SANTA STEFANO (1 HR AWAY)

TO MAP 28X

CASERA AIARNOLA

1 HR 10 MINS

PASSO SAN ANTONIO

55 MINS

DANTA DI CADORE

APPROXIMATE SCALE   0   1km
                     0   ½ mile

Still you follow Trail 164, past another turn-off (this time for Forcella Valdarin at the **Piazza de le Tabelle**, 1554m) and on through thinning forest past numerous small holiday cabins situated in hillside meadows. Keep to the main path (ie follow the left-hand trail) at the **Bivio per Pra della Monte**, and 10 minutes later you'll land on the main road at the **Passo San Antonio Dambel** (1476m) just north of *Hotel Passo San Antonio* (☎ 0435-650018; 1476m; L90,000 for room and board).

Taking the first left turn (signposted 'Sappada and S.Stefano') past the hotel, leave the road altogether by the 'Danta 3km' sign and walk on a wide track (signposted '51') through a forest popular with mushroom pickers. At the first junction, go right and under the low electricity cables which you can hear crackle and hum, and then after passing a string of houses on your right, switch to the path heading off to your left. Ten minutes later you'll pass the **Ave Maria Chapel**, then on a bend in the path a series of monkey bars, part of an exercise course running through this little stretch of forest. Not long afterwards, at the end of the path, take a short diversion up to the **Santa Barbara Church** (1437m), which affords lovely views over the village of **Costalissoio** on the other side of the valley, and **Costa** (to the left of Costalissoio and visible from the path just below Santa Barbara) as well as the roofs of **Danta di Cadore** immediately below you. Passing through the village between the church and *Sister's Bar* (a good place to stop and rest), walk down the Via Roma which is flanked by terraced houses whose shuttered windows all sport flower boxes, and at the end of the street turn left and make for the main road. Those who wish to finish their day here can stay at *Albergo Dolomiti* (☎ 0435-650085), with rooms starting at L80,000 per night. There's a cashpoint on the Via Roma.

Back on the main road, just beyond the **Cela Fernanda house** on the first bend in the road after the village, a sign points out a woodland path to Santa Stefano di Cadore. Judging by the way parts of it have been churned up, it's more of a track for off-road vehicles than walkers, but it's not a bad trail, and certainly a great deal more interesting (and quicker) than taking the main road. The first half of this path is easy to follow; by a wood cabin, however, the path becomes a channel and begins to peter out. Trees other than the ubiquitous pine now begin to flank the path, which has all but disappeared by the time it reaches a second large woodland cabin. Keeping this cabin to your left, follow the trail as best you can and five minutes later you should run into a tarmac pathway by a large house, a path that leads to **Santa Stefano di Cadore** (909m), the final destination on this trek.

SANTA STEFANO DI CADORE

This unassuming little town lies at the junctions of the Cadore and Padola Valleys. Lacking any noteworthy sights — the church, the centrepiece of the town, is rather ugly by the standards of this part of the world — and a little too

Santa Stefano
di Cadore

quiet and sleepy, Santa Stefano is not really the place to celebrate the end of a trek. Nevertheless, the town does have its advantages: there's a tremendous pizza **restaurant**, *La Notla*, at Via Venezia 8, just to the south of the Piazza Roma (the square in front of the church) and the *Union Pub*, 200m to the north on the opposite side of the road, serves a wide variety of local and imported beers. The people of Santa Stefano also seem rather fond of ice cream, and there are a number of *gelateri* in town, including *Il Gelato* on Via Udine.

Accommodation

There's a *campsite* 2km east of Santa Stefano, while the cheapest accommoda-

tion in the centre is provided by the numerous *appartementi* (starting at L30,000); ask at the tourist office one block south of the church (9am-12.30pm, 4-7pm, closed Tuesday; ring ☎ 0435-62230 for a list of them). Or, for those who wish to spend their last night on the trek in some style, there's the elegant three-star *Albergo Centrale* (☎ 0435-62246), at Piazza Roma 5, the finest in town. Rooms here, all en suite, start at L80,000 single, L115,000 double. The best **trekking shop** is Costan at 68 Via Udine.

Transport

To get away, catch the seven-times-daily **bus** to Auronzo (7.25am-6.05pm;

15 mins, L2900), from where you can catch further transport to Cortina, Venice and other destinations. Alternatively, catch a bus to Calalzo (8 daily; 30 mins) for **trains** to Venice (2 daily, currently at 9.50am and 8.40pm).

You'll need to buy your ticket before you board from either the tourist office or a tabacchi. All buses leave from the market square by the river, just a couple of hundred metres to the south of the Piazza Roma.

ROUTE Y: AN EXCURSION FROM RIFUGIO FONDO VALLE TO SESTO AND SAN CANDIDO   [MAPS 30–31]

[**Tabacco maps 017 and 010**] Many may sneer at the simplicity of this particular walk along the Val di Sesto, indeed, to call it a trek or even a hike would be overstating the matter. Where, the purists cry, are the heart-racing climbs and knee-trembling descents for which the Dolomites is justly famed? And where are those exhilarating (for some read 'terrifying') via ferrata, where your very life hangs by a piece of shaky iron-mongery hammered into the side of a cliff?

But while it's true that this gentle amble through hillside forest and meadow is hardly going to get the adrenalin pumping, if you're looking for a comfortable stroll between two of the most delightful Alpine villages in Italy, across fields and forests that are crawling with all creatures great and small, along a path that, though it never rises above 1600m in altitude, still manages to provide some spectacular views over the northern faces of a number of mountains including the Punta dei Tre Scarperi and the Croda dei Baranci, then the **Sentiero Meditazione** ('Meditation Path') between Sesto and San Candido is for you. The downhill march from the *Fondo Valle* through the Val Fiscalina to the start of the walk is also pleasant and restful.

The entire walk between *Rifugio Fondo Valle* and San Candido can be accomplished easily as a daytrip from the rifugio; if this is your plan, make sure you set off early, thereby allowing you time to enjoy the churches and historical buildings of Sesto and San Candido before the last bus back to *Hotel Dolomitenhöf* departs San Candido (currently at 3.38pm every day). Alternatively, you can choose to stay overnight in one of the villages en route, both of which are teeming with hotels and pensions.

From the *Fondo Valle*, Alta Via 5 continues its meandering way north and down, following roughly the course of the wide dry river bed. You'll pass stables, a house with frescoes of the muscular Ladin giants, Huno and Hauno, painted on its northern wall, and the rather grand *Hotel Dolomitenhöf* (☎ 0474-710364; summer prices start at L85,000 half-board; 1460m) eventually arriving at a car park opposite the hotel's driveway.

From the northern end of this car park a path continues north down the valley before dividing into two separate ways, Trails 1a and 12.

Map 30 – Rifugio Fondo Valle to Sesto 139

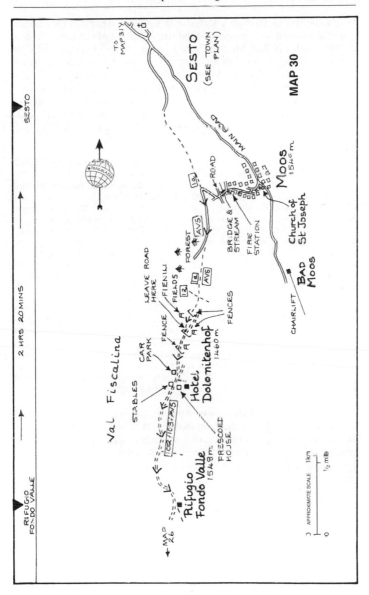

Follow the former through a series of three fields separated by wooden fences and dotted with pines, wooden fienili and purple crocuses. You'll see the chairlift at **Bad Moos** on your right just before the third field; by continuing along the path, in less than 15 minutes you'll cross the stream and arrive at the village of **Moos** (1339m). Turn left at the end of the street by the eighteenth-century **Church of St Josef**, walk along the main road for the next kilometre or so (it's not very busy, and you can always continue to follow Route 1a if you wish to get away from the traffic altogether) until you arrive at the village of **Sesto/Sexten** (1302m).

SESTO/SEXTEN

Dominated by the huge white **Church of San Vito**, Sesto is an enchanting little village with a number of mildly diverting sights to keep you there a little longer than you probably planned. Apart from the church itself, which was consecrated in 1384, there are the arcades in the nearby cemetery with its **frescoes** of the *Dance Macabre* by Stolz, and a memorial to Sepp Innerkofler (see p105).The huge state-of-the-art **tourist office** at the eastern end of town is rather special, with a comprehensive selection of books for you to browse through and on the first floor a picture-board exhibition (in Italian and German only) of the wildlife of the Dolomites. Upstairs, the library (Monday to Friday 10am-noon and 3-6pm) has **Internet** facilities (L5000 for 40 minutes). If you have any questions at all about trekking and the staff at the tourist office can't help you, give the guides at the **Alpine Schüle** behind the tourist office a try (daily, 5-7pm).

If you fancy spending a night in the village, B&Bs and private rooms start at about L30,000 in the summer season. One of the cheapest is *Egarter Hermann* at Via Dolomiti 22 (☎ 0474-710577), on the banks of the canal, with prices just L28,000 even in the peak season. Ask at the tourist office for other accommodation possibilities.

The Holzer **bus** company runs 14 buses daily from Sesto to San Candido and a similar number arrive from San Candido (15 mins). These buses from San Candido travel on to Moos (5 mins), and five daily travel on to the *Hotel Dolomitenhöf* in the Fondo Valle (15 mins from Sesto).

To join the **Sentiero Meditazione** which begins up the hill to the north of Sesto, take Via San Vito, the road to the right of the large sports shop in the centre of town, and right again up Larchenweg/Via del Larice. The tarmac road stops by a signpost, but the track continues up the hill where, by a stream, it passes the first of many carved tree trunks, a feature of this meditational path. A minute later you cross the road and continue past the houses along the tarmac path as it leads uphill. Leaving the tarmac on the hairpin bend, follow the path signposted to '*Gasthof Waldruhe*'. You are now on Route 4d, a trail that takes you under the ramp of a wonderful old barn, then past a house decorated with frescoes, before leading you into a magical, moss-carpeted pine forest. A second carved trunk, this one inscribed with quotations from Genesis (1:29 and 1:26), and a third one, (Mark 9:42), next to some ancient oil presses, decorate the trail. Between the two is a turn-off to some prehistoric stone slabs. Scarred with strange

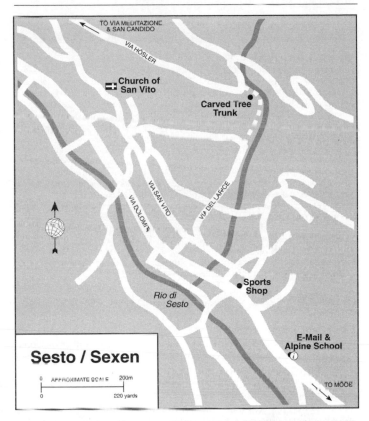

TO VIA MEDITAZIONE
& SAN CANDIDO

VIA HÖSLER

Church of
San Vito

Carved Tree
Trunk

VIA SAN VITO

VIA DOLOMITI

VIA DEL LARICE

Sports
Shop

Rio di
Sesto

E-Mail &
Alpine School

Sesto / Sexen

0   APPROXIMATE SCALE   200m

0   220 yards

TO MOOS

cuts and gashes, these large monoliths were supposedly used in Neolithic
times as a place of pagan worship. The stones lie a 15-minute walk away
from the main trail at the end of the path signposted 'Pietre Preistoriche'.

Back on the main trail, five minutes after a splendid wooden sculpture
of Christ you'll come across a small wooden chapel, the **Waldkapelle**
(1553m), built against the side of a huge boulder. The chapel dates back to
the World War I when the villagers in the valley were forced to flee to the
hills to avoid the heavy bombardment from the Italians (Val di Sesto being
part of Austria at this time). You can go inside the chapel and sign your
name in the visitors' book by the door. Just beyond the church lies another sculpted tree-trunk, this one bolted around the trunk of a living pine.

To reach San Candido, you have to take a turn-off to the left just
beyond the church and begin the long stretch downhill along Route 4

❑ **Val di Sesto/Sextental**
Demarcating the north-eastern limits of the Dolomites, the Val di Sesto runs between the mediaeval town of **San Candido** and the **Passo di Montecroce** some 15km to the south-east. Austrian until the end of World War I, it was given to the Italians as part of the 1919 peace treaty to become the eastern-most valley of the Alto Adige region. Nevertheless the valley remains distinctly Tyrolean in character in terms of language, architecture and ambience, and the Austrian border lies just a few kilometres to the east.

The major towns in the valley are **San Candido**, or Innichen, with a population nudging 3000, and Sesto (Sexten in German; population 2000), the latter of which gave its name not only to the valley but also to the range of huge mountains that flank its southern side, known as the Sexten Dolomites, and the national park, the **Parco Naturale Dolomiti di Sesto**, of which these mountains form the major highlights. The village in turn derives its name from a group of six houses located since the Middle Ages near the entrance of the north-south running **Valle Campodidentro** to the west of modern Sesto. Known as Sexta, these houses provided a sort of rest station for travellers journeying along the ancient trading route that passed through the valley. The village is also known as **San Vito** after the glorious fourteenth-century parish church that sits in its centre.

(later 4 and 5). It's a gentle walk of at least an hour, though it's enlivened by the presence of some weird and wonderful fungi, a number of wooden apiaries and, if you're very lucky, the possible sighting of a red deer or two grazing near the path.

Just a few hundred metres before San Candido, and just beyond a set of power lines, the path forks: take the right fork, then a left at a second one soon after. It's then only a matter of minutes before the onion dome and rectangular tower of San Candido's two most famous churches appear between the trees.

SAN CANDIDO/INNICHEN

Located at the junction of the Val Pusteria and Val di Sesto, San Candido (1167m) is a small but historically important town whose skyline, as you will notice when descending from the Sentiero Meditazione, is dominated by a number of ancient churches, all seemingly engaged in some bizarre ecclesiastical competition to see who can produce the most spectacular, gaudy and over-elaborate interiors. Most dazzling of all is the Romanesque **Parrocchiale di San Michele**, or Church of Saint Michael (6am-6pm), whose interior features some delightful frescoes by Christoph Anton Mayr.

Immediately opposite, the square-towered **La Collegiata** is a much older, larger and yet simpler construction dating back to the eleventh century. The beauty of this church lies in the details, including the faded frescoes in the

Map 31 – Sesto to San Candido 143

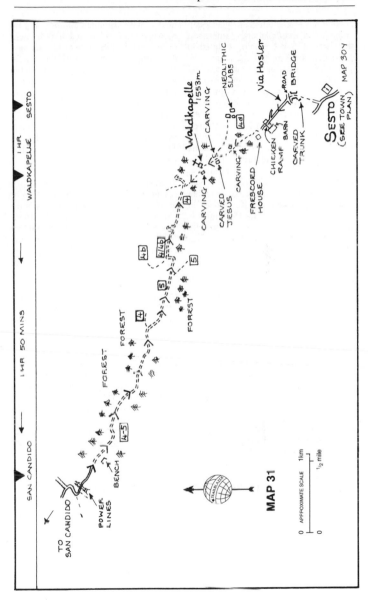

MAP 31

cupola, the fourteenth-century wooden crucifix and accompanying statues, and the statue of San Candido, sculpted in 1240, that now stands in the crypt.

Other interesting old churches and ecclesiastical museums include the dumpy Baroque **Cappelle Altötting e del Santo Sepolcro** with its dioramas of the Passion, which lies to the east of the train station, or the **Franciscan church and convent** at the western end of Via PP Rainer. Best of all, however, is the **Museo della Collegiata** (Tuesday, Friday and Saturday 5-7pm), a museum dedicated to the churches of San Candido which contains some exquisite works of devotional art. It's housed in the oldest monastery in the Dolomites, a Romanesque structure built by Benedictine monks in AD769. You can also visit the **Dolomythos Museum**, a colourful collection celebrating the wonders of the Dolomites, including information on the Ladin Culture and a large fossil collection, much of it assembled by the English geologist, Miss Ogilivie-Gordon.

Services
The **tourist office** (☎ 0474-913149), sitting in the shadow of La Collegiata, has information on all these attractions as well as on the accommodation in town.

Accommodation
Check out the good one-star *Patzleiner* (☎ 0474-913211) at 3 Via I. Mantinger, to the north of the bend in the Rio di Sesto, with spotless rooms ranging between the L35,000 and 40,000 mark, or the excellent-value two-star *Siebner-hof-Bergmann* (☎ 0474-913428), at 24 Via dei Tintori, with large comfortable rooms and including a huge breakfast for just L35,000 upwards. There are plenty of **banks** and ATMs in town, including the Banco di Bolzano e Trento, whose ATM accepts Visa, MasterCard, Cirrus and Eurocheque. The library behind La Collegiata has **Internet** access.

Transport
If you decide to return to Sesto/Moos or even *Rifugio Fonde Valle*, **buses** leave from behind the Cappelle Altötting. There are 14 buses a day heading down the Val di Sesto, and five to the *Dolomitenhöf*, the last one currently leaving at 3.38pm. There are also four buses daily to Cortina, via Dobbiaco and Misurina, and one (8am) that travels up to *Rifugio Auronzo*. S.A.D. also run buses to both Bressanone (7 direct everyday, or change at Brunico) and Bolzano (5 direct everyday, or change at Brunico).

The **train station** is a few hundred metres to the west of the Cappelle Altötting. Currently there is one train a day to Bolzano (12.58pm), one to Rome (6.40pm), five to Lienz in Austria, nine to Innsbruck (2hrs 30 mins), one to Trento (5.34am), 14 to Dobbiaco (4 mins) and four that travel all the way up to Munich (5hrs 30 mins).

ROUTE Z: RIFUGIO ZSIGMONDY-COMICI → AURONZO
[MAP 32]
[Tabacco map 017] This is easily the shortest finish to the west-east trail, taking just a few hours from the Val Fiscalina to the southern Dolomite town of Auronzo. Unlike the other two routes, however, this finale uses *Rifugio Zsigmondy-Comici* as its base in the Fiscalina, rather than the *Fondo Valle*. To get to *Zsigmondy-Comici*, take Route (i) above (see p125); this is preferable to walking up the Val Fiscalina from the

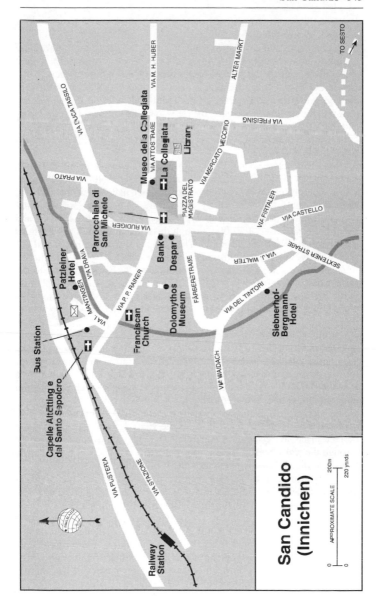

San Candido
(Innichen)

APPROXIMATE SCALE

0 — 200m
0 — 220 yards

TO SESTO

Railway Station

Bus Station

Capelle Altötting e
del Santo Sepolcro

Franciscan Church

Patzleiner Hotel

Parrocchiale di
San Michele

Museo della Collegiata

La Collegiata

Library

Bank

Despar

Dolomythos Museum

Siebnerhof-
Bergmann Hotel

PIAZZA DEL MAGISTRATO

VIA DUCA TASSILO

VIA PRATO

VIA DRAVA

VIA MANTINGER

VIA P. P. RAINER

VIA PUSTERIA

VIA STAZIONE

VIA WAIDACH

VIA RUDIGER

VIA ATTOS TRABE

VIA M. H. HUBER

ALTER MARKT

VIA FREISING

VIA MERCATO VECCHIO

VIA FIRTALER

VIA CASTELLO

SEXTENER STRAßE

VIA J. WALTER

VIA DEL TINTORI

FÄRBERSTRAßE

Fondo Valle, an exhausting two-hour climb, which you'd have to do if you took Routes (ii) or (iii).

Having got yourself to *Zsigmondy-Comici*, the path over the **Forcella Giralba** (2431m) and onto *Rifugio Carducci* is easy to discern: a light grey streak against the darker rocks littering the northern face of the **Croda dei Toni**. (This mountain is the Twelve O'Clock peak on the sundial; see p131 for details). It's a monotonous but brief 30-minute scramble up to the forcella, enlivened by views back down over the *Zsigmondy* and the Val Fiscalina. At the top, you'll have to say goodbye to this side of the Sesto mountains as you pass through the forcella to the greener **Via Alta Giralba**.

Squeezed between the Croda dei Toni (to your right as you head south) and Monte Giralba, *Rifugio Carducci* (☎ 0435-400485; 2297m) is a tiny, homely place in a rather exposed spot just below the forcella. Owned by the CAI, it is run by one family, as are many of the more remote rifugi, with the wife and two boys doing most of the cooking and serving. Beds are only L13,000, though this reflects the lack of amenities on site (no showers, for instance). The menu is similarly limited and has to be ordered in advance. Still, the dining area, heated by a wood-fuelled furnace, is pleasant, and the view south down the valley and on to the giant, snaggle-toothed lower peaks of the **Croda di Ligonto** (2766m) more than makes up for these disadvantages. They also have diagrams posted outside the rifugio to help you decipher which mountains you're looking at.

Within 40 minutes of leaving the *Carducci*, and after passing a giant boulder, in the shadow of which a family of marmots had chosen to make their home when I was last there, you leave the mountain meadows for forests of dwarf pines as the path zigzags towards and through three mountain streams. After the second stream the vegetation changes again, with tall alpine trees now replacing their diminutive cousins. Other non-alpine species such as the beech and oak also thrive in this area.

Soon you reach the small lawn of the **Pian de le Salere** (1380m), a perfect place to rest and recuperate. The path then continues south through the **Val Giralba Bassa**, following the course of the Rio Giralba from now on, and at one point crossing it on a sturdy wooden bridge.

Thirty minutes after leaving the Pian, you emerge from the woods at the foot of the hill by a number of large alpine chalets, and the now tarmac path heads down to the main Cortina—Auronzo highway. Look back, and you should be able to see the *Carducci* high on the hills above you. From the road, you can catch a bus to Auronzo, though you'll need to buy a ticket beforehand from *Pensione Cacciatori*, five minutes east (left) along the road. Or you can walk the two miles east, though it's all along the busy main road, much of it without any pavement. It is hardly exciting and can be quite hair-raising when the trucks drive by.

Map 32 – Rifugio Zsigmondy to Auronzo Highway 147

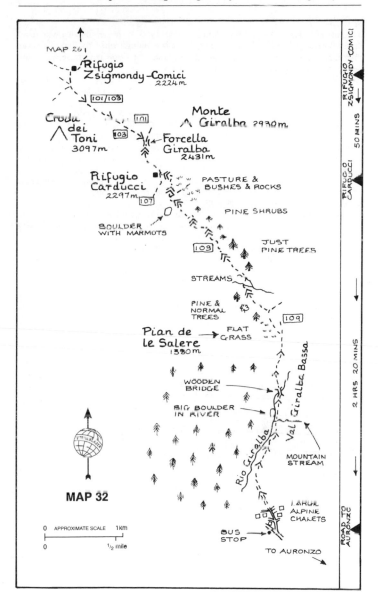

MAP 26

↑

Rifugio
Zsigmondy-Comici
2224m

101/103

Crodu
dei
Toni
3097m

Monte
Giralba 2930m

101

103

Forcella
Giralba
2431m

Rifugio
Carducci
2297m

PASTURE &
BUSHES & ROCKS

107

PINE SHRUBS

BOULDER
WITH MARMOTS

JUST
PINE TREES

109

STREAMS

PINE &
NORMAL
TREES

FLAT
GRASS

109

Pian de
Le Salere
1380m

WOODEN
BRIDGE

BIG BOULDER
IN RIVER

Val Giralba Bassa

Rio Giralba

MOUNTAIN
STREAM

MAP 32

1/ARUR.
ALPINE
CHALETS

0 APPROXIMATE SCALE 1km

0   1/2 mile

BUS
STOP

TO AURONZO

RIFUGIO
ZSIGMONDY-COMICI

50 MINS

RIFUGIO
CARDUCCI

2 HRS 20 MINS

ROAD TO
AURONZO

AURONZO

The medium-sized town (population 4500; 866m) of Auronzo is little more than a thin strip of houses sandwiched between a lake and the southern foothills of the Croda dal Campo. The forests around here used to provide the timber to make the galleys for the Venetian republic's fleet, though these days the town's economy and fame is based largely on the huge lake that stretches along the entire southern side of Auronzo. Though Auronzo looks as quaintly olde-worlde as any other settlement in these parts, the lake itself is actually a modern landmark, brought about by the building of the 55m-high **Santa Caterina Dam** which stands to the east of the town. The dam is named after the nearby sixteenth-century **church** that sits, forgotten and almost invisible, to the east of the town centre at the southern end of the **Ponte Tiziano**.

Of more interest, perhaps – and certainly nearer – is the **Church of Madonna delle Grazie**, a few hundred metres east of the town centre on the main road into town. The original church was built in 1738 by the inhabitants of Auronzo, in an attempt to inspire some divine intervention to end the hostility between themselves and the people of Dobbiaco in the Val Pusteria as to who controlled Misurina and Maraia. The tactic seemed to work, for in 1752, just 14 years later, the Venetian republic and the Austrians signed an accord that ended the dispute at a stroke.

There are any number of other churches in town, as well as an excellent **museum**, with sections on the flora, fauna and minerals of the Dolomites. It's open daily from 9am-noon and 4-7pm in July and August.

Services

Just a few hundred metres east of the museum is the helpful **tourist office** (☎ 0435-99603); alpine guides are on hand every evening from 5 to 7pm to answer any questions you may have about the trails.

If you're starting your trekking in Auronzo, you may be interested in Cartoleria Articuli Regalo on the main street, which has a good selection of Tabacco **maps**, and the Lavaredo **sports shop** at Via Dante No 23.

The Pellicano **supermarke**t is the place to stock up on food and there's a branch of the **camera shop** Foto Ottica on the same street. There is currently no Internet centre in town.

Accommodation

As ever in the Dolomites, this is easily available.

Try the extremely comfortable *Meuble Fontana* (☎ 0435-400049) right in the heart of the action at Via Ospitale 6, with single rooms starting at just L30,000 (doubles L50,000-plus), or the slightly more upmarket *Vecellio* (☎ 0435-9420) at Via Pais 7, with rooms on average only L5000 more.

If you fancy splashing out and celebrating the end of your trek in style, *Auronzo* (☎ 0435-400202) at Via Roma 30 is the most luxurious place in town, a three-star establishment with prices starting at L70,000 for a single, L110,000 double.

Transport

The easiest and quickest way to get to **Cortina** is to go via Misurina, though there is only one bus in the morning at 9.15am and one in the evening (at 2.52pm). From Misurina there are seven buses to Cortina (9.26am-5.20pm; 35 mins). Otherwise, the simplest way is probably to catch a bus to Calalzo, a train from there to Ponte nelle Alpi, and a second bus to Cortina from there.

To reach **Venice**, it's necessary to travel to Calalzo by bus, then change for the train. The initial journey takes 30

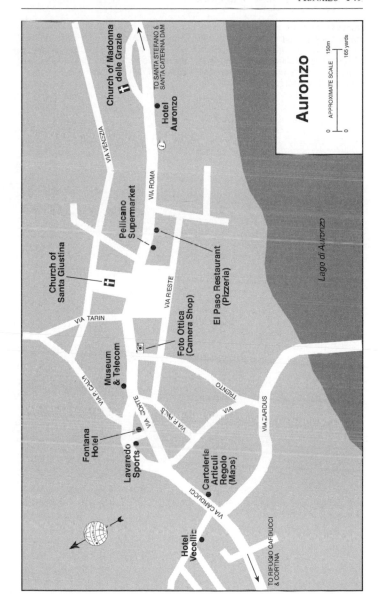

Auronzo

APPROXIMATE SCALE

0 ___ 150m
0 ___ 165 yards

TO SANTA STEFANO &
SANTA CATERINA DAM

Church of Madonna
delle Grazie

VIA VENEZIA

Hotel
Auronzo

VIA ROMA

Pellicano
Supermarket

Church of
Santa Giustina

VIA TARIN

VIA R'ESTE

El Paso Restaurant
(Pizzeria)

Lago di Auronzo

Foto Ottica
(Camera Shop)

VIA P. CALVI

Museum
& Telecom

VIA TRENTO

VIA CORTE

VIA R'US

VIA ZARDUS

Fontana
Hotel

Lavaredo
Sports

Cartoleria
Articuli
Regolo (Maps)

VIA CARDUCCI

Hotel
Vecellio

TO RIFUGIO CARBUCCI
& CORTINA

minutes, and there are 12 buses every day (5.55am-7.50pm), though only two are direct (at 8.55am and 7.55pm; 20-30 mins). From Calalzo there are two direct trains to Venice (at 9.50am and 8.40pm; 2hrs 30 mins), and seven others which require you to change in Ponte nelle Alpi or Conegliano. There is also one train daily from Calalzo to **Roma** (8.55pm; 10hrs), and about six to **Padova** (3hrs 20 mins).

PART 4: ALTA VIA 2

Facts about the walk

The Alta Via 2 (AV2) is one of the great European mountain trails. Taking anywhere between 10 and 16 days to complete (though I once met a group of Italians who claimed to have finished it in six, and, at the other extreme, a couple from Newcastle who had been returning to the Dolomites every year for the past four years in their attempts to complete it all), the trail is the longest alta via of them all, measuring approximately 150km from start to finish. Within these 150km you will find no less than eight of the major Dolomite mountain groups, including such well-known massifs as the glacier-covered **Marmolada** and the **San Martino**, as well as over **thirty mountain passes**, or forcella. The path also runs through three Italian provinces, Bolzano, Trento and Belluno, and three distinct linguistic regions too: the German-speaking Tyrol, the Ladin language of the central Dolomites and the Italian tongue dominant in the southern Alps. And having climbed up from the city of Bressanone to the lofty Alpe di Plose, the trail never once dips below 1300m until the final descent into Feltre; here, truly is a path that deserves the name 'alta via' or 'high route'.

The Trail is officially nicknamed the **High Route of the Legends**, since it passes through a number of mountain ranges that have become famous as the venue of innumerable legends and myths. From the Odle Massif, scene of many a Ladin story, to the Vette Feltrine, supposed haunt of witches, ghosts and demons, your entire itinerary is rich in folklore and fairytales, a few of which are recounted in the relevant places in this book.

To repeat the advice given in part one of this book: though no specific climbing or mountaineering skills are required to complete AV2, freedom from vertigo and a reasonable level of fitness are both essential. In some places the trail is furnished with metal ropes and ladders to help you negotiate a steep climb or a narrow or crumbling path. Again, no specialist skill is required, just a strong nerve. If, however, you have any via ferrata equipment (see p25) there'll be times when it could come in handy.

The last section of the walk, through the Feltrini mountains, is particularly tough on both the nerves and the knees with some exhausting climbing and a number of narrow and precarious trails. Rifugi are few and far between on this section too; as a result, locals and experts advise that you don't attempt this section alone or in bad weather.

For those who do have the requisite level of skill and mountain experience, and all the right equipment, there are a number of vie ferrate detours that one can take along AV2. You will find that these have been pointed out and described in detail in the appropriate places in the following chapter.

BRESSANONE/BRIXEN

Said to be the Tyrol's oldest town, mediaeval Bressanone (560m) sits at the confluence of the Rienz and Isarco rivers. It's a commercially advantageous location that has helped to guarantee Bressanone's prosperity throughout its thousand-year history, and today, with a population approaching 18,000, the town is South Tyrol's third largest. Though part of Italy, the town appears Austrian in everything except currency and, as with many settlements in this part of the world, every name, including place and road names, has

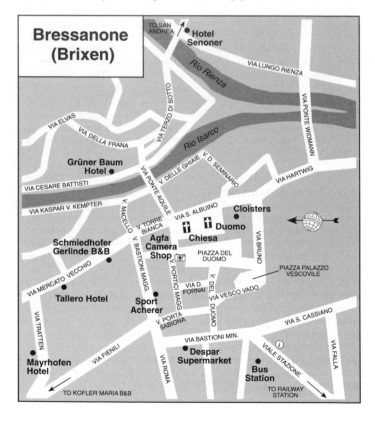

❏ **Tabacco maps**
Tabacco maps 030, 07, 015, 023 and 022 are required for this route. Purchase them before you set off, for maps are hard to come by on the trail itself.

two versions: one Italian and one German. The city's dominant landmark is undoubtedly the cathedral, or **Duomo**, with its Baroque interior and frescoes by the esteemed eighteenth-century Tyrolean artist Paul Troger. A stroll along the cobbled streets flanking the **Piazza del Duomo**, the city's central square, should also include visits to the eleventh-century **parish church** and its 72m-high **White Tower**, and the splendid Romanesque, fourteenth-century **cloister**. Other attractions in the town centre are marked on the plan on p152.

Services
The **tourist office** (☎ 0472-836401), at Viale Stazione/Bahnhofstrasse 9, has further information on the local sights and can help you find accommodation. If you need to purchase any **trekking equipment** before you set out, visit Sport Acherer on Via Bastioni Maggiore. There's an Agfa **camera shop** just to the west of the Domplatz at the eastern end of the Durchgang, and a Despar **supermarket** to the south on Via Bastioni Min

Accommodation
Bressanone has numerous accommodation possibilities, and compared to its neighbour in the Valle Isarco, Bolzano, offers far better value for money too. One of the cheapest options is to take a room at *Kofler Maria* (☎ 0472-831368) at 9 Via Pentolai, to the south-west of town, where prices start at just L22,000 per person including a decent-sized breakfast.

For just a few thousand lire more, however, you can stay in *Schmiedhofer Gerlinde* (☎ 0472-836352), another

B&B in a far more central location at 15 Via Mercato Vecchio (Altenmarktgasse 15).

As for the hotels in Bressanone, *Tallero* (☎ 0472-830577), further up the road from the *Schmiedhofer Gerlinde* at Via Mercato Vecchio 35, is basic but cheap (L30-55,000 per person), while the *Mayrhofer* (☎ 0472-836327), situated at Via Tratten (Trattengasse) 17, has spacious, good value rooms (about L60,000 per person).

The *Grüner Baum* (☎ 0472-832732) is a few notches above the others listed here, being a semi-luxury four-star hotel located in the prettiest part of the city at Via Stufels 11. Prices start at L80,000 per person in the low season, which may sound like a lot but actually represents exceedingly good value.

Transport
Bressanone is a transport hub, and you'll find **buses** here to all parts of the Tyrol and beyond.

Destinations include (with weekday frequencies given): Cortina (2 daily at 12.15pm, 1.20pm), San Candido (11 daily, though for most you'll have to change at Dobbiaco), the Alpe di Siusi (3 daily, last at 1.20pm), Bolzano (12 daily), Ortisèi, Santa Cristina and Selva (12 daily) and even Milan (every 30 minutes, 7.15am-7.15pm).

The **train station** lies approximately 1km south-east of the tourist office. Destinations include: Bologna (7 daily); Bolzano (20 daily); Innsbruck (19 daily), Milan (3 daily); Munich (8 daily); Napoli (daily); Roma (2 daily); San Candido (3 daily); Trento (2 daily); Venice (2 daily); and Verona (at least 14 daily).

BRESSANONE TO RIFUGIO PLOSE   [MAP 33]

[Tabacco map 030]   Though advertised as a trek between Tyrolean
Bressanone and the Renaissance town of Feltre, the official beginning of
AV2 is not actually Bressanone at all but *Rifugio Plose*, five kilometres
to the east of the city and some 1800m higher. As such, it is usual for AV2
trekkers to begin their journey by catching a bus up to the Bressanone
suburb of **San Andrea** (961m), and the cable car from there to the **Alpe
di Plose**, the terminal of which is just a 20-minute walk along Trail 7
from the rifugio. Buses from Bressanone's terminal to San Andrea currently leave thrice-daily, at 7.42am, 11.45am and 1.12pm.

However, there are those trekkers who maintain that the four-hour
25min walk up to *Rifugio Plose* is an integral part of the AV2, and for these
people we have described the walk below. It's not a bad hike, though it's
a rather tough introduction to the AV2, the path being relentlessly uphill
for virtually the whole way. So if you want to complete this section, read
on; if, however, you'd rather start at *Rifugio Plose*, don't let any trekkers
persuade you that by doing so you will have missed out on part of the AV2.
That simply isn't true.

To begin, from Bressanone's Domplatz head north over the iron
bridge known as the **Ponte Aquile**, then east (right) down Via Bassa
Angelo Custode and Via Terzo di Sotto through the most attractive quarter of Bressanone, a part that tends to be missed by many visitors.
Crossing the bridge at the end, continue straight ahead up Via Otto V
Guggenburg, the road to the left of *Hotel Senoner*; 250m along, there's a
sign indicating a path that leads right into a little copse before eventually
emerging by yet another bridge. Rather than cross the bridge, however,
turn right and take the path through the woods. The trail from here is
straightforward enough save for two forks in the woods, one almost
immediately after the other: take the left-hand path at the first fork (the
right-hand one, which is obstructed by a wooden barrier, leads into a
field), and the right-hand fork at the second. In both cases, there are waymarkings nearby to ensure you stay on the right trail.

Passing a **farmhouse** and attendant greenhouses, the path winds up to
a road. Turning left and heading up the hill from here past a field of
sweetcorn and some apple and pear trees, you'll soon come to a signpost
pointing right (south) into a field on route 4. The path zigzags a little after
this, before emerging on the road into the tiny Bressanone suburb of **San
Andrea**. This part of the walk from Bressanone should have taken you
about an hour and probably a little less if you had no trouble finding the
correct path, which isn't easy.

As you walk into town, ahead of you at the end of the road is the local
parish church. On your right, 100m before the church, is the Despar
supermarket, while one block to the west is the local **tourist office**. From

Map 33 – Bressanone to Rifugio Plose 155

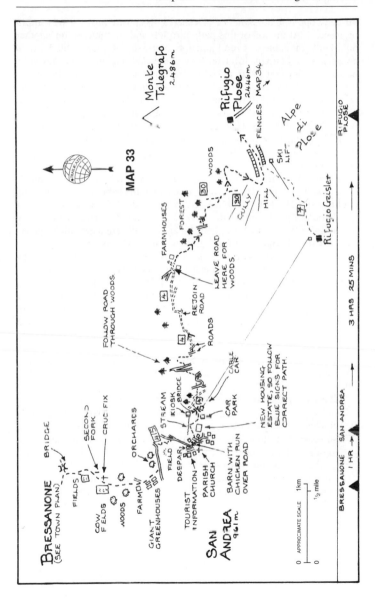

virtually opposite San Andrea's Despar, a signpost points the way uphill on Route 4. At the top of this path, turn left and continue up for another 50m until you come to a road junction. Normally, Routes 4 and 5 would continue straight up the hill from here to the cable car terminal. Currently, however, a housing estate is being built right across the path. It is to be hoped that a new, clearly marked trail will have been organized by the time you read this, but if it hasn't, cut diagonally left through the field above the road; then, when you come to a stream, turn sharp right through the forest (ie above the field you have just walked through). A path has been waymarked through this forest with a blue 's'. When you come to a fence turn left, and in a few minutes you'll be at the car park by the **San Andrea cable car**.

From now until you reach *Rifugio Plose*, you'll be following Trail 4. To join it, cross the bridge immediately below the cable car terminal, and continue straight on up the hill through the field to the kiosk by the chair lift. Turning right here into the woods, a few hundred metres further on you'll arrive at a sort of spaghetti junction of different woodland paths. Keep to Trail 4 which is quite well waymarked at least through this first stage, and before long you'll come to a road by a crash barrier. Cross the road and head into the forest on the other side. From now on the way-markings get a little less clear as Route 4 follows roughly the course of the mountain road, taking innumerable short cuts through the forest while the road zigzags back and forth. Most trekkers lose their way a couple of times during the next section, for the waymarkings become less frequent and there are dozens of other trails joining and leaving Route 4 through-out. Should this happen to you, there are two options: retrace your steps to the last waymarking and try a different trail from there; or wait until you hit the mountain road, and from there try to rejoin the trail, which is often signposted on the road.

The path eventually leaves the mountain road altogether, climbing higher and higher up the western slopes of **Monte Telegrafo** (2486m) into thicker forest. Fortunately, once you've left the road behind the path is also easier to follow with waymarkings more frequent; minutes after leaving the road, the path emerges from the forest onto heathland by a gully, where it takes a sharp turn to the right. You are now less than 30 minutes from the rifugio, reached via the fenced-off **ski piste** to your left.

Chilly *Rifugio Città di Bressanone alla Plose/Plose Hütte* (☎ 0472-521333; 2446m), located in the northern corner of the **Alpe di Plose** (Plose Plateau) and owned by the Bressanone section of the CAI, is one of the largest rifugi in the Dolomites and, thanks to its location, under-standably popular with day-trippers from the Valle Isarco. With its sou-venir shop, which also sells maps and books on the Dolomites, and size-able dining hall serving top-notch food, this rifugio is also one of the more professionally-run, though it still only charges the standard

Map 34 – Rifugio Plose to Passo di Eores 157

L32,000/16,000 (non-members/members) for a bed in a dorm. As an introduction to the comforts (and otherwise!) of the local rifugi, therefore, *Rifugio Plose* isn't bad.

RIFUGIO PLOSE → RIFUGIO GENOVA   [MAPS 34–35]

[Tabacco map 030] From *Plose* signposts point the way east on routes marked 4/6/7. Leave 4 and 7 for path 6 at the small saddle known as the **Forcella Luson/Lüsner Scharte** (2383m). This trail, having crossed a number of pistes, then metamorphoses back into Trail 4, a path you'll be following for the rest of this stage, (much as those who walked up from Bressanone did for the last stage). If you get confused with all the different trail numbers, just look out for the AV2 waymark, a large red triangle with the number 2 inside it, which appears now and again on the route. Trail 4 leaves the plateau, entering into ever-thickening forest where you'll find the first aided sections of the AV2, though they're nothing to be apprehensive about: save for one ladder to help you climb out of a

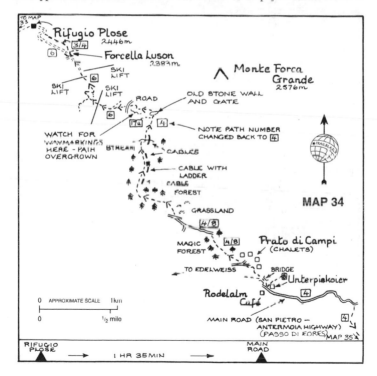

small gully, the 'aiding' takes the form of iron cables attached to the cliff by short stretches of the trail where the path is rather too narrow for comfort. For many trekkers, the cables are surplus to requirements and are seldom used.

Bending sharply to the left (east), the path eventually leaves the forest for the grassy southern slopes of the **Monte Forca Grande**, before plunging headlong into the dark, boulder-strewn and mossy stretch of woodland that sits above the **Prato di Campi** (or Gampenwiesen), a meadow sprinkled with a number of wooden holiday chalets. At its foot lies the mountain highway and the **Passo di Eores/Kofeljoch** (1860m), which separates the Plose from the Pùtia group.

Reaching the pass, continue on Trail 4 (often muddy) as it follows the line and contours of the highway eastwards while remaining a couple of metres below it. After a sharp right-hand bend in the road and just a few metres after the highway and Route 4 are reunited, the trail gives up trac-

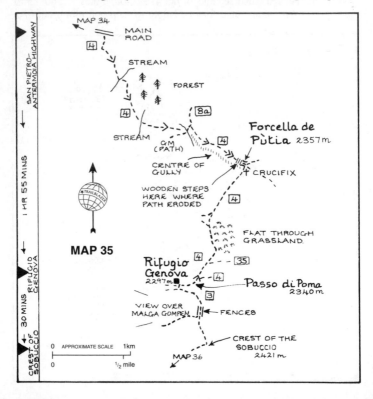

Map 36 – Rifugio Genova to Forcella della Roa 159

ing the road and heads off up the hill, through woods alive with the sound of birdsong. This is the beginning of the climb up to the **Forcella de Pùtia/Peitlerscharte** (2357m), an ascent that follows the course of the **Rio Sorte** up a rocky gully to the pass.

Turning hard right at the top, in 30 minutes you'll arrive at *Rifugio Genova al Passo Poma/Schlütler-Hütte* (☎ 0472-40132; 2297m), an ideal spot to finish your trekking for the day. Run by the CAI, the *Genova* nestles snugly below the small saddle known as the **Passo di Poma** (2340m) separating the Bonsoi and Col di Poma peaks, thus providing some lucky guests with an immense panorama to the west from their bedroom windows, with an equally impressive view available from the forcella, just a few metres away to the east. Beds in *Genova* cost the standard L32,000/16,000 for non-members/members.

RIFUGIO GENOVA → RIFUGIO PUEZ   [MAPS 36–37]

[**Tabacco map 030**] From *Genova*, AV2 begins by leading back east (on a different path from the one on which you arrived) up to the Passo di Poma. You are now on Route 3, and will remain so until after the **Forcella**

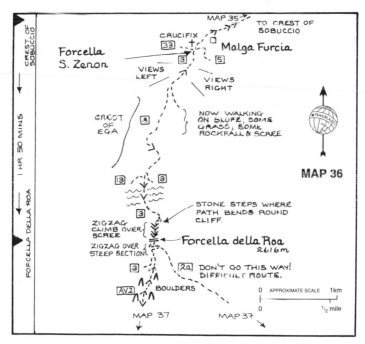

della Roa, over two hours away. Climbing fairly steeply to the crest of the **Subuccio/Sobutsch** (2421m), the trail then heads south-west, gently descending across grassy slopes to the **Forcella S Zenon** (marked on the Tabacco maps as the Furcela de Furcia; 2293m) and the junction with trails 5 and 33.

Ahead of you rises the massive spires and peaks of the Odle group. The trail now turns due south in the shadow of the elongated **Ega** crest, at the eastern end of the Odle group, before beginning the long climb towards the **Forcella della Roa/Roascharte** (2616m), the deep, distinctive notch in the cliffs ahead of you. A few minutes before you reach the foot of this brutal ascent, a second 'Trail 3' leaves the main trail to your left and descends to the floor of the valley. Needless to say, this path should be ignored. The correct path continues straight on, traversing numerous small patches of scree before rounding the foot of a rocky spur, whereafter the going gets much steeper and harder as you scramble across the loose rock splinters up to the forcella. It's a tiring ascent, but not a particularly dangerous one. Immediately after the forcella the path once again divides: in this instance, stick to the path wriggling down the slope ahead of you, rather than the path heading off to the left, which is a technically difficult route and for experienced mountain climbers only.

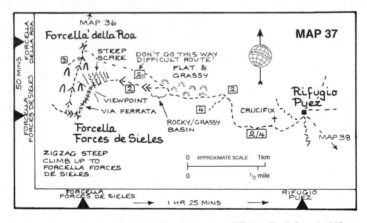

After a few minutes of zigzagging down the cliffside, Trail 3 and AV2 go their separate ways, the former switching right while the AV2 continues straight ahead on a well-waymarked track through a cluster of gigantic

---

(Opposite) Scrambling up a via ferrata through the Val Setus to the summit of the Sella Group. **(Overleaf)** The Laghi dei Piani (see p106), near the Rifugio Locatelli.

Map 38 – Rifugio Puez to Passo Cir 161

boulders to a second mountain pass, the **Forcella Forces de Sielles** or **Siellesscharte** (2505m).

For the final leg of this stage to *Rifugio Puez*, please turn to p88.

RIFUGIO PUEZ → RIFUGIO BOÈ [MAPS 38–39]

[Tabacco map 07] This stage takes you across a noiseless space on the southern side of Puez, eventually leaving this range altogether for the Sella group, a formidable crown of mountains encircling a high altitude plateau, and a favourite destination of mountain climbers and via ferrata addicts.

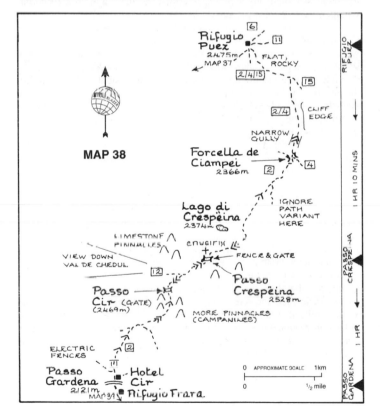

(**Opposite**) Ibex below Rifugio Biella.

But firstly, the descent from Puez. Heading south-east from the rifugio on Trail 2/4/15 (ie the path that passes above the nearby flagpole), follow Trail 2/4 only when it takes a southerly turn at a signposted junction. Continue along a cliff edge and down a steep but short gully and turn right to yet another signposted junction at the **Forcella de Ciampei** (2366m). Follow Trail 2 (the alternative, Trail 4, heads off east towards the village of Colfosco) and, ignoring the signposted variant that appears to your left soon after, descend into the small natural bowl known as the **Altipiano di Crespëina**, at the centre of which and all but invisible from the path is a small body of water known as the **Lago di Crespëina/ Crespëinasee** (2374m). Route 2 now takes you, after a 150m climb over sometimes loose stones (watch carefully for waymarkings) to the **Passo Crespëina/Crespëinajoch** (2528m), flanked on either side by spire-like weathered campaniles. Passing by a beautiful crucifix and through a small wooden gate, you are now walking on a well-trodden path scything through the scree at the upper end of the eerily silent **Val de Chedul**. Sheep often graze in these parts, and a sign here warns dog-owners to keep their pets on leads. The path curves round to the south-west and just 30 minutes after leaving Passo Crespëina you reach a second mountain pass, **Passo Cir/Cirjoch** (2515m).

Your path (still Trail 2) now picks its way through more campaniles and down south-west towards the **Passo Gardena/Grödnerjoch** (2121m), a relatively trouble-free path dotted with some colourful wild flowers. Passo Gardena is a bit of a non-event, consisting of little more than a hotel, *Hotel Cir* (☎ 0471-795127; L80,000 per person half-board), a rifugio, *Rifugio Frara* (☎ 0471-795225; L45,000 per person) and a couple of souvenir shops, but it is also an important crossroads for a number of mountain trails and a minor tourist destination in its own right, where hordes of foreign day-trippers can gawp at the lower slopes of Puez and Sella without ever leaving the confines of the tour bus.

Viewing it from the descent towards the Passo Gardena, the Sella group over the other side of the pass presents a seemingly impenetrable wall of sheer rock and scree. Yet the slender **Val Setus**, which is more of a steep gully than a valley hidden from view from Passo Gardena, provides non-mountaineers with a way into the very heart of the Sella. It is reached by following the ominously-numbered Route 666 which begins at the Frara car park, skirting round the slopes of the **Col de Mesores** (2615m) on its way to the mouth of the Setus.

Having arrived at the gully entrance, you'll notice that even this trail isn't easy. An exhausting zigzag over barren scree precedes a lengthy section of near-vertical via ferrata. Technically this section is a cinch but a head for heights, not to mention a certain degree of stamina, is required to reach the top. Do so, and you will have reached 2610m and climbed a fraction under 500m since leaving Passo Gardena. As a reward, the

Map 39 – Passo Cir to Rifugio Boè 163

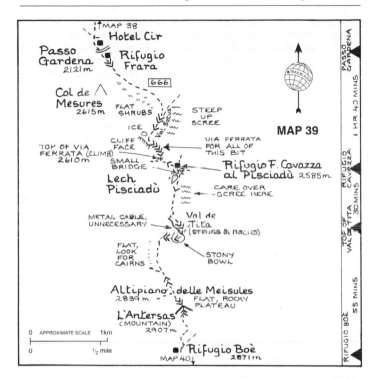

homely **Rifugio Franco Cavazza al Pisciadù/Pisciadù Hütte** (☎ ()471-836292; 2585m), just to the left at the top, is on hand to provide weary trekkers with essential nourishment to sustain them through the next leg of this stage, and very weary ones with a bed for the night (L32,000/16,000 non-members/members). The village that you can see in the valley to the north-west is **Colfosco**.

From *Pisciadù*, continue on 666 as it descends to **Lech Pisciadù**, keeping the lake to your right as you follow the trail around the upper western face of the **Cima Pisciadù**. Turning left, negotiate the steep **Val de Tita**: an aided climb, according to the Tabacco maps, though the wire cable now lies unused to the right of the new path. This short ascent brings you out by a small and shallow pond in a natural stony bowl, where the water has stained the rocky ground dark brown.

The path now turns right and climbs briefly over the 2900m mark as it rises up and out of the bowl before, mercifully, levelling out. Still on stony ground, follow the cairns now as they lead you south and down to a flat, rocky plateau, the **Altipiano delle Meisules** (2839m), crisscrossed by paths heading in all directions. Go straight ahead, up and over **L'Antersas/Zwischenkofel** peak that you see ahead of you; at 2907m it is the highest point on the trail so far. Continue on and soon you'll reach *Rifugio Boè* (☎ 0471-836217). Yet another CAI-owned rifugio, the *Boè* stands on a windswept saddle between the Col Turont and the Piz Lech Dlace. At 2871m, it's one of the highest and most remote rifugi in the Dolomites. For this reason, food is more expensive than at other CAI-owned rifugi, though the beds (L28,000/14,000) are just as cheap as elsewhere. Try to get here early to stake your claim to a place by the fire.

RIFUGIO BOÈ → MALGA CIAPÈLA   [MAPS 40–42]

[Tabacco map 07 and 015] Is there a walk in the Dolomites that can rival the stretch between the Passo Pordoi and the Lago di Fedaia, a path known since time immemorial as the **Viel dal Pan**? OK, so it's not really for thrill-seekers but even without the dominant presence of the Marmolada and its glistening, grumbling glacier this level stroll through a hillside meadow alive with butterflies and full of wild flowers is simply delightful – and a total contrast to the scenery of the previous stage.

But you have to get to the beginning of the Viel dal Pan first, and that involves a level hike of about an hour along the southern half of the Sella, followed by one of the most vertiginous descents in the Dolomites.

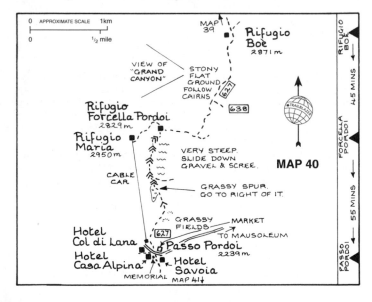

It begins at the tiny *Rifugio Forcella Pordoi* – which was closed when I last tried to visit but according to local reports is still going strong – and throughout the descent you find yourself not so much walking as sliding down as if scrambling down the side of a massive and very steep sand dune. Look up ahead occasionally and you'll notice the Marmolada looming up for the first time on this route.

Only near the bottom, as the path rounds a rocky outcrop, does the giddy gradient ease off a little. From the *Rifugio Forcella Pordoi* (2829m) to the pass is a drop of almost 600m; that's a gradient of about 1:2. If you'd rather not tackle this descent, you can climb to *Rifugio Maria* (2950m) and take the chairlift down to Passo Pordoi (2239m) instead.

PASSO PORDOI

This is a typical Dolomite settlement: that is to say, a place that wouldn't exist without tourists. Take away the chairlift, the hotels, the restaurants, souvenir shops and the semi-permanent market specializing in low-quality fleeces and other trekking gear, and you're left with nothing save a road, some great views to the west and east and a small **memorial** commemorating the building of the road by Vittorio dal Lago da Cles de Trento and Alfredo Riccabon da Cavalese between 1900 and 1909.

Just to the north-east of the pass, however, at the end of a little lane, is a mausoleum where the bodies of almost 9000 German and Austrian soldiers from both world wars are buried.

Of the hotels, *Col di Lana* (☎ 0462-601277) is the smartest, with prices starting at L70,000 per person; the CAI-owned *Hotel Casa Alpina* (☎ 0462-601279) on the other hand, is rather basic despite the distinctly un-CAI prices (L50,000/90,000 sgl/dbl).

The third hotel, *Savoia* (☎ 0462-601717), is probably the best of the bunch, though still not great value at L50,000 per night for bed and breakfast in the low season.

From the Passo there are four **buses** daily (three at weekends) to Arabba (9.10am, 10.25am, 3.40pm, 5.05pm) and three to Ortisèi (10.15am, 4.10pm and 4.55pm), from where you can catch further transport to the larger towns.

My advice is not to linger here, but walk past the entrance of *Hotel Savoia* to Route 601, which passes a small **chapel** above the road before it heads south to the start of the Viel dal Pan. The climb is an easy one; at the top, you can look south over a network of chairlifts running all over the southern side of the Sass Beccé. From the top, turn left past *Rifugio Sass Beccé* and the nearby *Rifugio Baita Fredarola* (2388m), and take the right fork on 601.You are now on the verdant Viel dal Pan, while confronting you to the south is the glacier-topped northern face of the Dolomites' largest mountain, the mighty Marmolada.

Assuming that viewing conditions are favourable on your trek, you should pause at *Rifugio Viel dal Pan*, a food and drinks only rifugio perfectly situated to allow you to enjoy a cold beer while gazing at the glacier. Don't get too comfortable, however: there's still some walking to be done. (And don't drink too much either: cashing in on there being no trees on the Viel dal Pan, the rifugio charges for the use of its toilet!)

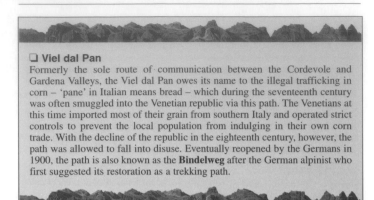

All good things must come to an end including the Viel dal Pan. But at
least with this walk you're given a choice of how to end. Having taken
the right fork marked 'Rifugio Castiglioni' down the hill, you'll see a
signpost which makes your options clear: right on *via difficile*, left on *via
facile*. My advice is to turn left, then take the steep, unofficial path that
leads off right soon after.

At the foot of this path is the **Lago di Fedaia** (2054m) and *Rifugio
Castiglioni* (☎ 0462-601117), a large, privately-run hostel with prices
beginning at L28,000 for a space in a twelve-bed dorm, (L32,000 with
breakfast).

After the delights of the Viel dal Pan, the final section of this stage is
one big anti-climax, at least if you choose the walker's route rather than
the via ferrata path, which is truly for experts only (see box on
pp170–171). Those planning to do the latter are advised to finish their day
here, spend the night at the *Castiglioni* and get an early start the next
morning. The rest, however, would be better off walking across the dam
to *Rifugio Dolomia* (☎ 0437-601221; two- or three-bed rooms, L45,0000
bed and breakfast) then along the southern shores of the lake to the life-
less *Rifugio Passo di Fedaia* (☎ 0437-722007; L40,000 per person). The
dark green section of the lake immediately to the west of the rifugio is, in
fact, the original lake before the dam was built and the body of water
increased dramatically. From there head down to the small cluster of
hotels known as **Malga Ciapèla** (1410m).

This last section from the *Fedaia* is a dull and laborious 90-minute
downhill trudge, most of it either on or near the road or the adjoining ski
piste. There are plenty of hotels in Malga Ciapèla but if money is a big
concern and you prefer the homely touch of a local B&B to the imper-
sonality of a big hotel, my advice is to stay above the main settlement at

Map 41 – Viel dal Pan   167

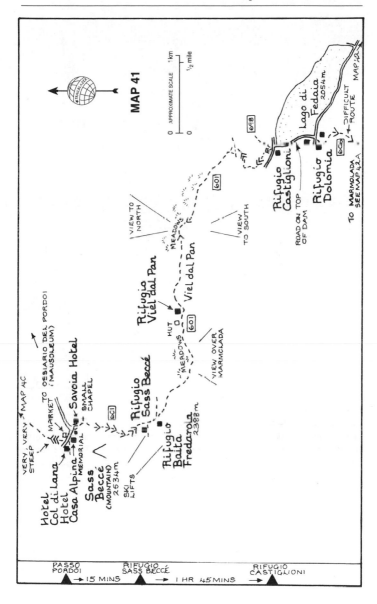

MAP 41

APPROXIMATE SCALE

Hotel Col di Lana
Hotel Casa Alpina
Savoia Hotel
VERY, VERY STEEP — MAP 40
TO OSSARIO DEL PORDOI (MAUSOLEUM)
MARKET
MEMORIAL
SMALL CHAPEL
Sass Beccé (MOUNTAIN) 2634 m
SKI LIFTS
Rifugio Sass Beccé
Rifugio Baita Fredarola 2388 m
Rifugio Viel dal Pan
HUT
MEADOWS
VIEW OVER MARMOLADA
Viel dal Pan
VIEW TO NORTH
MEADOWS
VIEW TO SOUTH
Rifugio Castiglioni
ROAD ON TOP OF DAM
Rifugio Dolomia
Lago di Fedaia 2054 m
DIFFICULT ROUTE
MAP 42
TO MARMOLADA SEE MAP 42A

PASSO PORDOI
RIFUGIO SASS BECCÉ
RIFUGIO CASTIGLIONI
→ 15 MINS
→ 1 HR 45 MINS →

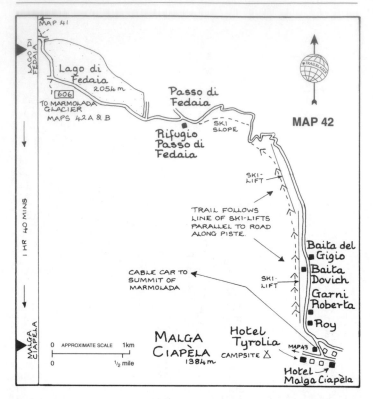

Baita del Gigio (☎ 0437-722059), a cosy little place serving very good food, with rooms starting at around L30,000 per person including breakfast. If you'd rather be a bit nearer the action (though there's very little action going on during the trekking season), try the ***Hotel Malga Ciapèla*** (☎ 0437-522987), which offers sizeable rooms with breakfast for L73,000 in the low season, rising to L123,000 during the August holidays. There's also a ***campsite*** at the western end of town. Malga Ciapèla also has a small shopping arcade, (follow the signs to *Bar Negozi*), including a **sports/trekking shop**, a café, tabacchi (that also sells stamps) and, round the other side of the hotel, an **ATM** that accepts Visa, MasterCard and Cirrus cards.

The cable car, incidentally, is actually a three-stage journey up to the Marmolada's *Rifugio Punta Rocca,* a very worthwhile journey if you have the time.

❏ The Marmolada

The Dolomite's tallest mountain is also, thanks to the glistening glacier that crowns the 'Queen of the Dolomites' on its northern side, one of its most recognizable. (Ironically, this 'Highest Mountain in the Dolomites' is not actually made of dolomitic rock at all but plain old limestone with traces of magnesium carbonate.) There are actually two high points on the Marmolada's vast mountain summit: the **Punta Rocca** (3309m), which was first conquered by the Englishman John Ball in 1860, and the **Punta Penia** (3343m), first scaled by possibly the Dolomites' most famous climber, the Viennese Paul Grohmann, in 1864.

Situated right on the front line during World War I, the Marmolada's glacier, the largest in the Eastern Alps, is riddled with galleries and tunnels excavated by the Austrians during the first year of fighting. It's incredible to think that a whole battalion of Austrian troops were sometimes housed inside this glacier during the First World War, battling not only against the Italians but also the elements: 400 men lost their lives, for example, in a single avalanche on the Marmolada during the bitter winter of 1916. As late as 1947 bodies of Austrian soldiers who perished in the First World War were still emerging from the glacial ice – usually in an excellent state of preservation.

Mountaineers and skiers flock to the Marmolada today. Climbers in particular head to the mountain's near-vertical southern face, where a 1000m-plus drop into a scree valley below awaits those who lose their battle with the mountain; while skiers come to ski on the gentle, year-round icy slopes of the glacier itself. Non-climbing trekkers, however, need not feel excluded, thanks to the installation of the **three-stage cable car** from Malga Ciapèla to the summit crest. At the end of the second and third stages there are view-points and restaurants, and even a small museum dedicated to the battles of World War I. The cable car leaves every half hour during daylight hours in summer.

ROUNDING THE MARMOLADA

On the following pages we describe two different routes round the Marmolada. The first, overleaf, is solely for experienced via ferrata tacklers with a full kit (ice pick included). It is a challenging path that takes you round the western side of the Marmolada, and offers, weather permitting, some pretty awesome views. Hopefully, those of you have opted for this trail spent a night at one of the rifugi by the Lago Fedaia, from where this trail begins.

Those who chose the soft option, however, as described on p172, should be under no illusions: the walk, though technically easier, is still long and exhausting.

❏ Traversing the western side of the Marmolada

The Marmolada is definitely one area of the AV2 where those willing and able to tackle a via ferrata have a better time of it than the walkers. While those who lack the necessary equipment or experience are forced to plod along a ski piste by a busy road to the east of the Marmolada, the via ferrata-ites have a much more beautiful, interesting and direct route around the western slopes of the Dolomites' biggest mountain. That said, this is a long trail, taking approximately eleven hours and involving an overnight stay en route in *Rifugio Contrin*. It's also rather a tricky one; only experienced climbers with the necessary equipment (rope, harness, helmet, crampons, glacier cream, sunglasses and an ice axe) should even contemplate attempting such a route, and then only in good weather. To begin, cross the dam to the cable car. Take the car (recommended), or climb in its shadow on Trail 606 up to the ruined Rifugio Col dei Bus, then scramble over shattered rocks to reach **Rifugio Pian dei Fiacconi** (2626m). Descending steeply in a westerly direction from here, the path then cuts a level swathe across ice, scree and snow to the notch in the north-west crest of the Marmolada. From here walk south (still on 606) to a narrow chasm between the Marmolada and the **Piccolo Vernel**, at the end of which lies the **Forcella Marmolada** (2896m).

❏ Traversing the western side of the Marmolada (cont)

A series of ladders leads off east from here to the summit of **Punta Penia** (3343m), the highest point on this – or indeed any other – trail in the Dolomites.

Returning to the forcella, continue straight on (south-west) for a couple of hours along the aided path over stones and rocks, then down along a series of zigzags to the **Val Rosalia**, at the end of which lies *Rifugio Contrin* (☎ 0462-601101; 2016m). Owned by the National Alpine Association, *Contrin* has room for 97 people, and charges standard CAI prices (L32,000/16,000) with breakfast an extra L8000.

Heading east from here through the Malga Contrin on path 607, the path now climbs once more up the Val de le Cirele; then after the junction with 612b, heads due south towards the **Passo delle Cirele** (2683m). There now follows a seemingly-interminable series of switchbacks over very fine, grainy scree as the trail plummets down to the **Val de Tas Cia**, the first area of rolling meadows and pastures on the trail since the Viel dal Pan. From here it's fairly plain sailing south along 607 to *Rifugio Fuchiade* (1982m), where you join up with the walker's trail.

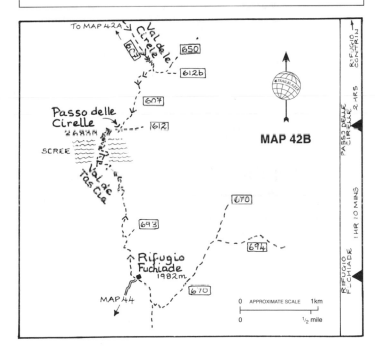

MALGA CIAPÈLA → RIFUGIO PASSO DI VALLES
[MAPS 43–45]

[**Tabacco map 015**] This is a long stage, though if you have the cash and volition you can break it up by staying at *Rifugio Fuchiade*, or one of the more expensive places in the Passo di San Pellegrino.

The day begins with a climb of the long and tortuous variety. From Malga Ciapèla, take the rough road (Trail 610) to the right (north) of *Hotel Tyrolia* that leads via a bridge and a campsite to a metalled road. Follow this road for about 20 minutes to a sign by a bridge over a dry stream pointing to Trail 689, a small path through a sweet-smelling pine forest. The path emerges eventually by the same road that you left 25 minutes before. Turning right at the junction, climb the slope through ever-thinning forest by following the sequence of curves in the road.

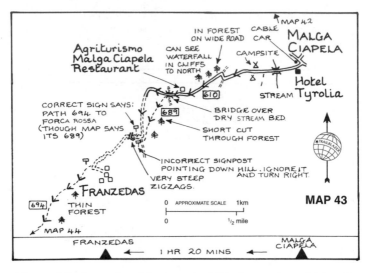

After a while the road straightens out and 35 minutes after rejoining the road you reach a signposted junction; continue on the road and it will lead you to the **Franzedas Farm** (1980m), a battered old farmhouse that could be used as shelter in times of emergency. Your path, however, (that is to say Route 689), heads off right through the pine shrubs towards the **Forca Rossa** (2499m). It's a gentle climb that steepens only towards the end. Note the slabs of brown and burgundy porphyry from which this peak is formed. At the top of the Forca Rossa there's a 'visitors' book' inside a small, rough wooden case, where you can sign your name for posterity.

Map 44 – Forca Rossa to Passo di San Pellegrino 173

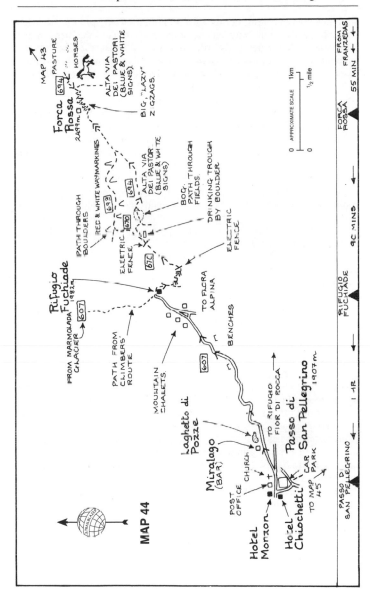

MAP 44

MAP 43

PASTURE

694 HORSES

Forca Rossa 2499m.

ALTA VIA DEI PASTORI (BLUE & WHITE SIGNS)

BIG "LAZY" Z GZAGS.

693

694

ALTA VIA DEI PASTOR (BLUE & WHITE SIGNS)

692

PATH THROUGH BOULDERS

RED & WHITE WAYMARKINGS

BOG. PATH THROUGH FIELDS

DRINKING TROUGH BY BOULDER

ELECTRIC FENCE

691

ELECTRIC FENCE

Rifugio Fuchiade 1982m.

607

FROM MARMOLADA GLACIER

PATH FROM CLIMBERS' ROUTE

TO FLORA ALPINA

BENCHES

MOUNTAIN CHALETS

607

TO RIFUGIO FIOR DI ROCCA

Laghetto di Pozze

Passo di San Pellegrino 1907m.

Miralago (BAR)

CHURCH

CAR PARK

POST OFFICE

Hotel Monzon

Hotel Chiochetti

TO MAP 45

AUSTRALIA ???

0 APPROXIMATE SCALE 1km
0 ½ mile

PASSO DI SAN PELLEGRINO ← 1 HR → RIFUGIO FUCHIADE ► 90 MINS → FORCA ROSSA ► 55 MIN → FROM FRANZEDAS

And now the fun begins. For the next 90 minutes to *Rifugio Fuchiade* it's downhill nearly all the way, on one of the two AV paths that head in that direction. Unfortunately, it's still not an easy walk, for after all the superlative efforts of the CAI in maintaining all the other trails and way-markings in the Dolomites, they let themselves down badly here. The red-and-white waymarked trail that picks its way through the boulders to the right isn't too badly marked, though there's no indication what number trail you're walking on; but the blue and white **Alta Via dei Pastori** ('Highway of the Shepherds') that heads off through boggy fields to the left peters out after a few hundred metres, and it's up to you to try to guess the way through the mud for 400m or so. My advice is this: if it's been raining or is slippery underfoot, it would be wise to take the 'boulder' path to the right. Otherwise, you're better off taking the Shepherd's Highway, which is slightly quicker and more interesting. The path curves round to the west through a small, flat (and marshy when wet) grassy patch, then after passing over more rocky terrain (which is where you will probably get lost) eventually emerges by a trough next to a large boulder on the fringe of a large swathe of pasture.

From there, a faint trace of a path is visible in the grass, a path that passes through a couple of fences, rounds a ridge and heads down right towards *Rifugio Fuchiade* (☎ 0462-574281; 1982m). This smart and busy little establishment has only eight rooms and because of its soaring popularity (due in no small part to its wonderful food) advance reservations are essential. Rooms cost L65,000 per person including a scrumptious Tyrolean breakfast.

From the *Fuchiade*, it's a fairly dull hour-long amble along a rough track to the settlement of **Passo di San Pellegrino** (1907m), a stroll enlivened by the presence of some picture-book holiday chalets (my favourite, the **Fiordamont**, lies 10 minutes from the *Fuchiade* to the right of the road). In the village there's a bar, the *Miralago*, by the small Laghetto di Pozze, and some hotels that are hives of activity in the ski season but seem to hibernate for the rest of the year. The nearest rifugio, *Fior di Roccia*, lies 3km east along the road. For this reason, and providing it's a clear day, a climb over **Monte Pradazzo** (2279m) to the next *passo* is advisable, particularly as the best rifugio in the Dolomites awaits you there.

It's not a particularly difficult ascent, though after an initial clamber through a lovely forest you'll have to walk on a ski piste for the last part, which is never very pleasant. Nor, for that matter, is the descent, which loosely follows a wide tarmac mountain road. And though the path across the summit of the Pradazzo is difficult to follow, for the terrain is undulating and rocky and workmen have done their best to obliterate all way-markings, as long as it is a clear day you should have no problems completing this section of the AV2.

Map 45 – Passo di San Pellegrino to Passo di Valles 175

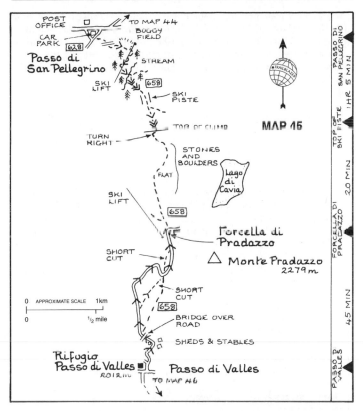

I'm afraid the summit is disappointing; indeed, nowhere in the Dolomites is the imprint of man's destructive hand more evident than on this small summit squeezed between the Marmolada and San Martino massifs. Which is a shame, for the fauna, both wild (marmots) and domesticated (sheep and cows), is still here, only now they graze in the shadow of electricity pylons and chairlift stanchions, to the grinding backbeat of heavy machinery (the small **Lago di Cavia** on the summit is owned by ENEL, the Italian electricity board). While crossing the plateau, watch out for waymarkings; they are few and far between, but there do seem to be enough to help you pick your way to the road leading down to the Passo di Valles. If it's hopelessly foggy at the top, turn right and walk underneath the chairlift cables, and this should lead you eventually to the mountain road and the beginning of the way down.

At the end of it all, nestling in the Passo di Valles, is *Rifugio Passo Valles* (☎ 0437-50270; 2012m), possibly the best value rifugio in the Dolomites. For only L21,000 in a spotless eight-bed dormitory (private rooms are also available), including a wonderful buffet breakfast and free (!) hot showers – not to mention a restaurant that stands head and shoulders above almost all others in this part of the world – this place is, quite simply, excellent.

PASSO DI VALLES → RIFUGIO PEDROTTI   [MAPS 46–47]

[Tabacco map 022] This is an action-packed stage to really test your mettle. Following a three-hour climb to *Rifugio Mulaz* on the northern rim of the **Pale di San Martino National Park**, a fairly straightforward and generally gentle ascent, though there are some assisted sections where you'll be hauling yourself over rocks using wire cables; it's then a further 4hrs 30 mins to the next rifugio, *Pedrotti*, along a far trickier trail. Unfortunately, at the time of writing, *Pedrotti* was closed for some very extensive renovations, so before you leave *Rifugio Mulaz* find out whether *Pedrotti* has re-opened. If not, or if this stage sounds too taxing to attempt in one go, a night at *Mulaz* is in order.

The climbing begins almost as soon as you leave the front door of the rifugio as Route 751 leads off east through long grass along the northern

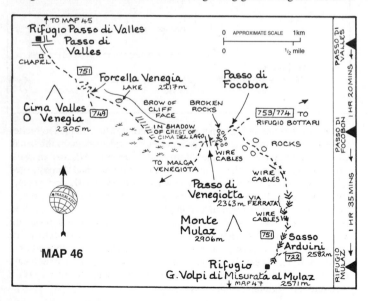

❏ The Pale di San Martino

The Pale di San Martino is a solid line of sheer cliffs, jagged peaks and moon-like plateaux extending for twelve kilometres south to north between the villages of Fiera and Passo Rolle. Like the other groups on the AV2, the Pale belongs distinctly to the Western Dolomites (see p37), having been pushed up as an unaltered whole during the collision between the African and European Continents (as opposed to the Eastern Dolomites, which crumpled and folded, leading to their less uniform, irregular shape). The **Cima della Vezzana** is the highest peak in the range at 3191m, though it is the summit just to its south, the **Cimon della Palla** (3186m), which, because of its isolation, more defined shape and greater symmetry, is probably the more famous.

The Pale is named after an eleventh-century Benedictine hospice, now, sadly no more, which was established for pilgrims crossing between Fiera and the Val di Fieme. That hospice was built in the Val Cismon, the valley immediately to the west of the Pale, and a town, San Martino di Castrozza, grew up around the hospice. Today that town still flourishes as a popular tourist destination and base for skiers and trekkers. Though the AV2 bypasses the town, those wishing to visit it can catch the cable car down from near *Rifugio Pedrotti*.

face of the **Cima Valles O Venegia**. Another steep but short ascent brings you to the brow of the cliff and the **Forcella Venegia**, where you should keep to Route 751 and turn left. Walking on level ground in the shadow of the crest of the Cima del Lago, with a minimum of effort you get to **Passo di Vengiotta** (2363m) which affords wonderful views north towards the Marmolada and the towns that live in its shadow, including **Falcade** and **Caviola**.

Continuing east and up the hill, you'll soon come to a series of three grassy spurs separated by shattered rocks followed, where the path turns south, by a section of the trail fraught with minor difficulties. If you've managed to complete the vie ferrate on the AV2 so far, however, these new obstacles should present few problems. The path, initially at least, can be difficult to discern but, when you start climbing on the rocks up towards the gully, look to your left and you should see waymarkings. Wire cables enable you to haul yourself up the last few metres of the gully, at which point the path turns abruptly right and begins to climb the massive grey lump of karstic rock ahead. The wire cables are now more useful as waymarkings than anything else; leaving them behind, the ascent continues up the mini-peak of the **Sasso Arduini** (2582m), with the much taller summit of **Monte Mulaz** (2906m) a permanent, brooding presence on your right. At the top of the climb, from left to right the **Cima** di Zopel (2813m), **Cima di Campido** (3001m) and, most impressively, the **Cima di Focobon** (3057m), rise up before you beyond the **Ghiaccio** (Glacier) **di Focobon**. The spartan, bleak but friendly *Rifugio Giuseppe Volpi di Misurata al Mulaz* (☎ 0437-599420; 2571m) is just a short, steep descent away to your right, CAI-owned and with standard CAI prices (L32,000/16,000). If you're stopping overnight at the rifugio, don't miss the opportunity to take the easy footpath from the rifugio up to the summit of Monte Mulaz, 45 minutes away.

From the *Mulaz*, the adventure into the heart of the almost lunar landscape of the Pale starts. The action begins as soon as you leave the rifugio via a trail round the back. While most trekkers head off west on trail 710, your trail, 703, goes south towards the **Forcella Margherita** (2655m).

The slope up to the forcella is short but incredibly steep, and if you've already examined it from the comfort of the *Mulaz* you'd be forgiven for thinking that only those with the vertical climbing capacity of houseflies would be capable of negotiating such an ascent. Not true, however, as you'll discover when you start the ascent and notice a sort of 'trail' scratched into the side of the cliffs. Nevertheless a bit of scrambling is required and you must be careful.

From the forcella the path hugs the eastern wall of the valley, traversing scree slopes as it makes its way towards the **Passo delle Farangole**, at 2932m the highest point, Marmolada diversions excepted, on this alta via and the highest point reached in this book. Such altitudes aren't gained without a struggle, however, and the via ferrata up to the saddle is a bit tricky, in particular, the first two metres or so that lead up to the via ferrata, where you have to climb up an outcrop with only one metal rung, a small cable and a few other rusty bits and bobs for assistance. Those who find it testing or indeed terrifying can take comfort in the fact that nothing else on this stage is likely to be as traumatic.

The wire cable leads all the way up to the forcella and down the other side to where a signpost points out the various options. Your route, Trail 703, continues down to the valley floor. At this point everybody loses the trail but no matter for a second path has been worn into the mountainside to your right, which joins up with the original a few minutes later.

As you progress along the path, the mountainside gradually grows more verdant and grazing deer are not an uncommon sight; peculiarly, however, there never seems to be any birdsong in this valley.

The path continues, falling slightly to the small **Val Strut** (marked by the turn-off for *Bivouac Brunner*) and on around the face of the **Cima del Comelle** (2951m); from there it heads off in a southerly direction, though thanks to the bend in the path it feels as if you're heading west. This part of the walk involves a lengthy but easy section of via ferrata as it traverses the **Valle Delle Galline** (a good head for heights is required

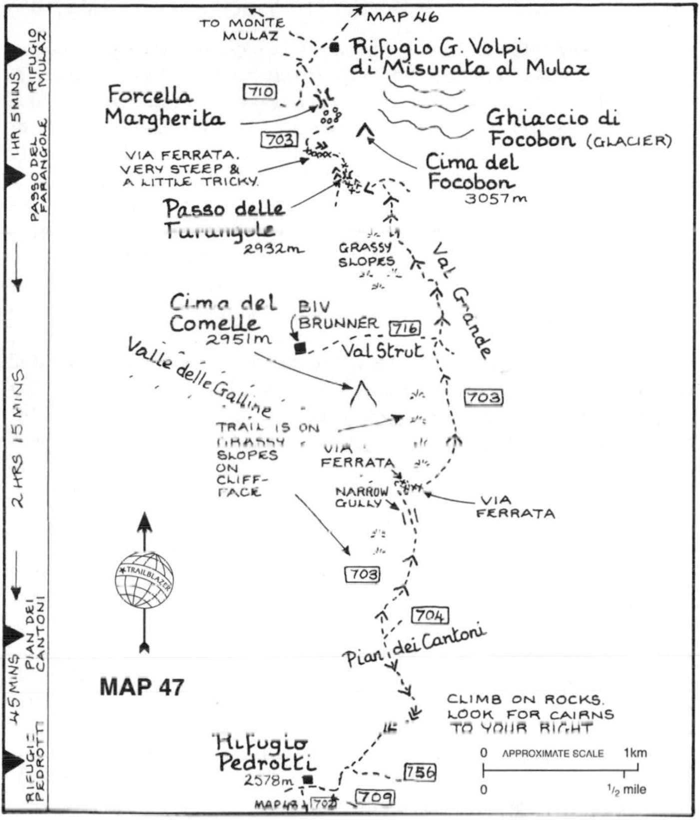

Map 47 – Rifugio Mulaz to Rifugio Pedrotti 179

Left margin (top to bottom):
RIFUGIO MULAZ / 1HR 5MINS / PASSO DEL FARANGOLE
2 HRS 15 MINS
PIAN DEI CANTONI / 45 MINS / RIFUGIO PEDROTTI

Map labels:
TO MONTE MULAZ
MAP 46
Rifugio G. Volpi di Misurata al Mulaz
Forcella Margherita
710
703
Ghiaccio di Focobon (GLACIER)
VIA FERRATA. VERY STEEP & A LITTLE TRICKY.
Cima del Focobon 3057m
Passo delle Turungule 2932m
GRASSY SLOPES
Val Grande
Cima del Comelle 2951m
BIV BRUNNER
716
Val Strut
Valle delle Galline
703
TRAIL IS ON GRASSY SLOPES ON CLIFF-FACE
VIA FERRATA
NARROW GULLY
VIA FERRATA
703
704
Pian dei Cantoni
MAP 47
CLIMB ON ROCKS. LOOK FOR CAIRNS TO YOUR RIGHT
Rifugio Pedrotti 2578m
756
MAP 48
702
709

0   APPROXIMATE SCALE   1km
0   1/2 mile

TRAILBLAZER

over this section), then drops down to the valley floor, where it joins Route 704 on the rocky floor of the **Pian del Cantoni** at approximately 2300m.

The climbing begins again soon afterwards, as signs direct you south towards the *Pedrotti*. Watch out for the waymarkings here, as the correct route turns sharp right just a few minutes into the climb: look for two cairns above you to your right, and aim towards them. Though the gradients are very steep, the karstic rock is easy to climb, being pitted with natural footholds and steps, and just 45 minutes after leaving the valley floor you'll see the signpost below the *Rifugio Pedrotti* (☎ 0439-68308; 2578m) also known as *Rifugio Rosetta*, coming into view ahead of you.

RIFUGIO PEDROTTI → RIFUGIO TREVISO　　　　　　[MAP 48]

[**Tabacco map 022**] From the *Pedrotti*, you have two choices: the simpler, but less interesting path 709 to the *Pradidali*; or our route, the invigorating, official AV2 route, Trail 702. Such is the hard nature of the stone on San Martino that trying to etch a path upon it is nigh on impossible. For this reason, the beginning of Route 702 is laid out like a garden path with stones flanking either side of the route. The path quickly begins to descend (owners of the relevant Tabacco map will have already noticed the mass of red zigzags at this point!), dropping almost 300m before rounding a grassy outcrop and traversing a rockfall. Just after a snowfield on the left, the first via ferrata tract of this stage begins, a largely-horizontal cable attached to the western wall of the **Cima Pradidali** (2774m) above the snow-bound valley floor. The cable finishes just before the forcella but the path up to the pass is easy from here. The pass is named the **Passo di Ball** (2443m) after the English mountaineer, John Ball, the first man to conquer Monte Pelmo and other Dolomite peaks and the first president of the British Mountaineering Society. *Rifugio Pradidali* (2278m), with its gorgeous views down the Val Pradidali, lies a knee-jerking 30 minutes downhill to your left and is visible from the pass. CAI-owned, prices are a standard L32,000/16,000 for a bed, with cheaper food prices for members too. The washing and toilet facilities are rather basic to say the least.

From the *Pradidali*, AV2 heads north-east along the western shores of the dried-up **Lago di Pradidali**, before turning sharp right (east) to begin its drawn-out climb over boulders and scree. The waymarkings are nothing more than red streaks on the rocks but they help you to negotiate the climb up to a signpost, which points the way up to the **Passo delle Lede** (2695m) on Trail 711. The initial part of this ascent is tricky, up a steep gully with shifting stones. Red waymarkings add a splash of colour to the left-hand wall of the gully, and you'd be wise to hug this side as you ascend, using your handgrip on the wall to stop you from falling backwards when the stones underneath your feet start their inevitable slide back down the hill.

At the top of this gully, after only a couple of strides, the path veers off to the right (south-east) over some easily climbable rock terraces. Having gained the forcella, and enjoyed the last close-up view of the Pale behind you, head down the hill across scree and meadow for 45 minutes towards ***Bivacco C. Minazio*** (2250m), a comfortable and well-stocked bivouac with a nearby source of fresh, drinkable water (follow the orange waymarkings). The path, initially at least, is no less steep on this side than the other, though the slope soon becomes more gentle. At the bivouac, the debris of an American airforce plane which crashed in 1957, killing all eleven passengers and crew, has been collected by the CAI of Padova and placed in a pile next to a plaque recording their names.

Map 48 – Rifugio Pedrotti to Rifugio Treviso 181

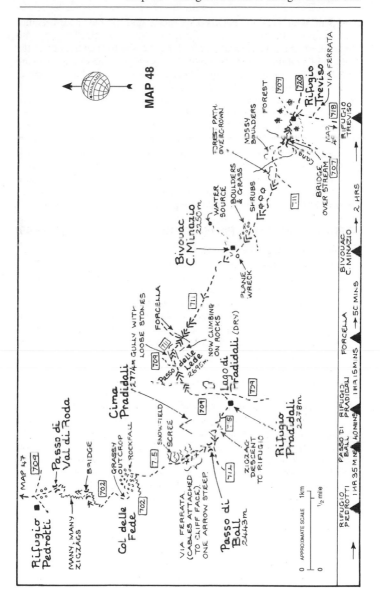

MAP 48

Rifugio Pedrotti

MANY, MANY ZIGZAGS

↑ MAP 47   709

Passo di Val di Roda

BRIDGE

702

GRASSY OUTCROP   ROCKFALL

Col delle Fede

702

VIA FERRATA (CABLES ATTACHED TO CLIFF FACE) ONE ARROW STEEP.

Passo di Ball 2443m

ZIGZAG DESCENT TO RIFUGIO

714

7.5   SNOWFIELD   SCREE

709

Cima Pradidali

2774m GULLY WITH LOOSE STONES

709   Passo delle Lede 2690m

7.5

Rifugio Pradidali 2278m

711

FORCELLA

NOW CLIMBING ON ROCKS

709   Lago di Pradidali (DRY)

711

PLANE WRECK

Bivouac C.Minazio 2250m

WATER SOURCE

BOULDERS & GRASS

SHRUBS

711

FOREST PATH OVERGROWN

MOSSY BOULDERS

FOREST

707   720

Rifugio Treviso

VIA FERRATA

718

MAP 49 RIFUGIO TREVISO

707

BRIDGE OVER STREAM

2 HRS

0   APPROXIMATE SCALE   1km
0   ½ mile

RIFUGIO PEDROTTI — 1HR 35 MINS → PASSO DI BALL — 40MINS → RIFUGIO PRADIDALI — 1HR 15 MINS → FORCELLA — 50 MINS → BIVOUAC C.MINAZIO — 2 HRS → RIFUGIO TREVISO

The path, which restarts between the plane and the hut, now becomes very steep – painfully so – as it zigzags its way downhill. Entering into thick forest, the path runs due east along the southern extremity of the **Pala dei Colombi**. A signpost points left again along an overgrown path to *Rifugio Treviso*. It's a path that leads down to a strange but enchanting area of large green mossy boulders, followed by an equally exquisite valley stream, the **Canali**. A stiff 200m climb up along a series of lazy zigzags lies between the delightful wooden bridge traversing the Canali and this stage's destination. *Rifugio Treviso* (☎ 0439-62311; 1631m) is in a wonderful location, squirrelled away from the world in the thickly-forested **Canali Valley**. Over one hundred years old, and today run by the descendants of the original owner (and overrun by a whole host of cats), the *Treviso* is a little too basic for some, (the washing facilities, for example, consist of one alfresco tap), but being part of the CAI network it's cheap and pleasant enough, and the tap water is potable.

RIFUGIO TREVISO → PASSO CEREDA   [MAP 49]

[**Tabacco map 022**] As you will find out on this stage, *Rifugio Treviso*, though it may not be the most comfortable place in the world, performs one vital function in that it splits up two rather protracted and painful downhill sections. That said, this stage's descent, though it still has the capacity to hurt, is a little shorter than yesterday's and not so relentless.

This stage also takes you, after a fairly lengthy climb, outside the Pale di San Martino National Park, whose borders run along the spine of the **Cima d'Oltro**. If it sounds like a lot of work, don't be misled: the ascent and descent apart, this stage is rather simple and, taking just under four hours, very short too.

Route 718, the path you will be following for the whole of this stage, begins behind the rifugio and heads off through the woods westwards down the valley. Ignore deviations both to the left (which leads to the Via Ferrate dell Canalone and is signposted in Italian 'for experts only') and also the unmarked path heading down the hill to the right, and instead follow the almost level trail as it meanders off through the forest until, just past the third rockfall, a signpost points upwards towards the **Forcella d'Oltro** (2279m) at the top of the boulder-strewn **Vallone d'Oltro**. It's a stiff but straightforward climb to the forcella, taking at least 45 minutes. At the top you'll be rewarded with a ptarmigan's-eye view over the villages of the **Val de Mis**, backed by the Feltrini Dolomites, where you will be walking in the next stage.

Initially, the descent into the valley is as steep as the ascent just completed, though after just 10 minutes or so a sharp right-hand bend brings you onto an almost horizontal path heading south-west under the cliff-face. It's a wonderful walk, reminiscent in many ways of the Viel dal Pan

Map 49 – Rifugio Treviso to Passo Cereda 183

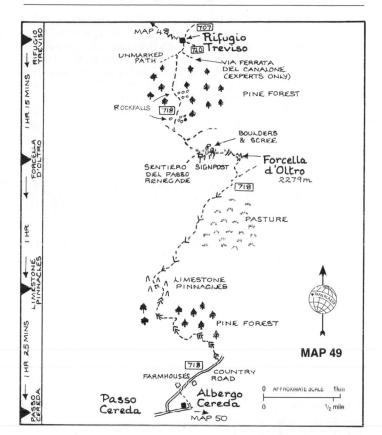

MAP 49

to the north of the Marmolada. The long grass, the butterflies and the plethora of wild flowers are common to both, though on this walk there are far fewer people but more deer and marmots instead.

The path undulates as it encounters successive mountain ridges and it climbs steadily. Eventually, after surmounting the highest ridge, you come upon a wonderful 'forest' of campaniles, those strange limestone towers eroded into slender spires by the passage of time. It's definitely worth a photograph or two. The *serious* descent to the Passo Cereda begins here, as the path picks its way south and south-west between the campaniles before eventually turning south-east and heading straight down through thick forest. The agony endured by the knees is mitigated near the bottom of the hill by a mountain road, flanked by some wonderful picture-perfect alpine farm buildings. Turning right onto the road, you'll reach the **Passo Cereda** and its homely rifugio just a few minutes later. *Rifugio Cereda* (☎ 0439-65118/65030; 1361m) is one of those flashy-looking privately-run rifugi located at busy mountain passes that always look as if they would be more expensive than they actually are (the *Rifugio Passo Valles* is another case in point). For L35,000 at the *Cereda* you get a bunk bed in a spotless dorm, with hot showers and a mighty breakfast included in the price. The food in the restaurant is highly recommended and the tap water is potable.

❏ Those who wish to give up at this late stage, because of lack of time, inclement weather or whatever, will be pleased to know that there are twice daily buses (No 503) to Fiera di Primiero.

PASSO CEREDA → RIFUGIO BÒZ   [MAP 50]

[Tabacco maps 022 and 023] The mountains of the Vette Feltrine are amongst the least-visited and wildest in the entire region. Few trekkers make it to this southern extremity of the Dolomites, and even many alta via walkers give up at Passo Cereda and take a bus from there.

The main problem with trekking in the Feltrini is water; there's either too much of it or too little. If the former, many of the paths are little more than muddy ledges and become dangerously slippery after rain, so **a crossing of the Feltrini should not be attempted in bad weather**; or, there will be too little, for despite the verdant façade the mountains present to visitors, there are in fact remarkably few places where you can find safe drinking water. There are also only two rifugi and one bivacco on the trail, and because most of the trail lies inside the national park, camping is forbidden. For these reasons any walk in the Feltrini needs to be carefully planned. And if it has been raining, or the forecast suggests that it will do over the next two days, let discretion be the better part of valour and join the others on the bus from Passo Cereda.

If the conditions are all right, however, don't miss the chance to visit this beautiful and fascinating range. Though the walking is probably the toughest on the trail, with the paths a little precarious and exposed in places, the rewards of venturing into this southernmost range are ample. The views over the Venetian Plain to the south are quite delicious, the alpine scenery magnificent, the trekking is often quite invigorating and the two rifugi are pleasant enough. Plus, of course, you'll have the satisfaction of knowing that, staggering into Feltre, you will have finally completed the longest alta via of them all.

❏ Vette Feltrine

Home to an exceptional range of flora and fauna, the *Vette Feltrine* ('Peaks of Feltre') are a modestly-sized range forming the westernmost part of the **Parco Nazionale Dolomiti Bellunesi**. Amongst the park's 1500 species of **plant-life** are such rarities as the small white crucifer known as the *Thlaspi minimum*, and a high-altitude lily (*Lilium carniolicum*) that lives only in the exposed southern slopes of the Feltrine. The park owes its botanical fecundity to its unique geographical position on the very southern edge of the Alps, which enabled it to remain free of ice during each of the Quaternary glaciations, unlike their larger cousins to the north. Thus the more ancient species have been able to survive and thrive here more than elsewhere in the Dolomites.

The **landscape** of the Feltrine is characterized by large areas of extended scree, particularly on the northern side of the range, karst valleys and peaks bearded with grasses and wild flowers, including the 2335m-Monte Pavione, one of the largest and most famous peaks in the range. Steep and sheer on the northern side, towards the south the gradients are a lot shallower as the slopes melt and merge into the Venetian Plain, affording AV2 trekkers sweeping views of their destination – not to mention a mercifully gentle descent.

Though you'll be very lucky to spot any of the rare plant species for which the range is famous, you may have more luck with the **fauna**. The park plays host to many mammals, including deer, badgers, beech martens, weasels, squirrels and hedgehogs and even, so it is said, a lynx or two. Despite persistent rumours, however, it is highly unlikely that any bears have returned to the park since being driven out by man in the nineteenth century.

The official AV2 route begins east along the road from Passo Cereda, and from there a turn-off by a *padreterno* (wine shop) leads south to the village of **Mattiuzzi**, at just a metre or so over 1200m, the lowest point on AV2. A quicker and more picturesque alternative is to take the path across the road from the rifugio. This trail takes you through woods and over streams, then down to a meadow where it joins up with the covered path of the official route. Follow this path uphill for the next 20 minutes as it winds through forested hillside, leaving it for a smaller forest track on your right just before the road finishes. (The signpost pointing out the trail warns that it is a '*sentiero difficile*'; it's a fair description but try not to let it put you off.) Before long, this forest track joins a dry – at least in good weather – boulder-filled stream-bed and follows its course up the side of the **Sasso delle Undici** (2310m). Though the path forces you to clamber over many of these boulders, the climbing is not technically difficult. Do watch out for the waymarkings though, for the path suddenly and unexpectedly takes a sharp turn left, leaving the gorge and traversing diagonally east. Crossing over two more dry beds, the path takes you to the top of a subsidiary ridge, where you'll have your first view of the **Intaiada Valley**.

From now on the way gets a little tougher. Turn sharp right at the saddle; after a few metres you come to an aided section of the trail where the path climbs gently to a second ridge. Ahead at this saddle you can see yet another ridge, this one surmounted by signposts marking the border of the national park; it lies about 40 minutes away, a distance that includes some pretty wearisome scrambling over loose stones and shale. The final climb to the **Forcella di Comedon** (2067m) is, by comparison, not a problem, for though the trail is just as steep, you'll be walking over stationary rock.

At 2067m, the Forcella Comedon is the highest point of the AV2 in the Feltrini, and from it you'll have fine views over the valley towns to the north (Sagron and Gosaldo), as well as the artificial **Lago della Stua** to the south.

Taking the trail to the right, you'll find the descent from the forcella down to the **Pian della Regina** no easier than the ascent that you've just completed, the trail quickly falling away to the right over shifting rocks and stones. On the *pian* itself, however, is *Bivacco Feltre-Walter Bodo* (1930m), one of the pleasantest in the Dolomites, with sleeping berths for 19 people and drinking water constantly available from the tap outside.

From the bivouac, you can see the trail heading off to the south-west all the way up to the **Col dei Bechi** (1960m), crossing streams (one of which supplies the bivouac with its potable water), climbing boulders and rounding, finally, a flower-filled section of the trail known as the **Pian del Re**, which requires some care.

From the Col, the path becomes a little narrower and the drop to your left much steeper as it follows a section of the trail called the **Troi dei Caserin**; a good head for heights is useful here. But again, don't worry unduly: in the places where the path is deemed too narrow, an iron cable has been fixed to the rocks. The trail continues its progress south-west through sunkissed meadows, winding down a grassy spur before returning to the southern face of the **Sass di Mura**, which it hugs for the next 2.5km. Immediately after the iron cable the path passes underneath an overhang, where the going underfoot is particularly slippery thanks to the constant drip of water from the cliffs above. You can opt to risk it and stay on the ledge at this point, or you can pass beneath it by taking the lower path to your left.

Soon after, you'll come to the sheer grassy sides of the Caserin. This particular stretch is especially precarious when wet, for the path is now just a mud track and a very narrow one at that. Take care, and in a few minutes you'll arrive at the **Passo Mura** (1867m), and a sign telling you that once again you are entering the **Parco Nazionale delle Dolomiti Bellunesi**. You have two options from here: turn sharp left and walk

Map 50 – Passo Cereda to Rifugio Bòz 187

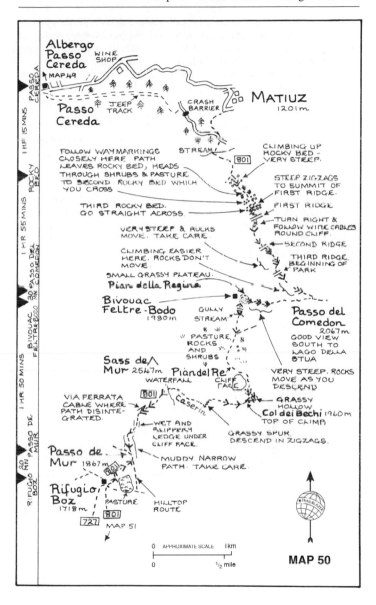

Albergo
Passo
Cereda   WINE
            SHOP
▲ MAP 49

PASSO CEREDA

Passo   JEEP
Cereda   TRACK

CRASH
BARRIER

MATIUZ
1201m

1 HF 15 MINS

FOLLOW WAY MARKINGS
CLOSELY HERE. PATH
LEAVES ROCKY BED, HEADS
THROUGH SHRUBS & PASTURE
TO SECOND ROCKY BED WHICH
YOU CROSS

STREAM

801

CLIMBING UP
ROCKY BED –
VERY STEEP.

STEEP ZIGZAGS
TO SUMMIT OF
FIRST RIDGE.

THIRD ROCKY BED.
GO STRAIGHT ACROSS.

FIRST RIDGE

TURN RIGHT &
FOLLOW WIRE CABLES
ROUND CLIFF.

VERY STEEP & ROCKS
MOVE. TAKE CARE.

SECOND RIDGE

CLIMBING EASIER
HERE. ROCKS DON'T
MOVE.

THIRD RIDGE.
BEGINNING OF
PARK.

SMALL GRASSY PLATEAU.
Pian della Regina

Bivouac
Feltre-Bodo
1930m

GULLY
STREAM

Passo del
Comedon
2067m
GOOD VIEW
SOUTH TO
LAGO DELLA
STUA

PASTURE,
ROCKS
AND
SHRUBS

Sass de
Mur 2547m

Piandel Re
WATERFALL   CLIFF
              FACE

VERY STEEP. ROCKS
MOVE AS YOU
DESCEND

VIA FERRATA
CABLE WHERE
PATH DISINTE-
GRATED.

801   Caserin

GRASSY
HOLLOW
Col dei Bechi 1960m
TOP OF CLIMB.

WET AND
SLIPPERY
LEDGE UNDER
CLIFF FACE.

GRASSY SPUR.
DESCEND IN ZIGZAGS.

Passo de
Mur 1867m

MUDDY NARROW
PATH. TAKE CARE.

Rifugio
Bòz
1718m   PASTURE   HILLTOP
                      ROUTE
801
727   MAP 51

TRAILBLAZER

0   APPROXIMATE SCALE   1km

0   1/2 mile

MAP 50

along the top of the ridge, enjoying the views of the Val di Alvis at your feet to your left, before dropping west down the grassy slope to *Rifugio Bòz*; or you can simply head straight for the rifugio by taking the more direct path (also on your left) that heads round the ridge and down.

Rifugio Bòz (☎ 0439-6448; 1718m), set in scenes of bucolic splendour, is run by the CAI and, like most of their huts, offers a rudimentary standard of accommodation (L32,000/16,000). However, the people who run it are very nice and the meals, for a high altitude rifugio, surprisingly good – it is such a treat once again to savour food that really tastes as if some time and care has gone into its preparation. They also provide free filtered water.

RIFUGIO BÒZ → FELTRE   [MAPS 51–52]

[**Tabacco map 023**] And so to the final stage of both the Feltrini mountains and the AV2. Like the first half of your walk through the Feltrini this stage is also packed with awkward paths requiring steady footing and a good head for heights. Stamina and preparation are important too: the next rifugio is six hours away from Bòz, and there is no water between the two, so make sure you carry plenty.

From the *Bòz*'s eastern gate, Route 801 turns smartly south into the forest; it's a trail that, though poorly signed and with few waymarkings, is relatively well used and easy to follow, and it will lead you, half an hour after leaving the rifugio, up the **Monte Colsent** ridge to the **Passo di Finestra** ('Window Pass'; 1766m). Go right from the passo along the **Via Tilman**, but after only 100m or so take another right turn up the cliff-face, a turn-off that isn't very well marked. At the top of the short climb is a narrow precipice that's been blasted into the rock. Take care on this narrow ledge (there are several plaques attached to the cliff-face commemorating trekkers who perished here) and it will lead you via a short aided section to the beginning of the climb up to the **Sasso di Scarnia** (2150m). It's a fairly convoluted ascent incorporating plenty of zigzags, a little clambering and scrambling, a couple of short passages with wire cables and two sections, each only a few paces long, where the path narrows sharply until it's little more than a slender isthmus with two huge vertical drops on either side. Little or no technical experience is required to tackle this ascent; as you can imagine, however, you do need a good head for heights.

At the end of this climbing you find yourself, approximately 80 minutes after leaving the Passo Finestra, on the south-eastern side of the Sasso, following a path that, having woven its way through a number of large boulders, is now heading south beneath an overhang in the Sasso's eastern face. Care is still needed here, for the stones are loose and the rock can be smooth and slippery, though before long you'll find yourself on

Map 51 – Rifugio Bòz to Passo di Pietina 189

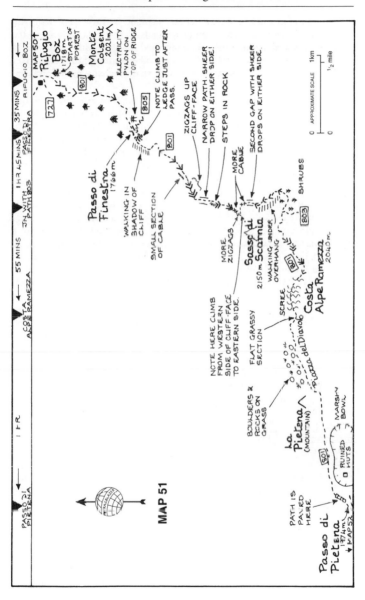

MAP 51

firmer ground as you head south to more verdant, fertile slopes filled with alpine shrubs and grass.The path now bends to the right, following the contours of the **Scarnia**. After the signposted junction with Route 803 (a handy short cut to Feltre), there follows another short uphill section over rocks as the *mulatteria*, or mule path (for that is what you are now on) continues its course westwards.

Tracing the northern rim of a scree-lined amphitheatre, the path then climbs up to a small grassy area filled with wild flowers known as the **Costa Alpe Ramezza** (2040m). At its western end just before the precipitous path along the walls of the Val Noana, trekkers are treated to a sumptuous view north, including the western edge of the **Pale di San Martino**, the valley town of **Fiera di Primiero** and, further up, the village of **San Martino**.

The path, while continuing west, now saunters in the shadow to the north of the ridge before dropping down to the weird, boulder-strewn plateau of the **Diavolo**. Picking your way through all this natural masonry, the path becomes much flatter as it passes along the northern side of a green, marshy bowl, rising only gently towards the **Passo di Pietena** (1974m). From this mini-saddle you can see your path leading all the way up to the **Passo Le Vette Grandi** (2040m) – the final high pass on AV2. It takes about 45 minutes to walk between the two passes, the trail bending round to the south and west along the perimeter of the **Busa delle Vette** before climbing out of the basin on a four-wheel drive track. Four minutes beyond Le Vette Grande lies ***Rifugio dal Piaz*** (☎ 0439-9065; 1993m), a classic CAI-owned rifugio with only dorm beds available (L32,000/16,000). Unusually for the Dolomites, some of the staff here speak excellent English. The green pyramid to the north-west of the rifugio is **Monte Pavione**, at 2335m the highest point in the Feltrini; it is visible if you walk a little way westwards.

As the last bus to Feltre from Croce d'Aune has left by mid-afternoon, most trekkers prefer to spend a night at the *Piaz* and then head off early the next morning. (If you can't bear the thought of spending one more night in a rifugio, I should say that I've always found hitching from Croce d'Aune very easy, with many day-trippers willing to provide AV2 trekkers with a lift, no matter what state they're in) Be warned, however: the walk between the *Piaz* and Croce d'Aune catches a lot of people out; expecting an easy descent, particularly after they see the beautiful old military road swinging away down the hill ahead of them, many mistakenly think this last section will be a doddle. It isn't.

Though there are no uphill sections and nothing dangerous about the walk, it's a knee-shaking 100-minute downhill assault that will leave you, by the time you trudge into **Croce d'Aune** (1016m), really exhausted. It is possible to take some short cuts off the road; indeed, after 15 minutes Route 801 leaves the road altogether in favour of a dirt track through the

Map 52 – Passo di Pietina to Croce d'Aune 191

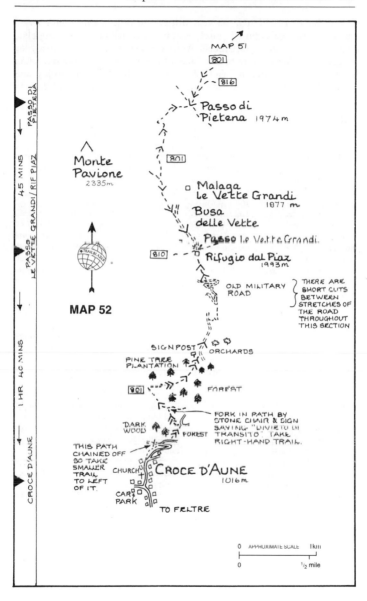

forest. Sometimes the path is very difficult to follow with a number of possible paths presenting themselves at certain junctions. If nothing else, at least the walk down to Croce d'Aune will persuade you to finish your walk here, rather than try to continue all the way down to Feltre. If you do decide to carry on, the walk is an interminably long and boring one along a highway, with only the twee little village of **Pedavena** (335m) as compensation.

FELTRE

A decidedly Italian town, subdued Feltre (272m) provides the perfect finish to the AV2 and a neat counterpoint to the Tyrolean towns of the northern Dolomites. Still surrounded by mediaeval city walls, this ancient Renaissance town has been destroyed and rebuilt on numerous occasions throughout its colourful history, though many of its most beautiful edifices, its churches, museum, frescoed palazzos and civic buildings, are largely original, having been built in the sixteenth century when the town formed part of the Venetian Republic. Today these architectural treasures provide the sightseer with plenty to occupy him or her at the end of the trek.

Accommodation

Unfortunately, Feltre is not good for accommodation. The cheapest place is **Da Berto** (☎ 0439-2852) at Via Liberazione 12, though it's not exactly luxurious and rather a let-down if you've been pining for a few home comforts during your trek. Prices start at L35,000/60,000 for a single/double including breakfast. Better value is provided by the two-star **Park Hotel** (☎ 0439-880088) at Via Santa Maria del Prato, with doubles starting at L40,000 per room in the low season. The three-star **Nuovo** (☎ 0439-89241) at Via Fornere Pazze 5 has a whole range of facilities, including mini-bar and TV in the rooms, which start at L65,000 per person. Finally, at the top of the tree is **Doriguzzi** (☎ 0439-83660) at Viale del Piave 2, a four-star place with all mod-cons; prices start at L75,000 for a single room in the low season.

For that slap-up **meal** you've been promising yourself for the last fortnight, look no further than **Ristorante Tiziano** at Piazzale della Lana 8/12, one block back from the main street, which conjures up some wonderful pizzas (L9000) and truly cold beer at L6000 a time.

Transport

Those going back to Bolzano or Bressanone should travel first to Trento (5 daily; 6am-5pm; 2hrs). The ticket, which you buy at the train station, includes bus travel from Feltre to Primolano, then a train from there. From Trento there are plenty of trains heading to all destinations in Italy, including San Candido, Bassano, and Venice, as well as through the Brenner Pass to Austria via Bolzano (45 mins) and Bressanone (1hr 15 mins).

Other destinations from Feltre include Padova (11 daily; 1hr 30 mins); Belluno (10 daily; 30 mins); Rome (daily at 10.29pm; 8hrs 30 mins); Treviso (55 mins), and Calalzo (5 daily).

(**Opposite**) **Top:** Cows grazing on the southern slopes of the Alpe di Siusi. **Bottom:** The market at Feltre.(**Overleaf**) A rainy day on the shores of Lake Misurina (see p121).

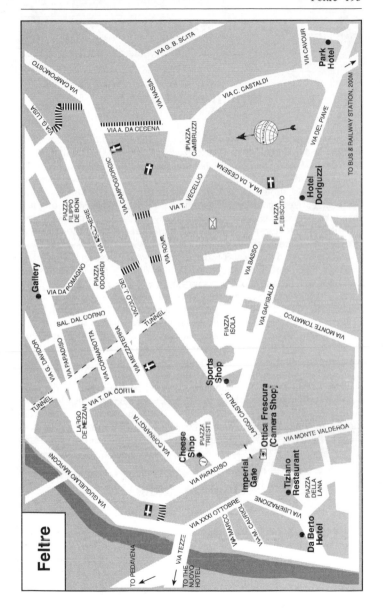

Feltre

PART 5: SHORT TREKS

Which short trek?

For the benefit of those who wish to savour the beauty of the mountains without undertaking a two-week trek, the following shorter trails have been devised. All of these trails start and finish at towns or on main roads, and as such all but one (the Croda da Lago route) have adequate public transport connections. Each lasts between **one and five days** and has been categorized according to the number of days required to complete them: the first section deals with simple day walks, the second with two-day trails, while the third and final section deals with those routes that take between three and five days to complete.

While many of these short walks at least partially overlap the two main trails described earlier, to a large extent they also complement these main trails. Some of them include ranges not covered by either of the longer trails, such as the **Brenta**, **Marmarole** and **Monte Piana** trails. In other cases, although the shorter trail covers a range that has already been featured in one of the longer treks, it does so by using a different path, thus providing a different trail and different scenery to the one already described. Don't forget, too, that the major trails can also be broken up into a wealth of smaller trails. In the introduction to each of the following sections I suggest at least two ways in which you may wish to do this, though of course there is nothing to stop you choosing your own section from a larger trail.

One further point: on these shorter trails we have designed the walks so that they'll not take more than four or five hours each day. Thus those pushed for time and of a suitable level of fitness may wish to combine some of the days, thereby combining two-days' worth of trekking into one.

One-day trails

Probably the finest and simplest one-day walk is the **Viel del Pan**, described in detail in the AV2 section on pp165–166. It only takes about two hours altogether yet is packed with exhilarating scenery and unobstructed views over the Dolomites' largest mountain. The easiest way to get to the start of the walk is to take a bus to Passo Pordoi from either the village of Canazei to the west, Arabba to the east or Passo Sella further north. Having arrived at the Lago di Fedaia at the end of the trail, you can either choose to spend the night there or catch one of the buses passing along the road to the north of the lake. Another excellent one-day walk is the trail between *Rifugio Col de Varda*, up the hill from the Lago di Misurina, and *Rifugio Auronzo*, in the shadow of the Tre Cime di Lavaredo. This trail passes through spectacular scenery along the **Sentiero Bonacossa**, and provides a perfect introduction to via ferrata. The walk is described on pp121–125, and both the Lago di Misurina, from where you can catch a ski-lift to the beginning of the trail, and *Rifugio Auronzo* are well served by buses from Cortina and Dobbiaco.

CRODA DA LAGO

[Tabacco map 03] This is a straightforward trail taking you round the mountain to the south of the Tofane group. It's included here because its simplicity and proximity to the town of Cortina makes it an ideal first walk for those who have just arrived in the Dolomites and have decided to use Cortina as a base. The total walking time is about five hours. Getting back from the walk can be a little tricky, particularly if you don't have a car, for there is no public transport. It is possible to hitch but set out early to leave yourself plenty of time to find a lift on the way back.

From Cortina, catch a bus heading west towards the Passo Falzarego, and alight at the tiny village of **Pocol**, six kilometres west of Cortina. A secondary road (marked as Trail 434) leads south-west from the main road towards Passo Giau. Having followed this road for 1500m or so, take trail 434 which branches off left (due south). This rough track soon peters out into a walking path, which climbs some 300m to meet up with Trail 437. Keep to Trail 434 as it rises and rounds the northern perimeter of the **Ciadenes** peak and enters the **Val Negra**, at the end of which is the surprisingly large Lago Federá and the accompanying *Rifugio Croda da Lago*.

Still on 434, the trail now takes you even higher on a gentle gradient up to the **Forcella Ambrizola** (2227m), with views across to the Pelmo and even as far as the Pale di San Martino to the south-west. At this point the route takes a sharp turn to the right (west) on 466, before joining 436 a couple of hundred metres further on. With the **Lastoni di Formin** massif to your right, the path takes you through a gorgeous, grass-covered high-altitude plateau. Still rising gently, it passes the tiny Lago delle Baste (on your left) before joining with Trail 465 at the **Forcella Giau** (2360m). From now on, it's downhill virtually all the way as you continue on Trail 436; at one point, the path divides into two, both signposted 436. It really doesn't matter which branch you take, though the right-hand trail is slightly longer, less steep and more scenic. At the foot of the trail is the road back to Pocol, from where you'll have to hitch.

ALPE DI SIUSI

[**Tabacco map 05**] This is a simple, four-hour walk around the largest high-altitude plateau in Western Europe. The walk begins with the chair-lift from Ortisèi, and ends with one to Santa Cristina, so ideally one of the villages in the Val Gardena should be your base. From the rear deck of the chairlift, this trek follows Trail 6 south, and then, when you hit the road, Trail 3 as it heads east across the Alpe di Siusi. (Note that on the plateau many of the signposts give the destination but not the number of the path. In this case, follow the sign to *Rifugio Saltria*.) Continue on Trail 3 as it loops north towards the **Monte Pana** through woodland and meadow on an uncovered road. From Monte Pana, you have the option of taking the chairlift back down or walking the extra hour down to Santa Cristina.

MONTE PIANA

[**Tabacco map 03**] Of both historical importance, and of interest purely for the breathtaking panoramas encountered along the way, this is an excellent one-day trail that can be done on its own or as a diversion from the west-east route. The trail begins just to the north of the **Lago di Misurina**, on the road signposted to the Tre Cime (Trail 122). After a few hundred metres, a smaller paved road branches off left, and it is this path you should take as it winds up to *Rifugio Bosi* (2205m). Towards the top the path becomes steeper and the paving deteriorates until it's just a muddy track. Nevertheless, this is a fairly straightforward 90-minute trek which should provide no difficulties.

Having explored the plateau, visited the open-air **museum** and enjoyed the panorama, you can either return the same way or head north towards *Hotel Tre Cime di Lavaredo*. The easiest way to do this is to con-tinue due north from the rifugio across the **Alpe dei Castrati**, then turn sharp right on Trail 6a until it joins up with Trail 103. From here, go left and amble down to Trail 10/102, which will lead you down to *Hotel Tre Cime di Lavaredo* (as described on p104).

THE BRENTA GROUP

Despite the Brenta's reputation as a Mecca for via ferrata-ites, this route is very simple and involves no difficult vie ferrate at all. It's also a surpris-ingly quiet route with few trekkers. Long may it stay that way. Be warned, however, that there is currently no Tabacco map to the Brenta, so you'll have to rummage around the bookshops to find a locally produced map.

The trail begins at **Madonna di Campiglio**, reachable by bus from Trento. Having arrived, look for the Monte Spinale chairlift and use it to take you up to the rifugio of the same name. From here, head off east on

Trail 331 past a small *laghetto* to *Rifugio Graffer* (2261m). You'll reach a junction with Trail 316 which you should take towards **Passo del Grostè** (2442m), a further 30 minutes on from the *Graffer*.

From the pass, continue east, this time on trail 301, which you will be following all the way to Andalo. The path bends south-east across a karstic plateau, with natural 'steps' similar to those near *Rifugio Biella* (see p100). Passing the junction with Trail 314 and heading through the wide forcella separating the **Monte Turrion Basso** and **Monte Turrion Alto**, you cross the fields of the **Campo Flavona** and climb up to the **Passo della Gaiarda** (2242m). From here, it's merely another 45 minutes down to *Rifugio Malga Sopra* (1861m), which appears suddenly along the trail.

From the rifugio it's a further two hours downhill to Andalo, a pretty and easy walk through woods and along a lengthy series of rock ledges. You'll be glad of the metal cord attached to steady yourself, for the drop is a sheer one.

If you've managed to follow 301 all this way you'll soon emerge at the village of **Pegorar**; the larger village of **Andalo** lies directly below you, from where you can catch buses and trains back to Trento.

Two-day trails

For many trekkers the **Sella Group** is the quintessential Dolomite massif. A wreath of spectacular pinnacles surrounding a barren high-level plateau, this place is simultaneously appealing and forbidding. The best trail across the Sella is that described on pp162–165, though you'll need to do a little via ferrata to reach the plateau, and as such this is not recommended for complete novices.

Similarly, a crossing of the lush **Puez-Odle range** (see p86–92) is also heartily recommended for the wonderful panoramas it provides along the way, and the extraordinary colours of the Puez rock; but this, too, contains a small knot of via ferrata that, while not technically difficult, should not be attempted by first-time mountain trekkers unless they have the necessary equipment and are accompanied by somebody with some experience.

Other recommended two-day stretches that form part of the larger trails include a crossing of the **Vette Feltrine** (see pp184–192), the section of the west-east trail from *Rifugio Col de Varda* to the *Fondo Valle* (pp121–128), or, for the very fit, a crossing of the Fanes group from **La Villa to Cortina** (pp94–97 & pp107–112), though three days is probably better for this.

THE SASSOLUNGO TRAIL

[**Tabacco map 05**] This walk around the western border of the Alpe di Siusi takes us you through the Sassolungo group, or Langkofel ('Long stone') in German. The entire trail could feasibly be completed in one day, though if you have the time a two-day hike is recommended allowing you more hours to appreciate the views over the Alpe di Siusi.

From *Rifugio Passo Sella* (easily reached by bus from the Val Gardena, Val Badia or Val di Fassa), head south on 4-594, a dirt track that soon develops into a simple walkable path named after the last king of Saxony, **F August Weg**, who was a keen rambler. After a few hundred metres the path reaches a junction, where you must take a sharp right turn (west) past the privately-owned *Rifugio Friedrich August* (2298m). The path now levels out as it rounds the **Grohmann summit**, so-called after the legendary Austrian mountaineer, before arriving at *Rifugio Sandro Pertini* (2300m), named after a popular Italian president. Less than an hour away is *Rifugio Sasso Piatto*, occupying the south-eastern corner of the **Alpe di Siusi**.

Beyond and to the north are the white-capped Austrian mountains. North is the direction you should head too, along Trail 9 which quickly reverts to Trail 527 as it loops round the western and northern faces of the Sassopiatto. The last section of this trail, up to the junction with Trail 525, crosses large stretches of scree, though the path is clearly marked and secure. Bending right (south), the path now enters the high-altitude **Vallone di Sassopiatto**, performing a series of short zigzags as it winds its way up to *Rifugio Vicenza* (2251m), the ideal place to end the first day's trek. Snugly located between the sheer walls of the Sassopiatto and Sassolungo, the rifugio is over 10 years old, though it was rebuilt in 1910 after an avalanche crushed the original building.

From the *Vicenza*, the path continues south-east for 90 minutes up and through the silent *vallone*, across scree and boulders to the bustling *Rifugio T. Demetz* (2681m), the terminus for the cable-car from Passo Sella. The rifugio sits by the **Forcella Sassolungo**, and so provides trekkers with glorious views west (back down the *vallone*) and south-east towards the Marmolada.

From the rifugio, you can either follow Trail 525 back down to the Passo Sella or, if you don't think your knees can take the pounding caused by this steep descent, catch the cable-car instead.

FANES

[**Tabacco Map 03**] This walk starts and finishes on the Cortina—Dobbiaco road at the tiny settlement of Fiames, about 5km north of Cortina. At the *Albergo Fiames*, take the forestry track on your left. This follows the main road for about two kilometres before heading uphill through woods. After crossing a two streams and rounding the Col Rosa you soon reach the **Ponte Outo** (1380m), a bridge across a deep ravine. Continue straight on (west) beyond the bridge, ignoring Trail 401 that leads off up the Val Travenanzes, and taking the short cut by the signpost to the **Alpe di Fanes** rather than the winding jeep track.

You are now in the **Val di Fanes**. Rejoining the jeep track and short-ly after passing a small plaque marking the 1916 Austrian front, you reach the entrance to the national park; the track now bends slightly northwards as it meets up with the AV1. Passing the **Lago di Limo** (2159m) and its accompanying *passo*, you soon reach the hotel-like *Rifugio Fanes* and the nearby *Rifugio Lavarella*: as good a place as any to stop for the night, it being about 4hrs 30 mins since you headed off.

The next leg of the loop, from *Rifugio Fanes* to *Rifugio Fodara Vedla*, is described as part of the west-east route on pp97–99. From Fodara Vedla, your path (now Track 9) leads due east along a stream past the (usually dry) **Lago di Fodara** (1990m) and on via a series of gravelled zigzags to the Vallone Scuro and *Rifugio Ra Stua* (1668m), where you'll drink the finest hot chocolate in the world. (This rifugio, however, provides no accommodation.) From there, continue on down to the starting point of this trek, and then on to Cortina.

Three- to five-day trails

When it comes to three-day trails the choices are endless. I particularly like the walk from **La Villa** in the Val Badia to *Hotel Tre Cime di Lavaredo* in the Val di Landro, which forms part of the west-east trail and is described on pp94–104. The four-day crossing of the **Pale di San Martino** (pp176–182) is also almost unbeatable with plenty of spectacu-lar vistas and some quite lengthy vie ferrate too.

For five-day trails, **Cortina to Santa Stefano di Cadore** via the Tre Cime is a spectacular, exhausting trial of stamina and nerve (it includes the hardest via ferrata in this book, see pp116–136); the alternative fin-ishes (to San Candido or Auronzo) are less demanding and a day shorter.

ANTELAO AND MARMAROLE

[**Tabacco map 16**] This trek around mountains not covered in either of the main trails takes around three days. This region of the Dolomites is known as the **Cadore**, and for 500 years supplied Venice with the timber to make its ships. Cut down from the vast forests that once covered these mountains, the logs were floated downstream on the Piave River all the way to the Venetian lagoon. A lot of wood was required for this as the shipbuilding yards produced a galley a day during their heyday. Later, the Cadore was just one of the many territories given up by the Austrians during their retreat at the start of World War I. Along the trail you'll notice the ruins of a number of fortifications, all destroyed by the Austrians before they left.

Beginning at charming little **Pieve di Cadore**, the birthplace of the artist Titian whose statue graces the centre of town, you'll need to hike (30 mins) up to the nearby hillside hamlet of **Pozzale** (buses also ply this route). In Pozzale, look out for CAI signs pointing west on Trail 253 to *Rifugio Antelao* via the **Forcella Antracisa** (1693m), a straightforward but steep ascent through forests of beech and spruce. This stretch of the walk takes a couple of hours or so, depending on how long you take to admire the superb views. The bivouac hut by the forcella was closed when I last checked. From the forcella the path (now Trail 250) widens to a 4WD track as it heads towards the *Antelao* (1796m). With the next rifugio a good five hours away at least, you will probably want to rest here for a night and start out early the next day. From the rifugio you can see the distant **Antelao** peak to the west, and it is in this direction that the path now heads, towards the **Forcella Piria** (2096m), where there are more stunning views of the Antelao.

Fifty metres beyond the forcella, take a sharp right turn and descend to the start of Trail 258, which will take you through the gorgeous **Val Antelao** and down to the **Val d'Oten** (3hrs from the forcella) and the main road to Calalzo. Don't go south along this road; go north to the **Bar alla Pineta**, and on to Trail 260, part of the Alta Via 5, which will take you via a protracted series of zigzags to *Rifugio Chiggiato* (1911m), a further two hours on from the Val d'Oten.

From behind the *Chiggiato,* Trail 262 branches north then north-east, skirting the south-eastern side of the **Marmarole** along a fairly level path through meadows dotted with dwarf pines. There is a fixed cable by a narrow stretch of path which is nothing to get too worked up about. Incidentally, Pope John Paul II also walked this way, as testified by a plaque above the first cable. The path slowly descends now to *Rifugio Baion* (1828m); another hour's walk north-east along Trail 272 will bring you to *Rifugio Ciareido* (1969m), formerly a military barracks and now a very cosy refuge with some really good food. From the *Chiggiato*, it's approximately 3hrs 30 mins.

The final leg of this walk is straightforward, involving a 30-minute trudge down a wide 4WD track to *Rifugio Marmarole* (1788m), then a much longer walk of two hours or so, either on the 4WD track or, on the much quicker, steeper and more scenic Trail 33 down to the town of **Lozzo di Cadore**, from where you can catch buses back to Pieve.

APPENDICES: ITALIAN WORDS & PHRASES

Useful Italian words and phrases are included below. Although many people in the Dolomites speak German, it is true to say that whilst German-speakers nearly always speak Italian too, the Italian-speakers rarely know much German. The same is true for the signposts: if they're written in just one language that language will be Italian.

NUMBERS

1	*uno*	11	*undici*	30	*trenta*
2	*due*	12	*dodici*	40	*quaranta*
3	*tre*	13	*tredici*	50	*cinquanta*
4	*quattro*	14	*quattordici*	60	*sessanta*
5	*cinque*	15	*quindici*	70	*settanta*
6	*sei*	16	*sedici*	80	*ottanta*
7	*sette*	17	*diciasette*	90	*novanta*
8	*otto*	18	*diciotto*	100	*cento*
9	*nove*	19	*diciannove*	1000	*mille*
10	*dieci*	20	*venti*	1,000,000	*un milione*

ITALIAN-ENGLISH VOCABULARY

abete	fir tree
alpeggio	a small, high-altitude farm used for making dairy products
alpinismo	mountaineering
alta via	high-level walking route
alto	high
aperto	open
avanti	ahead
basso	low
becco	pointed mountain peak
betulla	birch tree
biglietto	ticket
biglietteria	ticket office
bivacco	unstaffed mountain shelter
bosco	woodland
burrone	cliff or precipice
caduta massi	falling rocks
caldo	hot
camera	room
camera singola	single room
camera a due letti	double room
camera con bagno	room with bath
camera con doccia	room with shower
campaniles	limestone steeples or towers formed by centuries of erosion by wind or rain.
campeggio	camping ground with facilities
campo	field

canale	rocky valley
canalone	larger version of canale
carta	map
cartina	map
cascata	waterfall
castagno	chestnut
castello	castle
chiave	key
chiuso	closed
cima	mountain peak
colazione	breakfast
colle	hill
corda	rope
difficile	difficult
discesa	descent
dislivello	gradient
doccia	shower
escursione	walk or hike
est	east
faggio	beech
fienile	haystack
fiore	flower
fiume	major river
forcella	saddle between two mountains
frana	landslide
freddo	cold
fulmine	lightning
funivia	cable car
galleria	tunnel
gestore	rifugio manager
gettone	token
ghiacciaio	glacier
ghiaione	scree slope
giornaliero	daily
grotta	cave
incidente	accident
laghetto	small lake
lago	lake
larice	larch
letto	bed
malga	alpine hut used in production of cheese and butter
meridionale	southern
mezzo	half
mezza pensione	half-board
montagna	mountain
mulattiera	mule path

nebbia	fog
neve	snow
nord	north
nuvoloso	overcast
occidentale	western
orario	schedule
oratorio	shrine by the side of a path
orientale	eastern
ospedale	hospital
ovest	west
parcheggio	car park
parete	rockface
passerella	footbridge
passo	mountain pass
pensione	small hotel
percorso	route
pericolosissimo	very dangerous
pericoloso	dangerous
pernottamento	overnight stay
pian	plain
pineta	pine forest
pino	pine tree
pioggia	rain
piovoso	rainy
ponte	bridge
prato	meadow
previsioni del tempo	weather forecast
pronto soccorso	first aid
punta	mountain summit
quercia	oak
quota	altitude
rifugio	mountain refuge
ripido	steep
rocca	ruined castle
rudere	ruins
salita	climb, ascend
scarpone	walking boots
seggiovia	chair lift
sella	saddle
sentiero	footpath
settentrionale	northern
sinistra	left
smottamento	scree
soccorso	help
stazione ferroviaria	railway station
strada	road
sud	south

tempesta	storm
tempo	time, weather
temporale	thunderstorm
tenda	tent
torre	tower
torrente	small river
valanga	landslide or avalanche
val	valley
valle	valley
vallone	large valley
vento	wind
vetta	mountain peak
via ferrata	path equipped with iron cables, ladders etc
zaino	rucksack

ENGLISH-ITALIAN VOCABULARY

accident	*incidente*
ahead	*avanti*
altitude	*quota*
ascend	*salita*
avalanche	*valanga*
bed	*letto*
beech	*faggio*
birch	*betulla*
boots (walking)	*scarpone*
breakfast	*colazione*
bridge	*ponte*
camping ground	*campeggio*
car park	*parcheggio*
castle	*castello*
cable car	*funivia*
cave	*grotta*
chair lift	*seggiovia*
chestnut	*castagno*
cliff	*burrone*
climb	*salita*
closed	*chiuso*
cloudy	*nuvoloso*
cold	*freddo*
daily	*giornaliero*
dangerous, very dangerous	*pericoloso, pericolosissimo*
descent	*discesa*
difficult	*difficile*
east	*est*
eastern	*orientale*

field	*campo*
fir tree	*abete*
first aid	*pronto soccorso*
flower	*fiore*
fog	*nebbia*
footbridge	*passerella*
glacier	*ghiacciaio*
gradient	*dislivello*
half-board	*mezza-pensione*
haystack	*fienile*
help	*soccorso*
high	*alto*
hill	*colle*
hospital	*ospedale*
hot	*caldo*
key	*chiave*
lake, small lake	*lago, laghetto*
landslide	*valanga, frana*
larch	*larice*
left	*sinistra*
lightning	*fulmine*
low	*basso*
manager (of rifugio)	*gestore*
map	*mappa, carta, cartina*
meadow	*prato*
mountain	*monte, montagna*
mountain pass	*passo*
mountaineering	*alpinismo*
mule path	*mulattiera*
north	*nord*
northern	*settentrionale*
oak	*quercia*
open	*aperto*
path	*sentiero*
peak (of a mountain)	*vetta, cima, becco, punto*
pine forest	*pineta*
pine tree	*pino*
plain	*pian*
precipice	*burrone*
railway station	*stazione ferroviaria*
rain	*pioggia*
rainy	*piovoso*
river	*fiume* (large), *torrente* (small)
road	*strada*

rockface	*parete*
room	*camera*
single room	*camera singola*
double room	*camera a due letti*
room with bath	*camera con bagno*
room with shower	*camera con doccia*
rope	*corda*
route	*percorso*
rucksack	*zaino*
ruined castle	*rocca*
ruins	*rudere*
saddle (of a mountain)	*forcella, sella*
schedule	*orario*
scree	*smottamento*
scree slope	*ghiaione*
shower	*doccia*
snow	*neve*
south	*sud*
southern	*meridionale*
steep	*ripido*
storm	*tempesta*
tent	*tendo*
thunderstorm	*temporale*
ticket	*biglietto*
ticket office	*biglietteria*
time	*tempo*
timetable	*orario*
token (for phone etc)	*gettone*
tower	*torre*
tunnel	*galleria*
valley	*vallone* (large), *val, valle, canale* (rocky valley floor)
walk	*escursione*
waterfall	*cascata*
weather	*tempo*
weather forecast	*previsioni del tempo*
west	*ovest*
western	*occidentale*
wind	*vento*
woodland	*bosco*

FOOD GUIDE

For details about rifugio food see pp58-9.

Italian	**English**
acqua	water
acqua frizzante	sparkling water
acqua natural	still water
arancia	orange
birra	beer
bistecca	beefsteak
brodo	broth
burro	butter
caffé	coffee
cioccolata	chocolate
cioccolata calda	hot chocolate
calzone	folded cheese and tomato pizza
coniglio	rabbit
contorni	vegetables
cotoletta	veal, pork or lamb chop
cotoletta alla milanese	wienerschnitzel (breaded pork cutlet)
crema	cream
dolci	desserts
fagioli	beans
(ai) ferri	grilled
fettuccine	ribbon-shaped pasta
filetti	fillet
formaggio	cheese
(al) forno	roasted
frutta	fruit
funghi	mushrooms
funghi porcini	boletus mushrooms
gelato	ice cream
gnocchi	small flour and potato dumplings
insalata	salad
latte	milk
maiale	pork
manzo	beef
mela	apple
melone	melon
minestra in brodo	noodle soup
minestrone	thick vegetable soup
mirtilli	bilberries
mista	mixed
pancetta	bacon
pane	bread
panna	cream
patate	potatoes
patate fritte	chips
patina in brodo	noodle soup

pesce	fish
(al) pesto	crushed garlic, basil, oil and parmesan dressing
pollo	chicken
pomodori	tomatoes
prosciutto	ham
ragù	sauce made with mince and dried vegetables
riso	rice
sale	salt
salsa	sauce
salsiccia	sausage
speck	cured, smoked ham
succo	juice
tè	tea
tonno	tuna
uova	eggs
verdure	vegetables
vino	wine
vino bianco	white wine
vino rosso	red wine
vitello	veal
würstel	frankfurter
zucchine	courgettes
zuppa	soup

INDEX

Sahara Overland – a route & planning guide
Chris Scott
544 pages, 45 maps, 280B&W & 26 colour photos
ISBN 1 873756 26 7, *1st edition*, £19.99, US$29.95

This new guide covers all aspects Saharan, from acquiring doc-
umentation to vehicle choice and preparation; from descriptions
of the prehistoric art sites of the Libyan Fezzan to the ancient
caravan cities of southern Mauritania. How to 'read' sand sur-
faces, guidance on choosing a reliable guide, using GPS – it's
all here along with 35 detailed off-road itineraries covering over
16,000kms in nine countries, from Egypt's Western Desert to
Mauritania's Atlantic shore – Morocco, Mauritania, Libya, Mali,
Tunisia, Algeria, Niger, Chad, Egypt.
> *'As addictive as it is informative'* **Global Adventure**
> *'THE essential desert companion for anyone planning a
> Saharan trip on either two wheels or four.'* **Trailbike
> Magazine**

Istanbul to Cairo Overland *Henry Stedman*
320 pages, 44 maps, 23 colour photos
ISBN 1 873756 11 9, *1st edition*, £10.06, US$17.95

Where to stay, where to eat, what to see and all modes of overland transport on this route through Turkey, Syria, Lebanon,
Jordan, Israel and Egypt. Arabic script for all hotels and place
names.
> *'Useful and enjoyable to read'.* **TNT Magazine**

Australia by Rail *Colin Taylor*
256 pages, 50 maps, 30 colour photos
ISBN 1 873756 40 2, *4th edition*, £11.99, US$19.95

Previously published as *Australia and New Zealand by Rail*, this
guide has been re-researched and expanded to include 50 strip
maps covering all rail routes in Australia plus new information for
rail travellers.

Trans-Siberian Handbook *Bryn Thomas*
432 pages, 48 maps, 32 colour photos
ISBN 1 873756 42 9, *5th edition*, £12.99, US$19.95

First edition short-listed for the **Thomas Cook Guide book
Awards**. Fifth edition of the most popular guide to the world's
longest rail journey. How to arrange a trip, plus a km-by-km guide
to the Trans-Siberian, Trans-Manchurian and Trans-Mongolian
routes. Fully updated and expanded to include extra information
on travelling independently in Russia.
> *'The Trans-Siberian Handbook is a must.'* **The Sunday Times**
> *'Definitive guide'* **Condé Nast Traveler**

Adventure Motorcycling Handbook *Chris Scott*
288 pages, 28 colour & 100 B&W photos
ISBN 1 873756 37 2, *4th edition*, £12.99, US$19.95

Every red-blooded motorcyclist dreams of making the Big Trip –
this comprehensive manual will make that dream a reality.
Timbuktu to Kathmandu or Patagonia to Mongolia, whether
you're planning your own Big Trip or just enjoy reading about
other people's adventures, this book is guaranteed to illuminate,
entertain and, above all, inspire.

The Inca Trail, Cuzco & Machu Picchu *Richard Danbury*
256 pages, 32 maps, 24 colour photos
ISBN 1 873756 29 1, *1st edition*, £9.99, US$16.95
The Inca Trail from Cuzco to Machu Picchu is South America's
most popular hike. This practical guide includes 20 detailed
trail maps, plans of eight Inca sites, plus guides to Cuzco and
Machu Picchu.
'Danbury's research is thorough...you need this one'.
The Sunday Times *'...difficult to put down...This book is essential.'*
International Travel News (USA)

Trekking in the Moroccan Atlas *Richard Knight*
256 pages, 53 maps, 30 colour photos
ISBN 1 873756 35 6, *1st edition*, £11.99, US$17.95
The Atlas mountains in southern Morocco provide one of the
most spectacular hiking destinations in Africa. This new guide
includes route descriptions and detailed maps for the best Atlas
treks in the Toubkal, M'goun, Sirwa and Jbel Sahro regions.
Places to stay, walking times and points of interest are all included, plus town guides to Marrakesh and Ouarzazate.

Trekking in the Everest Region *Jamie McGuinness*
256 pages, 38 maps, 20 colour photos
ISBN 1 873756 17 8, *3rd edition*, £9.95, US$15.95
Third edition of the guide to the world's most famous trekking
region. Includes route guides, Kathmandu and getting to Nepal.
Written by a professional trek leader.
'The pick of the guides to the area.' **Adventure Travel**

Trekking in Langtang, Helambu & Gosainkund
Jamie McGuinness, 256pp, 35 maps,14 colour photos
ISBN 1 873756 13 5, *1st edition,* £8.95, US$14.95
This third guide in the **Nepal Trekking series** covers the region
north of Kathmandu. Comprehensive mapping, where to stay
and where to eat along the trails. Written by a professional trek
leader.

Trekking in the Annapurna Region *Bryn Thomas*
256 pages, 50 maps, 26 colour photos
ISBN 1 873756 27 5, *3rd edition,* £10.99, US$16.95
Fully revised third edition of the guide to the most popular walk-
ing region in the Himalaya.
*'Good guides read like a novel and have you packing in no time.
Two from Trailblazer Publications which fall into this category are*
Trekking in the Annapurna Region *and* Silk Route.' **Today**

Trekking in Ladakh *Charlie Loram*
256 pages, 70 maps, 24 colour photos
ISBN 1 873756 30 5, *2nd edition*, £10.99, US$18.95
Since Kashmir became off-limits, foreign visitors to India have
been coming to this spectacular Himalayan region in ever-
increasing numbers. Fully revised and extended 2nd edition of
Charlie Loram's practical guide. Includes 70 detailed walking
maps, a Leh city guide plus information on getting to Ladakh.
'Extensive...and well researched'. **Climber Magazine**
'Were it not for this book we might still be blundering about...'
The Independent on Sunday

Trekking in the Pyrenees *Douglas Streatfeild-James*
256 pages, 80 maps, 30 colour photos
ISBN 1 873756 21 6, *1st edition*, £10.95, US$16.95
NEW EDN June 2001 with increased coverage of Spain:
ISBN 1 873756 50 X, *2nd edition*, £11.99, US$18.95
All the main trails along the France-Spain border from the
famous GR10 coast to coast hike and the most scenic sections
of the GR11, to many shorter routes. 80 route maps include
walking times and places to stay.
'Readily accessible, well-written and most readable...' **John Cleare**
'Very informative ..Take this one with you'. **Country Walking**

❏ OTHER GUIDES FROM TRAILBLAZER PUBLICATIONS

For more information about Trailblazer and our expanding range of guides,
for where to find your nearest stockist, for guidebook updates
or for credit card mail order sales (post free worldwide) visit our Web site.

www.trailblazer-guides.com

ROUTE GUIDES FOR THE ADVENTUROUS TRAVELLER

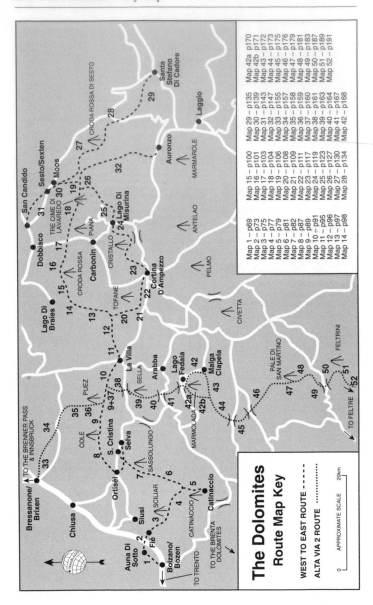

The Dolomites

Route Map Key

WEST TO EAST ROUTE - - - - -

ALTA VIA 2 ROUTE ··········

APPROXIMATE SCALE

20km